A CULTURAL HISTORY
OF DISABILITY

VOLUME 6

A Cultural History of Disability
General Editors: David Bolt and Robert McRuer

Volume 1
A Cultural History of Disability in Antiquity
Edited by Christian Laes

Volume 2
A Cultural History of Disability in the Middle Ages
Edited by Jonathan Hsy, Tory V. Pearman, and Joshua R. Eyler

Volume 3
A Cultural History of Disability in the Renaissance
Edited by Susan Anderson and Liam Haydon

Volume 4
A Cultural History of Disability in the Long Eighteenth Century
Edited by D. Christopher Gabbard and Susannah B. Mintz

Volume 5
A Cultural History of Disability in the Long Nineteenth Century
Edited by Joyce Huff and Martha Stoddard Holmes

Volume 6
A Cultural History of Disability in the Modern Age
Edited by David T. Mitchell and Sharon L. Snyder

A CULTURAL HISTORY
OF DISABILITY

IN THE
MODERN AGE
VOLUME 6

Edited by David T. Mitchell
and Sharon L. Snyder

BLOOMSBURY ACADEMIC
LONDON • NEW YORK • OXFORD • NEW DELHI • SYDNEY

BLOOMSBURY ACADEMIC
Bloomsbury Publishing Plc
50 Bedford Square, London, WC1B 3DP, UK
1385 Broadway, New York, NY 10018, USA
29 Earlsfort Terrace, Dublin 2, Ireland

BLOOMSBURY, BLOOMSBURY ACADEMIC and the Diana logo are
trademarks of Bloomsbury Publishing Plc

First published in hardback in Great Britain 2020
This paperback edition 2024

Series design: Raven Design
Cover image: Patient and Therapist © Craig Smallish/Getty Images

A catalogue record for this book is available from the British Library.

A catalog record for this book is available from the Library of Congress.

ISBN: HB: 978-1-3500-2929-3
       HB Set: 978-1-3500-2953-8
          PB: 978-1-3504-3667-1
       PB Set: 978-1-3504-3676-3

Series: A Cultural History of Disability

Typeset by Integra Software Services Pvt. Ltd.
Printed and bound in Great Britain

To find out more about our authors and books visit www.bloomsbury.com
and sign up for our newsletters.

CONTENTS

LIST OF FIGURES

NOTES ON CONTRIBUTORS

Owen Barden is Associate Professor in Disability Studies at Liverpool Hope University in Liverpool, UK. He is a core member of the Centre for Culture and Disability Studies and a comments editor for the *Journal of Literary and Cultural Disability Studies*. He has published on a variety of topics, including relationships between disability, dyslexia, technology, literacies, and learning, as well as research methodology. His more recent work has focused on the historical construction and representation of learning difficulties.

Fiona Kumari Campbell currently is Professor in the School of Education and Social Work, University of Dundee, Scotland, UK. She was Deputy Head of School (Learning and Teaching Scholarship) at the Griffith Law School, Australia until July 2014. Previous to this, she was Convenor of Disability Studies, School of Human Services and Social Work, Griffith University (2001–10), Australia. Fiona is an adjunct professor in disability studies at the Faculty of Medicine, University of Kelaniya, Sri Lanka, a person with disability and associated with several minority groups. Fiona has written extensively on issues related to Global South theory; disability—a philosophy of ableism, disability in Sri Lanka, and dis/technology, and she is recognized as a world leader in scholarship around studies in ableism. After the successful publication of *Contours of Ableism: The Production of Disability and Abledness* (Palgrave) in 2009, she is working on three book manuscripts: *#Ableism: An Interdisciplinary Introduction to Studies in Ableism*; *Textures of Ableism: Disability, Voice and Marginality*; and *Jewlanka: Footprints of Jewish Presence in Sri Lanka from Ancient Times to the Mid-1950s*.

Theodora Danylevich earned her PhD in literary and cultural studies from The George Washington University, Washington D.C., USA in 2018. She is at work on a manuscript that looks at the ways in which disabled and denigrated women in American literature, art, and film from the beginning and the end of the twentieth century compose a "sick archive" that bears witness to the sexist and racist violence of the nation. She teaches in the Women's and Gender Studies program at Georgetown University, Washington D.C., USA where her courses are a part of the university's Disability Studies minor. She also holds an MA in Communication, Culture, and Technology from Georgetown and teaches technical writing. In a previous life, she was a poet.

Anne McGuire is an Assistant Professor in equity studies at the University of Toronto, Canada. Drawing on cultural perspectives in disability studies, critical race, queer theory, and feminist science and technology studies, her research reads twenty-first century spectrum approaches to health and illness against a backdrop of neoliberal social and economic policies. She is the author of *War on Autism: On the Cultural Logic of Normative Violence*, which was awarded the 2016 Tobin Siebers Prize for Disability Studies in the Humanities. With Kelly Fritsch, she is co-editor of a 2018 special issue of *Feminist Formations* on "The Biosocial Politics of Queer/Crip Contagions."

Rod Michalko has taught sociology and disability studies in several Canadian universities, the most recent being the University of Toronto. He is the author of numerous articles, and his books include *The Difference that Disability Makes* and *The Mystery of the Eye and the Shadow of Blindness*, as well as *The Two in One: Walking with Smokie, Walking with Blindness*. He is also co-editor with Tanya Titchkosky of *Rethinking Normalcy: A Disability Studies Reader*. Rod is currently involved in writing fiction from the perspective of blindness. *Things Are Different Here* is his first collection of short stories, and he is currently completing his first novel, *My Thick Persian Rug*. Rod lives with his partner, Tanya Titchkosky, in Toronto.

Zahari Richter, MA MS, is an artist, debate coach, and English PhD student at The George Washington University, Washington D.C., USA. Zahari's publications have focused on queer theory, disability theory, cultural history, internet studies, and phenomenology. Zahari's interdisciplinary interests range from digital humanities, media studies, science and technology studies, beat literature, and transgender poetry. In their free time, Zahari enjoys Pokémon Go, Nintendo Switch, folk punk, and hiking.

Bee Scherer, PhD (Groningen 2002), is the founding director of the Intersectional Centre for Inclusion and Social Justice (INCISE; http://incise.center) and a professor of religious studies and gender studies at Canterbury Christ Church University, UK. Bee's current research focuses on transfeminism, disability, gender and sexuality, and social justice in transnational Buddhist and Asian contexts. The founder of the interdisciplinary Queering Paradigms Social Justice research and activism network and conference series (http://queeringparadigms.com), Bee is also the editor of the *Queering Paradigms* and *QP in Focus* book series (https://www.peterlang.com/abstract/serial/QP) for Peter Lang, Oxford. Bee's latest audiobook, *Essentials of Buddhist Philosophy* (2018), is available for download from Wise Studies (http://wisestudies.com/product/essentials-of-buddhist-philosophy-with-bee-scherer).

Tanya Titchkosky is Professor of Disability Studies in the Department of Social Justice Education at the Ontario Institute for Studies in Education of the University of Toronto, Canada. Tanya's books include *The Question of Access*, as well as *Reading and Writing Disability Differently* and *Disability, Self and Society*. With Rod Michalko, she is co-editor of *Rethinking Normalcy: A Disability Studies Reader*. Her work is currently supported by a Canadian Social Sciences and Humanities Research Council Insight Grant, "The (Dis)Appearance of Disability in the Academy," where she traces the meaning made of disability and the relations sustained or omitted through this making.

Samuel Yates is a professorial lecturer and artist at George Washington University and American University, where he teaches courses in disability studies, cinema, and drama. He is examining disability aesthetics and contemporary theater in his current project *Cripping Broadway: Disability and the American Musical*. As a doctoral candidate, Samuel received ASTR's Helen Krich-Chinoy Dissertation Fellowship and GWU's Dean's Dissertation Fellowship to support his research on the relationship between a performer's athleticism, disabled embodiment, and commercial theater. He holds a Humanity in Action Senior Fellowship for his work on performance and traumatic memory, and is a George J. Mitchell Scholar. Samuel has collaborated with theaters such as the Abbey Theatre, the Eugene O'Neill Theater Center, The Samuel Beckett Centre, and Woolly

Mammoth Theater. His published work can be found in *Radical Contemporary Theatre Practices by Women in Ireland* (Carysfort Press), *Studies in Musical Theatre, The Matter of Disability* (U Michigan, 2019), and *Musical Theater Today*.

VOLUME EDITORS

Sharon L. Snyder's career includes a range of work as an author, artist, activist, and filmmaker. Her books include *Narrative Prosthesis: Disability and the Dependencies of Discourse* (2000), *Cultural Locations of Disability* (2006), and *The Biopolitics of Disability: Neoliberalism, Ablenationalism, and Peripheral Embodiment* (2015). She has also edited three collections: *The Body and Physical Difference: Discourses of Disability* (1997), *A History of Disability in Primary Sources*, volume 5 of *The Encyclopedia of Disability* (2006), and *The Matter of Disability* (2019), as well as authored more than thirty-five journal articles and chapters. She has curated a museum exhibit on disability history at the National Vietnam Veterans Memorial Museum, curated disability film and arts programming for festivals and conferences, and created four award-winning documentary films: *Vital Signs: Crip Culture Talks Back* (1995), *A World without Bodies* (2002), *Self Preservation: The Art of Riva Lehrer* (2005), and *Disability Takes on the Arts* (2006).

David T. Mitchell is a scholar, editor, history and film exhibition curator, and filmmaker in the field of disability studies. His books include the monographs *Narrative Prosthesis: Discourses of Disability* (2000), *Cultural Locations of Disability* (2005), *The Biopolitics of Disability: Neoliberalism, Ablenationalism, and Peripheral Embodiment* (2015), and the collections *The Body and Physical Difference: Discourses of Disability* (1997), *A History of Disability in Primary Sources*, volume 5 of *The Encyclopedia of Disability* (2006), and *The Matter of Disability* (2019). He curated *The Chicago Disability History Exhibit* (Vietnam Veterans Memorial Museum, 2006) and assembled the programs for the Screening Disability Film Festival (Chicago, 2006), as well as the DisArt Independent Film Festival (Grand Rapids, MI, 2015). His four award-winning films include *Vital Signs: Crip Culture Talks Back* (1995), *A World without Bodies* (2002), *Self Preservation: The Art of Riva Lehrer* (2005), and *Disability Takes on the Arts* (2006). He is currently working on a new book and feature-length documentary film on disability and the Holocaust, tentatively titled *Disposable Humanity*.

SERIES PREFACE

As general editors of *A Cultural History of Disability*, we are based on either side of the Atlantic—in the Department of Disability and Education at Liverpool Hope University, United Kingdom and in the School of Social Sciences at Liverpool Hope University, United Kingdom, and in the Department of English at George Washington University, USA—but we are unified by our work and interests in disability studies, with a particular emphasis on culture and cultural production. This being so, the genesis of the project was in cultural disability studies, from which grew discussions about history that led us in many fruitful directions (e.g., Longmore 1985; Davis 1995; Garland-Thomson 1997; Mitchell and Snyder 2000; Kudlick 2003; Snyder and Mitchell 2006; Burdett 2014a; Coogan 2014; Doat 2014; Tankard 2014; Rembis 2017). The name mentioned more than any other was that of Henri-Jacques Stiker, whose work was prominent in our thoughts at the proposal stage, and as such resonates here. The method in his most famous book, *A History of Disability*, "ranges from close readings of literary texts as exemplary of dominant myths to discussions of the etymology of disability terminology to medical taxonomies of specific conditions and test cases to an examination of current legislative initiatives" (Mitchell 1999: vii). The real interest, as Stiker states in an interview published more than thirty years after the first edition of his book, is not "History with a capital H like trained historians do," but "grand representations, systems of thought, the structures beyond history" (Kudlick 2016: 140). The spirit if not the letter of this method is adopted in *A Cultural History of Disability*, our focus being how disability has been portrayed in various aspects of culture and what these representations reveal about lingering and changing social attitudes and understandings.

A Cultural History of Disability is indebted to contemporary disability activism and to other movements for social justice. As David Serlin writes in the introduction to an important anthology on the intersections of disability and masculinity,

> Within academic culture, tectonic disciplinary and intellectual shifts of the 1960s and 1970s gave rise to the fields of ethnic studies and critical race theory, women's and gender studies and men's studies, LGBT studies and queer studies, and disability studies, and crip theory. Scholars in these fields have not always been in alignment, of course, but they do increasingly recognize each other as workers and activists in adjacent and overlapping fields of critical inquiry, cultural production, and social justice. (Serlin 2017: 8)

Many chapters in *A Cultural History of Disability* are thus deeply and necessarily intersectional, attending to gender, race, sexuality, nation, and other axes of human difference. In the process, the project attends to multiple modalities of disability experience, past and present. In presenting such an interdisciplinary and theoretical project, we therefore depart from the kind of history of disability that, for example, focuses on the story of so-called special schools from the perspective of their governors

(Burdett 2014b), or the history of major medical advances (Oshinsky 2005), in favour of one that delves into the underpinning social attitudes faced by disabled people beyond and long before such institutions or advances.

We are keenly attuned as well to the many ways in which disability has been *represented*. A "*system* of representation," according to Stuart Hall, "consists, not of individual concepts, but of different ways of organizing, clustering, arranging, and classifying concepts, and of establishing complex relations between them" (Hall 1997: 17). From this cultural studies perspective, a cultural history of disability is attuned to how disabled people have been caught up in systems of representation that, over the centuries (and with real, material effects), have variously contained, disciplined, marginalized, or normalized them. A cultural history of disability also, however, traces the ways in which disabled people themselves have authored or contested representations, shifting or altering the complex relations of power that determine the meanings of disability experience.

In formal terms, *A Cultural History of Disability* is a six-volume work on renderings of disability from Antiquity to the twenty-first century. The set of volumes is interdisciplinary insofar as it engages scholars with interests in disability studies, education, history, literature, cultural studies, drama, art, and several other related fields and disciplines. Each volume covers one of six historical periods: Antiquity (500 BCE–800 CE); the Middle Ages (800–1450); the Renaissance (1450–1650); the long eighteenth century (1650–1789); the long nineteenth century (1789–1914); and the modern age (1914–2000+). These individual volumes are edited by accomplished scholars who provide an outline of the major ideas and themes concerning disability in their given historical period.

The internal structure of the six volumes is notable. Following the period-specific introduction, each volume comprises eight chapters whose principal titles correspond throughout the set. This means that many themes can be traced across all six volumes— and thus across all six historical periods. The overarching themes of the eight chapters in each volume are tentatively listed as atypical bodies; mobility impairment; chronic pain and illness; blindness; deafness; speech; learning difficulties; and mental health issues. All of these themes are manifestly problematic, on account of the terminology and apparent focus on impairment rather than disablement or disability, not to mention categorization that swerves from the fact that many disabled people have multiple impairments. Accordingly, many of the volume editors and chapter contributors have creatively and critically worked with and beyond these problematics. The eight-part categorization across time is ultimately extended not in a positivistic but in an analytical mode, offering not sameness but a critical difference across the historical periods under review. "Learning difficulties," for example, materialize quite differently under modes of industrial or neoliberal capitalism (with their demands for a particular kind of productivity and speed) than they do in Antiquity or the Middle Ages, when "learning" and education were stratified more obviously according to caste or gender. Deaf people have not always conceptualized themselves as having a distinct language or inhabiting a "minority" identity; such a conceptualization clearly requires particular historical conditions that have only begun to germinate in the past three or four centuries. These two examples illustrate that, if somewhat simplistic, the overarching themes of the project assist readers who are keen to understand more about how disabled people are represented in culture and how ideas and attitudes have both resonated and changed down the centuries.

Historical changes in ideas and attitudes have been at times merely adaptations of a more general pattern; they have, however, at other times been more akin to what are often understood as "paradigm shifts," which fundamentally alter or reinvent the conditions in which human beings are located or rescript the underlying assumptions that give rise to how we apprehend the world. The concept of a paradigm shift comes—perhaps paradoxically for a cultural history of disability—from the history of science; Thomas S. Kuhn famously used the term to describe what happens when advocates for new scientific approaches or models (those Kuhn termed "young Turks") overturn what they perceive as the outdated views of those who came before them (Hamilton 1997: 78). As Peter Hamilton explains, however, where other systems of representation or "aesthetic domains of painting, literature or photography differ from sciences is their essentially multi-paradigmatic as opposed to uni-paradigmatic nature" (Hamilton 1997: 80). Paradigm shifts in the history of disability have thus been about *pluralizing* the ways in which disabled experiences might be apprehended or have been apprehended over the centuries.

For example, the activist invention of "disability identity" itself, in the twentieth century, could arguably be understood as an example of a paradigm shift that generated completely new vocabularies, multiplying the ways in which we might understand the embodied experience of disability. From this multi-paradigmatic perspective on embodiment, we can recognize that disablement on an attitudinal level involves a historical and changeable metanarrative to which people who have impairments are keyed in social encounters (Bolt 2014). Tracing these multiple paradigms across and through the cultural patterns of history, as well as noting the discontinuities between periods, can greatly enhance our critical understandings of the present. In turn, the new vocabularies of contemporary activism can enhance our critical understandings of the past. Indeed, only *with* the activist vocabularies of the present have we been able to conceive of disability as something that might have a cultural history worthy of being studied and debated.

A Cultural History of Disability demonstrates particular interest in the etymology of disability terminology (in keeping with the method exemplified by Stiker). In English, "disability" as a term appears to date from at least the sixteenth century, according to the *Oxford English Dictionary* (Adams, Reiss, and Serlin 2015: 6). The political scientist Deborah A. Stone linked the term to the needs of an emergent capitalist order, which newly demanded "able-bodied" workers, but which also needed to differentiate between those who would be sorted into what she identified as a "work-based" system and those who would be placed in a "needs-based" system. For its own consolidation, the emergent capitalist order needed to prioritize the former and stigmatize the latter, and Stone argues that "the disabled state" was charged (from the time "disability" circulated widely as a term) with the sorting, prioritizing, and stigmatizing (Stone 1984). Of course, various other examples of disability terminology have circulated both before and after the period Stone surveys. Often those other terms—*freak, retard, idiot*, and even *handicapped*, which until recently in English was dominant in many locations—have served to reinforce deep stigmas against disabled people and to valorize able-bodiedness and able-mindedness. At other times, various terms for what might now be understood through a disability analytic have functioned quite differently, and the early volumes of this series provide thorough considerations of the languages of disability that were available, say, in Antiquity or the Middle Ages. Contemporary activists have put forward disability as an identity and as the preferred term in many locations, as against "handicap" and so many other discarded terms, both the negative and the *seemingly* positive terms Simi Linton calls "nice words" (terms activists generally perceive as patronizing, like *differently abled* or *physically challenged*) (Linton 1998: 14). For decades, in ways similar to the world-transformative reclamations in the queer movement, activists have also played with the ways in which formerly derogatory words such as *crip* might be resignified in culturally generative ways

(McRuer 2006; Bolt 2014). Disability terminology, although sometimes overlooked, thus reveals much about changing ideas and attitudes.

Languages besides English have of course similarly been the staging grounds for vibrant conversations about disability terminology. Many Spanish speakers roundly reject *minusválido* (literally, less valid) or *discapacitado/a*; some activists and artists, particularly in Spain, have put forward the preferred term *persona con diversidad funcional* (person with functional diversity). Although the revision of these terms has had a more uneven reception across Latin America, the very existence of such debates testifies to ongoing and vibrant conversations about language—critical debates that resonate in Japan (Valentine 2002) and India (Rao 2001). The anthropologist Julie Livingston uses "debility" for her important work on Botswana, since no word in the languages spoken there translates easily into "disability," even though a concept is needed for encompassing a range of "experiences of chronic illness and senescence, as well as disability per se" (Livingston 2006: 113). The international and historical scope of these debates is immense.

What we begin to explain here is that *A Cultural History of Disability* is not meant to provide readers with the history of disability. *The history of disability* is in fact, from one perspective, the history of humanity, and as such too vast for any collection, no matter how extensive, illustrative, or indicative of key periods and moments. From another perspective, what we think we understand in our own moment as "disability" varies immensely across time and space, which is why this set of volumes ultimately presents multiple and variegated *histories* of disability. *The* cultural history of disability thus is not something we could or would endeavor to document, not even with the esteemed editors and authors we have gathered to conduct this research. Rather, what we offer here is *a* cultural history that leads readers down various and sometimes intersecting paths. The cultural history this set of volumes presents is an interdisciplinary one that is driven by an appreciation of disability studies and thus disability theory, recognizing that disability as an *analytic*—like a feminist or queer analytic—can be brought to bear on many different topics and cultural contexts, even if other time periods have conceptualized bodies and minds using very different language from our own.

David Bolt and Robert McRuer, General Editors

REFERENCES

Adams, Rachel, Benjamin Reiss, and David Serlin (2015), "Disability," in Rachel Adams, Benjamin Reiss, and David Serlin (eds.), *Keywords in Disability Studies*, 5–11, New York: New York University Press.

Bolt, David (2014), *The Metanarrative of Blindness: A Re-Reading of Twentieth-Century Anglophone Writing*, Ann Arbor: University of Michigan Press.

Burdett, Emmeline (2014a), "'Beings in Another Galaxy': Historians, the Nazi 'Euthanasia' Programme, and the Question of Opposition," in David Bolt (ed.), *Changing Social Attitudes Toward Disability: Perspectives from Historical, Cultural, and Educational Studies*, 38–49, Abingdon and New York: Routledge.

Burdett, Emmeline (2014b), "Disability History: Voices and Sources, London Metropolitan Archives," *Journal of Literary and Cultural Disability Studies*, 8 (1): 97–103.

Coogan, Tom (2014), "The 'Hunchback': Across Cultures and Time," in David Bolt (ed.), *Changing Social Attitudes Toward Disability: Perspectives from Historical, Cultural, and Educational Studies*, 71–9, Abingdon and New York: Routledge.

Davis, Lennard J. (1995), *Enforcing Normalcy: Disability, Deafness, and the Body*, New York and London: Verso.

Doat, David (2014), "Evolution and Human Uniqueness: Prehistory, Disability, and the Unexpected Anthropology of Charles Darwin," in David Bolt (ed.), *Changing Social Attitudes Toward Disability: Perspectives from Historical, Cultural, and Educational Studies*, 15–25, Abingdon and New York: Routledge.

Garland-Thomson, Rosemarie (1997), *Extraordinary Bodies: Figuring Physical Disability in American Literature and Culture*, New York: Columbia University Press.

Hall, Stuart (1997), "The Work of Representation," in Stuart Hall (ed.), *Representation: Cultural Representation and Signifying Practices*, 13–74, London: Sage Publications.

Hamilton, Peter (1997), "Representing the Social: France and Frenchness in Post-War Humanist Photography," in Stuart Hall (ed.), *Representation: Cultural Representation and Signifying Practices*, 75–150, London: Sage Publications.

Kudlick, Catherine (2003), "Disability History: Why We Need Another 'Other'," *American Historical Review*, 108 (3): 763–93.

Kudlick, Catherine (2016), "An Interview with Henri-Jacques Stiker, *Doyen* of French Disability Studies," *Journal of Literary and Cultural Disability Studies*, 10 (2): 139–54.

Linton, Simi (1998), *Claiming Disability: Knowledge and Identity*, New York: New York University Press.

Livingston, Julie (2006), "Insights from an African History of Disability," *Radical History Review*, 94: 111–26.

Longmore, Paul (1985), "The Life of Randolph Bourne and the Need for a History of Disabled People," *Reviews in American History*, 13 (4): 581–7.

McRuer, Robert (2006), *Crip Theory: Cultural Signs of Queerness and Disability*, New York: New York University Press.

Mitchell, David T. (1999), "Foreword," in Henri-Jacques Stiker (ed.), *A History of Disability*, vii–xiv, Ann Arbor: University of Michigan Press.

Mitchell, David T. and Sharon L. Snyder (2000), *Narrative Prosthesis: Disability and the Dependencies of Discourse*, Ann Arbor: University of Michigan Press.

Oshinsky, David M. (2005), *Polio: An American Story. The Crusade That Mobilized the Nation against the 20th Century's Most Feared Disease*, Oxford: Oxford University Press.

Rao, Shridevi (2001), "'A Little Inconvenience': Perspectives of Bengali Families of Children with Disabilities on Labelling and Inclusion," *Disability and Society*, 16 (4): 531–48.

Rembis, Mike (2017), "A Secret Worth Knowing: Living Mad Lives in the Shadow of the Asylum," *Centre for Culture and Disability Studies YouTube Channel*, May 10, https://www.youtube.com/watch?v=Ls5BgJ2x8U0 (accessed May 17, 2017).

Serlin, David (2017), "Introduction," in Kathleen M. Brian and James W. Trent, Jr. (eds.), *Phallacies: Historical Intersections of Disability and Masculinity*, 1–21, Oxford: Oxford University Press.

Snyder, Sharon L. and David T. Mitchell (2006), *Cultural Locations of Disability*, Chicago: University of Chicago Press.

Stone, Deborah A. (1984), *The Disabled State*, Philadelphia: Temple University Press.

Tankard, A. (2014), "Killer Consumptive in the Wild West: the Posthumous Decline of Doc Holliday" in David Bolt (ed.), *Changing Social Attitudes Toward Disability: Perspectives from Historical, Cultural, and Educational Studies*, 26–37, Abingdon and New York: Routledge.

Valentine, James (2002), "Naming and Narrating Disability in Japan," in Mairian Corker and Tom Shakespeare (eds.), *Disability/Postmodernity: Embodying Disability Theory*, 213–27, London and New York: Continuum.

Introduction

What We Talk About When We Talk About Disability

DAVID T. MITCHELL AND SHARON L. SNYDER

When readers review the table of contents for *The Cultural History of Disability in the Modern Age*, they may initially experience a sense of disorientation or even uncanny discomfort with the overarching presentation of chapters. This sense of an all-too-familiar and yet, at first glance, not overly promising potential might result from one of three different initial reactions: (1) the apparent "medicalized feel" of the topic headers as potentially indicative of a prevailing diagnostically oriented methodology not commonly associated with Disability Studies over the past thirty years or so; (2) the semi-"euphemistic" feel of the organizing themes that structure each chapter as if attempting to rhetorically hedge around the devaluation commonly associated with each disability group in question rather than breach a more direct politicized and/or historicized line of inquiry; and/or (3) the apparent transhistorical orchestration of these entries across massively distinct historical, cultural, and economic periods. Perhaps the best way to enter into this introduction on the "Cultural History of Disability in the Modern Age," then, is to address each concern at broader length and move to an explanatory overview of how the chapters attempt to address each problem that we undertake both as a collective think tank of theorists and as individual authors.

Let us begin by addressing each of the discomforts cited above before moving on to an explanation of our collective and individual modes of address and then concluding with a series of three close readings on what literary disability has to offer to our historical understanding of the subject. Each volume features eight parallel entries that feel relatively "medicalized" in orientation—atypical bodies, mobility impairment, chronic pain and illness, blindness, deafness, speech, learning difficulties, and mental health issues. A shared taxonomic impetus of deficit might be argued to guide these chapter titles. There is also an uncharacteristic focus on single disability groups that might suggest a cordoning off of differences into their own discrete diagnostic categories and a resistance to a more flexible "stretchiness" that has increasingly characterized work in the field (McRuer 2018: 19). In other words, to partition the cultural subject matter in this manner appears to remove their intersecting shared history of stigma and material, cognitive, sensory, and psychiatric devaluation from our methods of approach. They represent the "big six" diagnostic categories, along with the catchall classifications that bracket looser nomadic groupings of "atypical bodies" and "mental health issues."

Second, the entries resonate with a feeling of a tenuous euphemistic quality often associated with cultural efforts to identify differences that are necessarily pathologized and yet, to hide that founding undesirability, they suggest the artificiality of a promise: "mobility impairment" might prove an encounter with temporary barriers rather than systemic architectural exclusions; "learning difficulties" could suggest a mild hiccup in the cognition potentiality of the subject to be supplemented by the provision of special auxiliary aides; "deafness" and "blindness" pose a limitation somewhere short of "profound" and as losses to be shored up by the compensatory overdevelopment of other "intact" senses with technologies; "chronic pain and illness" might do little more than send one to the local pharmacy for some remedy purchasable in today's for-profit medical market such as a pill or cream rub for joint and muscle discomfort akin to Big Pharma's production of a deadly drug such as Vioxx (removed from the market for increasing heart attack risk in 2004) (Marcus 2016); "mental health issues" might refer to a simple shift in policy approach and access to a treatment facility as an example of greater flexibility in "health care" provision; "atypical bodies" might be misunderstood to serve as a junk category for the embodied, sensory, and mental leftovers not covered in the panoply of diagnoses surrounding it.

These questions of taxonomy—how one qualifies and categorizes characteristics of variable embodiment among the species Human—may at first suggest participation in some full-blown Foucauldian power/knowledge address of anomalous characteristics akin to the hierarchical taxonomies that organize flora and fauna in the vegetable and animal worlds (Foucault 1990: 159). The Modern Age mantra has been: diagnose, prescreen, prostheticize, segregate, euphemize, normalize, profitize, integrate. How to deal with populations that have proven so *narratable* and yet never quite—in disability historian Henri-Jacques Stiker's terms—*integral* to what it means to be Human (1999: xi)? Thus, to resignify the title of one of Raymond Carver's most well-known books: What do we talk about when we talk about disability (2015)?

Third, in addition to the medicalized and euphemistic "feel" of these content-based categories, the structural organization across the six volumes overall positions all taxonomies identified as necessarily operative in the various centuries/cultures/histories to which they "belong." Even in the twentieth century, such a longitudinal uniformity cannot be viably argued, as World War I gave advent to terms of trauma such as "shell shock," while World War II forwarded concepts of "war neuroses," and the Vietnam War delivered the multifactorial disorder, "post-traumatic stress syndrome" (Biernoff 2017: 76). Likewise, many of these war-induced diagnoses were also made applicable to other civilian populations such as immigrant children separated from their parents who were prosecuted for trying to immigrate across borders for asylum and greater economic opportunity, as Fiona Kumari Campbell discusses in her chapter on "mobility impairment." Or African-Americans seeking to cope with the loss of family members from police violence, as is currently going on in the USA in the summer of 2018, as examined in Theodora Danylevich's chapter on "chronic pain and illness." Those who apply such diagnoses know that these are not one and the same condition, but questions of shared symptomatology continue to guide ways of thinking about the management of trauma and their presumed material embodiment as symptoms, as is examined by Zahari Richter in their chapter on "speech disability."

Thus, the cataloguing technique of maintaining a uniformity of entries across volumes suggests that such impairments might be recognized as fully transhistorical and thus potentially universalized in applicability. Consequently, to enter into this volume or any of the others that precede it chronologically is to anticipate an encounter with a relatively static encyclopedic affair—one on the order of the most exhaustive treatments of any subject and potentially exhausting and repetitive above all else. The eighteenth-century French philosopher, Denis Diderot, along with John le Rond d'Alembert, authored the first volume of their *Encyclopédie* and, following various imprisonments, confiscations, and censorships by the government, religious authorities, and publishers, released the final folio volumes in 1772 (1750). As the primary composer of the *Encyclopédie*, Diderot once critiqued himself and other likeminded compilers of exhaustive ordering projects by commenting, "Watch out for the fellow who talks about putting things in order! Putting things in order always means getting other people under your control" (Diderot 2004). In Diderotian fashion, taxonomy is regarded with a great deal of suspicion in Disability Studies as a result, ordering discordant bodies into a more coherent lesser chain of being resonates with a sense of collusion in pinning down bodies for easier access, sequestration, study, and subordination. Assessments of the fallout from such imperatives of sequestration can be found to be actively operative in Rod Michalko and Tanya Titchkosky's chapter on "blindness" and Owen Barden's examination of "learning disability." In fact, such resistance to ordering as an act of the exercise of power infuses all of the chapters to come and, in fact, represents a shared approach to disassembling rather than reinstating such taxonomic efforts in our collective's overall shared methodology.

Nevertheless, these chapters do follow a loose ordering logic in that there is basic adherence to a chronology of ideas, practices, and events at stake; however, the overriding goal is to follow out how disabled subjectivities come to be fashioned as known bodies despite existing in the margins of cultural interests (Mitchell and Snyder 2015: 98). This is not to say that progressive teleologies of self-possession are documented in the pages to come, but rather that uneven, sporadic expression of a coming-into-being as disabled subjects marks one primary objective in each chapter. All of these chapters necessarily (and purposefully) fail at any ultimate arrival of expression of such subjectivities, yet there is something that ties them together in their shared frustration with the conscious, active exclusion of disabled peoples' perspectives that binds their methodologies and intents. Further, not just disability "identities" are at work here, as the chapters all theorize how this fashioning of subjectivities gives rise to a wellspring of conversations across diverse disciplines, organizations, policy networks, and publics, as can be found in Samuel Yates' chapter on "deafness" and Bee Scherer's anti-taxonomic analyses in the chapter on "atypical bodies." We might refer to this overarching structuring function as disability's impetus for narrativity—not only the bodies that we talk about, but the way we talk about them has to be addressed for adequate comprehension of such a diffuse experiential subject (Burton 1995: 207). Thus, the chapters serve as documents of "the difference engine" that disability represents in the Modern Age (Gibson 1995).

What we talk about when we talk about disability involves undertaking a grand dishevelment in its contours, operations, coherency, approach, and existence in the world. A better way to explain the approaches to come in this volume are that the authors talk about how others talk about disability, rather than participating in further ordering conversations of universality or new masteries of sense-making subjectivities themselves. At times, disability becomes a screen in these chapters without an essence; or, rather, its essence is one made up of discursive flotsam that proves inherently alienated from the lives discussed, as demonstrated in Richter's chapter on the ambivalent machinations of material vs. psychiatric sources for explaining stuttering and other speech anomalies. In fact, alienation might be said to be the point, in that what we talk about when we talk about disability as an existence is often to be set far away and distant from those authorizing the discussion. Titchkosky and Michalko provide an important series of examples as to how and why blindness cordons off its experiential subjects into a discordancy of non-sense-making, and Owen Barden addresses a similar argument in his analysis of knowledge regimes regarding the supervision and history of exclusions of individuals with cognitive disabilities. Whether perverse, distended, malformed, pathologized, defended, or even championed as another way to live, the point of so many of these conversations is the sealing off of disability from a proximity to the discussant standing safe in his/her own professional, public normative identity. Campbell's discussion of mobility as an unstated qualification of citizenship expertly demonstrates this professional partitioning of disability from normalcy, as well as Theodora Danylevich's analysis of racialization's intersections with various presumptions of psychiatric disability and nonapparent disability (i.e. the "fiction" of chronic pain) as an impetus for cultural expulsions and tactical misunderstandings. Further, Anne McGuire's chapter on "mental health problems" underscores the degree to which neuroatypicality results in justifications for overmedication, internment, and even murder of the psychiatric subjects in question.

Consequently, disability is a source of cultural anxiety to be sure throughout the Modern Age, and one that causes great consternation for nearly all assayers of pathologized difference. Despite the presumed vanquishing of metaphysical overlays of divine injustice, the provision of pensions to wounded veterans, or the falling away of schemes to garner wealth without work, disability comes to languish under a promise of medical fulfillment that will somehow destroy the need for those in need of support to continue their neediness. Whether these anxieties are born out of estrangement, fear of one's own bodily vulnerability, the exercise of small fiefdoms of professional, private, and public power, or the need to subordinate in order to inflate and/or make charitable as an object worthy of others' investments, the product is most commonly a reinstatement of a founding distance within the object itself rather than with the definers and their portable projection screens of differentiation and devaluation in need of fixing. One can witness such historical distances being instantiated in Yates' discussion of the collapsing of accessibility that occurs for deaf and hearing-impaired individuals with the advent of sound technology in film and in the violence against trans people of color discussed in Danylevich's chapter. Further, McGuire provides an analysis of the cultural sequestration of gay and lesbian people occasioned by the inclusion of the category "homosexual" as a sexual perversion or psychiatric pathology in various iterations of the *Diagnostic and Statistical Manual*. Likewise, Richter explores how speech disability serves as an all-purpose opportunity for disciplines as diverse and seemingly opposed as psychology, phenomenology, medicine, literary criticism, linguistics, political science, etc., to venture into concepts of dysfluency as definitive symptomology.

What we talk about when we talk about disability is preemptive of a defining value that might adhere in the subject's existence, and in taking such an approach, the authors here show that what is being warded off is knowledge itself in exchange for the cultivation of a purified medical and social object endowed by the scrutiny and, most commonly, the skepticism of others. Such a sequestration from influence by disabled people is central to Michalko and Titchkosky's analysis of the experiential and alternative subjectivities spawned by experiences of blindness. One of the overarching takeaways from this volume is that the Modern Age threw so much effort into practices of walling off bodies—a great confinement of a rhetorical, therapeutic, and carceral kind that is quite different from Foucault's diagnosis of earlier sequestration practices—that paying attention to particular modes of disability exclusion have much to tell us beyond more general studies of imprisonment, banishment, and neglect for social marginals" (Foucault 2005: 57).

Scherer's documentation of the ways in which those occupying atypical bodies are discounted as unsuccessful deployment of normalcy's static patterns of presentation and Danylevich's discussion of the imprecisions of chronic pain diagnoses (or, more typically, non-diagnoses) and their highly gendered implications for women's, trans, and intersexed access to health care both resonate with bodies that cannot be admitted to an alternative species of the Human (Weheliye 2014: 45). Those who in fact might contribute to the conversation were the conversation to be an exchange about alternative existences, active adaptations, and routes of counter-existence are bereft of that which makes the implementation and oversight of Modern norms so quintessentially bereft of their own defining value. In this regard, Richter's chapter exposes how voluminous discourses of speech disability go on without any consultation of the experiential subjects outside of a few celebrity figures who come to stand in as the ur-subject of a multivarious fluency impediment of expression. What we talk about when talk about disability, then, is a structuring difficulty of exchange because the object of the conversation might hold some key that we do not wish to find awaiting us under the mat outside the door of the Human. What we talk about when we talk about disabilities is, most importantly, the historical documentation of a series of ways to avoid the conversation. Barden demonstrates how racial presumptions of intellectual inferiority by colonial/imperialist nations ultimately feed into strategies for partitioning off those considered insufficiently rational, and Scherer's atypicality of embodiment departs from cultural imperatives to maintain an inflexible gender binary at all costs.

0.1. MODERN AGE PROBLEM SET: "BECAUSE EVERYTHING HAS A PERFECTLY REASONABLE EXPLANATION"

The group of essays collected here on disability in the Modern Age began its collective deliberations on how to anticipate and address these methodological and content problems by thinking about the massively difficult task of writing a theoretically driven history of any of these "condition groups" in the twentieth/twenty-first centuries. First, we wanted to acknowledge that the volumes are conceived (at least on the face of things) as a conservative, not particularly Disability Studies-based impairment group model (atypical bodies, deafness, blindness, mobility impairment, speech disability, pain and chronic illness, mental health problems). We used this partitioning organizational structure as an opportunity to make the volumes seem "traditional" in relation to disabilities as they are typically thought of in liberal management circles and policy wings, while really wanting to create the opportunity for thinking in depth about histories, therapeutic management/economic/political contexts, alternative social communities, and the richness of creative texts in relation to these flat diagnostic experiential categories. We (the editors) suggested thinking about an essay such as disability theorist Celeste Langan's "Disability Mobility" as a kind of model for how one might innovate within an approach to a seemingly restrictive category of impairment (2001). Langan's essay (while not quite as historically expansive or internationally engaged as this volume's chapters) uses US filmic texts of the late twentieth century with a theoretical framework that parses the difference between "equality" and "liberty" combined with a history of disability rights activism in relation to accessibility of public transportation and the overlap of race, class, gender, and disability populations who are economically bound to one form of slow, unreliable, impediment-ridden, and economically accessible transport (i.e. the public bus) if they hope to participate in the public sphere. She also uses an impairment grouping, "Mobility Disability," in order to show how expansively one might conceive of restricted movement in public spaces as a productive interpretive rubric for political intervention. Further, "Mobility Disability" makes an interesting turn near the conclusion in finding "alternative democracies" at work in the limited confines of the plodding, deterministically routed public bus circuit to which many disenfranchised groups must resort as their only means of mobility (Langan 2001: 477).

Next, we outlined three "problem" areas to consider in approaching the chapters: (1) the North American and UK-centric mooring of our author group; (2) the need to cover intersections of race and disability, as that crossing has struggled to be articulated in Disability Studies; and (3) the matter of globalization and how to address a world that is turning out to be not so "flat" (Friedman 2005: 8). All of these areas represent problems for the volume as a whole and do not belong to any individual chapter/author to solve. The first matter—the North American/UK-centric mooring of our author group—was just a reminder to all of us that it will be easy to overrepresent Canada, the UK, Australia, and the USA in this mix of commentary, and that we might all strive to make our analyses as international in scope as possible. Whether we avoided this problem is left for the reader to decide.

The second matter—the need to cover race/disability texts—is an attempt to reckon with the common elisions of race in Disability Studies and the parallel trepidation about approaching disability in Critical Race Studies (Watts and Erevelles 2004: 272). Racialized experiences of disability have been overlooked in that global slavery of African peoples resulted in multiple forms of violence against black bodies as a result of the ravages of The Middle Passage, forced labor, inadequate food and housing, denial of public education, and continuing inaccessibility to adequate health care (Schalk 2018: 51). Thus, these chapters attempt to wrestle with questions of disability across racialized communities, particularly with respect to the ongoing neglect of the communities of people of color due to police violence, racism, widespread poverty, and excessive proximities to toxic environments.

The third matter—globalization—involves an attempt to encourage authors to grapple with the fact that while products/capital move more easily than ever before across borders, bodies (particularly disabled bodies) are "possibly more fixed than ever." In relation to this last area of address, the chapters in this volume discuss disability as an automatic immigration prohibition as well as the pursuit (or impossibility of the pursuit) of therapies, medications, hormones, surgeries, and global aid, and in being situated as such, this emphasis opened up ways of thinking about disability's impact and nonapparent centrality to border crossings—more likely framed as refusals based on inability to be gainfully employed. Further, consider the rise of for-profit prosthetics industries that dump their unused/unwanted equipment on global outposts. Particularly those devalued geographies ravaged by earthquakes, hurricanes, volcanic eruptions, and other environmental disasters largely associated with human-made climatic toxicities (Mitchell and Snyder 2015: 54). These questions come up in a variety of ways, from rising mercury levels in animal populations consumed by humans, to widespread use of pesticides on crops and in vacation areas, to the massive impact of the overreliance on combustion engines, to greenhouse gases emitted in such vast amounts as to result in the melting of the polar ice caps (Taylor 2017: 17). All of these economic, diasporic, and environmental changes impact people with disabilities across all communities and nations in significantly adverse ways. Thus, the chapters in this volume contend that disability exacerbates susceptibility to such earthly embroilments and also tends to situate disabled people in greater proximity to harm through the various abandonments they experience. The irony of these exposures is that they come at a time in late twentieth-century multicultural, neoliberal capitalism when nations are openly celebrating their humane embrace of disabled people through various social support and integration schemes while at the same time raiding health care coffers and underfunding welfare and other caretaking support systems to balance beleaguered treasuries due to militarization and tax cuts for the wealthy at the same time (McRuer 2018: 4).

Our conversations on the challenges of globalization and representation next moved to a discussion of periodization and how we believe that, since the previous volume is devoted to the "long nineteenth century," our volume might take the beginning of World War I as its basic starting point. Further, this decision was not to exclude discussions of works pertinent to this history from prior moments, and in fact, many of these chapters follow their respective histories out by gesturing to key works not just of the 1910s, but also to prior centuries potentially covered elsewhere in these volumes. However, we agreed to use World War I as a historical informal ground zero to guide us through where the bulk of the chapter histories might situate themselves. After all, World War I was the historical beginning point for so many basic disability attentions previously ignored as inevitably mortality-dealing, from bladder infection treatment by antibiotics, to the development of facial prostheses for the aestheticization of war wounds, to the evolution of cane travel training due to mass blindings by mustard gas exposures (Biernoff 2017: 87). Therefore, one way to conceive of the chapters that make up this volume was to think about major historical ruptures in modern history as the motivating background for disability approaches in the primary works discussed.

Such traumatic historical touchstones might include incarceration practices, World Wars I and II, Aktion T4 and the Holocaust, the dropping of the atomic bomb by the USA on Hiroshima and Nagasaki within three days of each other, and the intranational partitionings of Germany, Korea, India, Pakistan, and Vietnam. The latter's military occupation by France and then the USA came particularly on the heels of the fallout of the domino theory of communism that sacrificed more than 53,000 American lives and somewhere near 1.1 million Vietnamese lives (Ward and Burns 2017: 1). In contemporary moments, one might consider the deinstitutionalization movements of the 1960s and 1970s, the rise of the prison–industrial complex, the end of Apartheid in South Africa, the HIV epidemic and the closing of the bathhouses, the neocon 1980s with its selling off of the public commonwealth, the burgeoning of for-profit medicine and rehabilitation, the passage of disability rights laws (the Americans with Disabilities Act, ADA, Disability Discrimination Act, DDA, etc.), cataclysmic climate change, diffusion of environmental toxicities, animal rights movements, the emergence of global Right to Die movements, (and then recent formal ratifications at the level of states and nations), and the histories of tech particular to each entry. We (the editors) also pointed out that tech as a pragmatic access consideration and representation as an interpretive approach are artificially held out as separate phenomena and that we wanted to avoid this problem in the more integrative approach offered throughout these histories. This is despite the fact that expanding modes of access inevitably pressure the creative address of newly forming market audience bases for all genres. This discussion also led to a discussion about the fact that new genres come into play in the "Modern Age" that are not present in the previous volumes' histories, such as film, social media, video games, etc. So, the object group of our analyses could be fully realized only in relation to adopting more expansive Cultural Studies-based approaches.

Finally, we discussed matters of audience. The obvious decision would be to write for the general research-familiar reader with a basic knowledge of Disability Studies. Our primary concern with regard to the matter of audience address involved the ways in which such approaches do not always lead to the most interesting writing or new theorizations of knowledge. Rather, what we sought to achieve was a volume of engaging essays that aim for originality of insight over homogeneity of content. Thus, we encouraged "idiosyncrasy" over formulas of presentation and content, assuming to some extent that readers who enter into these chapters will have significant familiarity with the basic touchstones of the history and representation of the "condition" category in question. In Langan's essay mentioned above, there is an attempt to lay out terms and basic arguments about disability rights history with respect to accessibility of public transportation, but her analysis tends toward moving readers through original readings and insightful turns of analysis that take "mobility disability" from a wheelchair-user's perspective of architectural exclusion to wider-ranging racial and economic categories of social analysis. The contributors to this volume set out the parameters of each chapter in some strict ways with regard to historical coverage and open up the question of methodological choices as part of the approach to deepening the topic overall. This, we believed, would help lay bare the thought process without having to make the writing voice less overtly "pedagogic" and/or overly "introductory."

Taking into account all of these considerations proves well beyond the reach of any individual chapter, but our goal is to cumulatively address as many concerns as possible over the course of the volume *in toto*. As the exasperated narrator in Stanley Elkins' *The Magic Kingdom* announces multiple times in response to queries from his caretaking and charity-minded characters about why disabled children have to experience the fate of being, well, "disabled": "Because everything has a perfectly reasonable explanation" (2000: 72). To be certain, the irony intended by Elkins in articulating that impossible promise of "everything [having] a perfectly reasonable explanation" sits at the forefront of a project such as this one, specifically with respect to disability, where the Modern Age has consistently approached the question of the meaning of disability as answerable by unearthing a defining undesirability of the majority of conditions considered. While multifactorial causes are difficult to apprehend, treating symptoms as causes has proven more common.

We know, for instance, that too much iron in the blood (hemochromatosis) is an undesirable situation, yet we know little about why the mutation leading to this condition occurs. Various forms of bloodletting form the treatment protocol for such iron-overloading disorders. Such disorders likely prove to be either adaptations for northern European consumers of red meat diets and/or imperfect cellular mutations for resistance to the bubonic plague. (Moalem and Prince 2008: 2). We know, for instance, that sickle cell anemia in persons of African and Middle Eastern origins is a condition that "limits" life expectancy, yet only recently have we theorized that such mutations that lead to this condition were likely responses to malaria, as they protected the body by making the transport of the disease in red blood cells less efficient (ibid.: 82). We know that the condition of esophageal atresia/tracheoesophageal fistula (EATF) has to be surgically corrected in order to create a workable passage from throat to stomach for food and liquid ingestion, yet there has a been a resistance to mapping demographic susceptibilities that might be related to rising mercury levels in fish. Surgeons largely know that pulling together the ends of unconnected esophageal passages to form a working foodway does not work without getting the cellular metabolism of the esophageal cells to grow first (the

Foker process), but the former, less workable correction is still performed more often than the latter, more time-consuming and financially cost-intensive treatment, despite it consciously leading to a significantly lowered quality of life (Mitchell and Snyder 2015: 195). Each of these impairments has its own history, its own mutational adaptation pattern, and its own embodied "logic" of alternative pathways for viability, yet we treat surface and symptom in each case while narrating the disorder as a failure of normative development rather than an adaptive reorganization of organisms. Thus, while "everything may have a perfectly reasonable explanation," the Modern Age has been overly quick to assign failed etiology of development from the normative as the cause without giving enough attention to the historical conditions that bring about such adaptations as necessary for successful treatment and lowered degrees of stigma. While a mutation at one moment of time might have extended the survivability of an organism, the residual effects in a later period may prove alternatively ineffective or noxious. Thus, adaptations for survival may, in turn, result in the need for their own treatment regimes in subsequent generations. The treatment may be necessary, but pursuit of causes matters as well. Because humans can often fail to see the cause (i.e. that everything does not have an immediately recognizable reasonable explanation), they diagnose and treat symptoms while leaving larger questions behind, such as the demographic proximity of EATF to industrial toxicities. The pursuit of causes is ultimately about the politics of how and why bodies respond in the first place.

We attend to a largely Darwinian theory of adaptation that discards uncovering the reason for disabilities in favor of a haphazard organismic expression (adaptive mutation) that is often narrated as maladaptive or dysfunctional (Gould 2002: 144). In other words, we jettison readings of disability as the imprecision of a guiding misfire in an otherwise static organism or the metaphysical plan of otherworldly design in favor of a more historically diffuse, empirical adaptability model, yet underscored by an unknowability as to why we approach disability as undesirable deviation from normal. To throw out the question of overarching design (divine or otherwise) is to give greater credence to the idea that humans do not know why disability happens in most cases, and that, most importantly, we know almost nothing about how differences in one regard may prove advantageous to the species in the long run. Thus, the essayists in this volume are skeptics at best of founding causes and, in particular, of pretending to know whether disability is an adaptation to another even more deleterious situation for the organism or social order in question. Each writer approaches his/her/their diagnostic population in a manner that gives unknowability its best chance to yield new meaning. They adhere to a strict sense of what Alison Kafer refers to as "futurity": we cannot know disability futures without actively thinking them into being and calling on their productive potential against the grain of most cultural thought in the Modern Age (2013: 5).

In part, the necessity of a more proactive thinking of futurity is attested to by the relative paucity of ways of imagining disability futures by the contemporary discourses examined throughout the chapters to come. To reckon with insufficiency of imagination and meaning is to open up the task of needing new formulas. Certainly, to a significant extent, these historically oriented chapters give readers an opportunity to know what they *do not* want as constitutive of the futurity of the world that they seek but has not yet arrived (Munoz 2009: 1). For instance, it would be more desirable to address the causes of rising mercury levels and the impacts of acid rain in certain areas rather than ignoring demographic patterns as the medical industry surgically corrects one anomalous body at a time. This individualistic approach to disability in medical circles is one primary way of cutting off the discipline from undertaking more active, pragmatic, and pressing politics.

Medicine tends to cannibalize its past and the sociology of the present "disorders" it treats, while literature and theory seek to make repressed histories and material agencies resurface in the present. The collective point for theorists in this volume is to make all of history contemporary history not because history will unfold again in its repetitive form, but rather that recognizing the practices/beliefs that led to previous catastrophes might help us to avoid them occurring again by building in preventative measures to anticipate such catastrophes in our current systems.

Despite the fact that we all know so well that this claim to possession of an empirical knowledge base about the origins of disability cannot be true (i.e. that there is no perfectly reasonable explanation of why disabilities exist), the collective also pressures a shared belief that this lack of founding cause in dysfunction is at the heart of the promise of disability. We put on certainty as a pose in the guise of our role as experts, or writers, or academics, or professionals, or chroniclers, even as experiencers of disability, etc., yet one cannot possibly know a topic in its shifting, sliding essence at base. The authors in this volume fully recognize their limitations as they approach these overviews of disability as a various and varied subject inevitably escaping its localization and/or universalization of meaning. Efforts to objectify and make empirical come into serious question, as well as the elusive certainty of definition itself. In this sense, our collective project was to produce an anti-*Encyclopédie* against the fashion of Diderot, although we also sought to contain some of the heresy for which his massive undertaking is so well regarded. Thus, part of the explanation that "everything has a perfectly reasonable explanation" is that this insistence on a secure foundational meaning is far from the case, and we do not seek to reproduce it in the chapters that follow. Instead, we desire the "stretchiness" of disability to surface and manifest the capacious nature of human difference that physical, cognitive, psychiatric, sensory, sexual, and nonapparent differences represent.

0.2. "[DISABILITY] IS A FISH": THREE TWENTIETH-CENTURY LITERARY DISABILITIES

The point here, of course, is not to dismiss disability to vaporous apparitions of discursive cultural fantasy; however, in the basic, constructivist social model of disability that has dominated approaches since the 1990s, the primary attention has been placed upon a shifting logos of disability. Deconstructionist methodologies are fully on display in the chapters to come, but the authors do not settle for the exposé of cultural phantasms as an endgame. As one learning-disabled narrator in William Faulkner's 1930 novel, *As I Lay Dying*, poetically and semiliterately explains by thinking about the culturally accrued meanings, historical dynamism, impairment altering functionality, and decomposing corporeality of his now dead mother, Addie Bundren: "My mother is a fish" (1990: 84). In making such an enigmatic claim, the speaker, Vardaman Bundren, employs a metaphor that suggests his ultimate inability to know the essence of one as intimate as even one's own mother. Such a failure of comprehension occurs even while carting her lifeless body across rugged terrain to arrive at a promised final resting spot in the town of Jefferson, Mississippi, miles away from the family home where she desires to be buried. This dying request occurs in spite of the difficulty it will place on the family to get her physical body there (economically, physically, geographically, socially, aesthetically, narratively, etc.). In this modernist moment, like so many modernist works, there is no private world left, as it has been utterly upended by the coming of the open embrace of the for-profit market in disability and death. Carting Addie Bundren's body across the state of Mississippi's post-slave, un(der)reconstructed geography makes all who come into contact with the family aware of the uncomfortable presence of this "white trash family," as the mother's body is actively decomposing and the pungent smell of her death telegraphs their arrival far ahead of any physical encounter.

The ill-fated trip produces disability and death as it costs the family the lives of an entire mule team, further physically disables Cash (his previously broken and mis-repaired leg is broken again), and ultimately turns out to be an excuse for Addie's husband and Vardaman's father, Anse, to replace his decaying natural teeth with a new pair of false teeth and a new bride after she lends him a shovel to bury his prior wife's body. One gets a sense from these chapters that disability plays host to countless opportunities for others, while being portrayed as the object of care that strains the nation's/medical systems' resources. For Vardaman, the mother's defining multifacetedness eludes his ability to recreate a coherent picture of her defining complexity and incoherency. Thus, what he knows is merely a rough approximation of knowledge standing in for true apprehension of his material, psychological, historical, and socially derided subject.

This problem of impartial knowing and the dishevelment of disability narrativity that can be caused even across apparently discrete taxonomic categories is already a product of the Modern Age to which this volume is devoted (Bérubé 2016: 2). One must work retrospectively from contemporary orderings of disability to a well-earned skepticism about truth claims on all fronts when a routinely despised social object such as disability is concerned. *Thus, this volume could be said to pay homage to a foundational disordering that exists at the basis of what we know of disorder itself.* In turn, the chapters to come do not argue that we cannot know anything about disability origins (congenital and/ or environmental etiologies), symptomatologies (presentations, secondary conditions, bodymind involvements), nor even functionalities, treatments, or cures. Rather, we collectively treat these influences as fully contingent, unfinished, "sent before [their] time" in ever evolving dynamic processes of adaptive difference (Shakespeare 2004: 1). Thus, as with Vardaman's metaphor of a slippery fish standing in for the elusive being of his mother, disability's coherence is rendered incoherent—i.e. a narrative cut up (pastiche) for cultural consumption that cannot be re-membered into a recognizable whole by the Modern Age.

As with Vardaman, who tries to grasp the slipperiness of his topic as it wriggles out of his hands and jumps back into the stream from which it came, our particular scholarly collective approached these chapters through mixings of chronology that might well be told in a more teleological way—contemporary to modern and back, residing among what Samuel Yates in his chapter on deafness refers to as the "in-between spaces" where ambiguity more explicitly resonates as most reliable in its radical contingency. There is no knowing without this understanding of a retroactive chain of meaning, as Žižek and other philosophers have insisted for language's delayed meaning-making chain (1989: 3)—likewise with the historical understandings governing these chapters on disability in the Modern Age.

Disability poses its own retroactive problem in that decisions to kill disabled infants with congenital cognitive impairments, carried forward from at least Ancient Greece (as advocated in the contemporary philosophy of ethics by Peter Singer and others), attempt to skirt the dilemma of retroactive value in human lives by arguing that mortality-dealing noninterventions (that which Ogden Nash refers to as "sins of omission") should happen because the disabled individual in question has no future concept of herself/himself/

themselves (Singer and Kuhse 1988: 1). In fact, the extinguishing of severely disabled lives can be justified by Modern Age utilitarianism before too much meaning can accrue and challenge the thought that such a member of the species Human will not develop a sense of self in history. In other words, all beings gather history and hold some sense of futurity, but killing in advance presumably is justified based on the violent refusal to see value in others, as they inevitably do and will. Conscious euthanasia is akin to the contemporary outrage of making a preemptive strike on devalued global populations—as George W. Bush once thematized US imperialism abroad: "we fight them over there so we don't have to fight them here." Disability is a fish, and the mercury levels are rising in the sea of the Modern Age in which it swims, to a point where continued cultural capture poses a risk to consumers of all stripes and depths.

Thus, this volume at base pursues an exposé of efforts to accrue historical meaning in relation to disability and disabled individuals—that which we will term in the shorthand notation of *non-normative experiences* and/or *bodyminds*—as an urgent problem with which to wrestle: how to know a thing as various as disability across something as massive and discordant as the "Modern Age" (Price 2011: 11), particularly in that the "Modern Age" has made one of its central objectives "knowing disability." In that impossible sense, then, we would argue that these chapters share a sense of humility and impossibility in their projects. Yet it is more than this, in that they bring their own experience of disability that has placed them in the kind of intimate relationship that prompts Vardaman to openly wonder: How can this phenomenon of a mother be known at base when it is so definitively various? Why must my relationship to knowledge through extreme intimacy be curtailed and humbled?

Or, in another quintessential modernist moment that resonates in an opposing direction, the chapters in this volume attend to disability's variousness, as in Virginia Woolf's portrayal of the artist Lily Briscoe's effort to paint a portrait of Mrs. Ramsey. In her war novel, *To the Lighthouse*, Lily can only resolve the riddle of Mrs. Ramsey in a fractured, cubist-like realization that distorts perspective and denies coherency (1981: 8). Ultimately, even the most pared-down domestic agent such as her hostess cannot be grasped straight on: "She saw it clear for a second, she drew a line there, in the centre …. Yes, she thought, laying down her brush in extreme fatigue, I have had my vision" (ibid.: 209). To draw a line down the center and call something finished is to splinter it into a representation that can only be called "undone" or, at least, unfinished and forever fractured in its finitude. Woolf depicts Lilly as the best of the "New Women" who desire careers during World War I and who experience significant depression and the fear of obscurity in the market of the Modernist male dominated, abstractionist movement.

Ultimately, *To the Lighthouse* pays homage to the materialist struggle of women painters and artists trying to break into fields of influence. Woolf herself went into manic episodes and had to undergo quiet therapy rounds for "visions" she continued to have in her bedridden convalescence that forbade her pen and paper and the strenuousness of a "writing life." It is difficult to see in retrospect how we should read Woolf's grappling with depression given the press of the war on her psyche—a fractionalization of Europe under perpetual warfare from the late nineteenth century onwards. Is this a disorder or, parallel to what Joan Didion once claimed regarding a diagnosis with MS as a "reasonable response to the times" (2009: 49)? Perhaps this uncertain bridging between Woolf's psychiatric experience and the idea of a market-driven depression offers a model encounter with the uncanniness of difference that proves the closest approximation of disability called forth by the commentaries to come.

Yet, disability's status as one of the baseline definitions of human variation serves as a definitively varied, variant, noncompliant, and nonconforming category. Certainly, one cannot comfortably situate such differences as "coherent" across ages, bodies, borders, and histories! Further, in addition to these structuring questions overall, there exists the question of "the Modern Age" itself; one that serves as a parameter for this volume's specific entries, for "the Modern Age" poses its own set of difficulties in establishing the overarching expectations of an ambiguous historical periodization project: Which version of the Modern, and how Western in orientation? Does the Modern in question here reference back merely to the age of Mechanical Reproduction, the slightly earlier Gilded Age of second-wave industrialization, or a wider circumference of coverage stretching back to the Early Modern period at the close of the Middle Ages as Foucault might situate it (Foucault 2005: 3)? Alternatively, is "disability" a product of the Modern Age itself, particularly given that most historians define the designation as no older than pensions for impaired veterans of the US Civil War (Stone 1984: 49)? As readers move on to the individual entries under each heading, she/he/they will quickly recognize how these potential structuring problems lead to innovative alternatives and an enrichment of Disability Studies approaches.

The chapters included in this volume on the *Cultural History of Disability in the Modern Age* assess the historical and cultural conditions of potentiality at work in the shaping and unshaping of disability as a twentieth- and twenty-first-century project. As the term "disability" does not enter into the discourse of nations prior to the US Civil War, development of the concept (largely in relation to pensions paid out to disabled veterans for a predetermined lost labor level of incapacity resulting from war injury) is nearly parallel to this volume's historical articulation. As Disability Studies historian, David Y. Yuan, explains, financially and medically supporting Civil War war wounded combatants on both sides (North and South) effectively served as a material and symbolic act of triage to heal a torn nation (Yuan 1997: 71–87). Supplementing disabled veterans' lives, bodies, and minds damaged by violence, then, proved akin to filling in a lack experienced at the level of the country itself; thus, disability arrives in a deployment of full symbolic power on behalf of a massive supplementation mission far beyond any body served. To understand this strange alternating capacity of disability to work at the macro and micro levels, forms of redemption exist across all of the writings collected here in relation to some of the most disparate forms of difference: mobility impairment, learning difficulties, chronic pain and illness, deafness, blindness, speech disability, atypical bodies, and mental health issues.

Yet, the setting of the Civil War as the site of disability's etymological surfacing in US history also situates the concept of repair and percentage of labor lost alongside of the tolls of racial slavery. Slavery, like disability and for disability as an inevitable outcome of enslavement itself, has been part of a highly repressed national history and an active unwillingness to come to terms with state histories of violence (Schalk 2018: 45). Susanne Knittel, a scholar in the field of Comparative Literature and Memory Studies, defines the "historical uncanny" as a specific tragedy or life-changing event that represses so much feeling that the trauma of the event continues to reverberate in the present, even if the original event is erased, forgotten, or actively suppressed (2014: 9). To solidify this point, Knittel uses the public commemoration of disabled Aktion T4 victims who were mass murdered by the Nazis during World War II in the gas chambers at the psychiatric institution of Grafeneck during the years 1939–40 (ibid: 41). The killings at Grafeneck are an example of a historical event that is little known but continues to exert pressure on contemporary German culture. This discussion of the historical uncanny as a past event that is so powerful it continues on in the present operates in a similar vein to Toni Morrison's use of the word "rememory" in her neo-slave novel, *Beloved* (2004: 169). "Rememory" marks things that happen to others in such a lasting way that the incident or place remains and exerts a powerful claim on the present—it fractures and impairs one's sense of the experience of here and now. The power of rememory asks something of those who bump into it, even if the event did not happen through direct experience or witnessing.

In *Beloved*, the characters struggle with the historical memory of slavery, including combinations of active erasure and conscious efforts to repress the slave past as literary devices of the "historical uncanny." As Sethe tells her remaining daughter, Denver:

> The picture is still there and what's more, if you go there—you who never was there—if you go there and stand in the place where it was, it will happen again; it will be there for you, waiting for you. So, Denver, you can never go there. (2004: 169)

While a rememory appears at first to be a neutral potential in the past, what Sethe goes on to explain is that severe trauma makes a "thought picture" linger on and pressure the present. In this case, the trauma is provoked by experiences in slavery. The memory of slavery *impairs* all of the characters, and Beloved's multiple disabilities stand as one of the most powerful examples of the impact of trauma in the novel. Similarly, chapters such as Owen Barden's overview of "learning disability," Bee Scherer's chapter on "atypical bodies," Fiona Kumari Campbell's chapter on "mobility impairment," and Theodora Danylevich's chapter on "chronic pain and illness" all seek to explore how racial, disabled, and slave histories are intertwined such that they cannot be effectively teased apart.

In order to analyze *Beloved*'s approach to disability, we might follow Sami Schalk's recent argument that such a braiding of racial and disability stories is necessary: "Using the history of slavery as my example, I contend that scholars must read representations of disability in neo-slave narratives as constitutive of both the discursive use of (dis)ability to justify the enslavement of black people and the physically and mentally disabling repercussions of racism for black subjects in the antebellum period and beyond" (2018: 36). For example, slavery takes its toll on each character in *Beloved* in its own way. This is true especially for Sethe, who is connected to her place of residence at 124 despite its active haunting and threats to her cognitive and physical well-being. Throughout the novel, Sethe's *traumatic* experiences of being forced into submission as "contraband humans" (Morrison 2004: 16), whipped while pregnant such that the scars form a chokecherry tree on her back (ibid.: 188), raped of her mother's milk by Schoolteacher's assistants (ibid.: 16), committing infanticide to keep her children from being returned to slavery (ibid.: 184), objectified and divided up on notepaper for her human and animal characteristics (ibid.: 188), and exchanging sex for letters on her daughter's gravestone (ibid.: 149) all come back to haunt her in the form of her dead baby daughter, Beloved.

When Beloved first surfaces from a nearby stream in a mysterious manner, the narrator describes her appearance in the following way: her breath "sounded like asthma .... Her neck, its circumference no wider than a parlor-service saucer, kept bending and her chin brushed the bit of lace edging her dress" (ibid.: 193). Further, Beloved's behavior is likened to women who have drunk too much champagne, "their straw hats with broken brims are often askew, they nod in public places; their shoes are undone" (ibid.: 184). Morrison's descriptions of Beloved as physically disheveled and her exhibition of erratic mannerisms recall ways that disabled bodies work as deviant and vaguely threatening to a public's sense of normalcy—such non-normative bodies call attention to themselves. Yet, it is not always apparent what detail is out of place—or in Morrison's terms "askew"—in order to catch the attention of the viewer; something seems out of place, but what that something is may be hard to define.

In part, such a non-normative presentation accorded to Beloved's arrival signifies the undesirable nature of slavery and the havoc that systems of human exploitation wreak upon the bodyminds of the enslaved. Beloved's appearance in this scene literally erupts into Sethe's field of vision and calls attention to her ungainly physical character—one who represents something very much akin to Knittel's theory of the "historical uncanny" as a "vertiginous intrusion of the past in the present" (2014: 50). All along, as Morrison's narrator explains, what most stands out in Beloved's presentation is an uncanniness of affect in that "amid all that she was laughing"; further, Beloved had "new skin, lineless and smooth, including the knuckles of her hand" (2004: 50). This luminosity of appearance suggests something newly born in the world—a sudden, unanticipated surfacing of the past in the present—and her arrival immediately starts to make demands on the living in relation to its uncanny appearance and appetite for attention. Disability in this sense might be argued to operate as a productive agent that forces an encounter with the violent past and the inferiorizing effects of physical/cognitive/psychiatric/sensory/sexual difference.

As the novel's plot deepens, Beloved's physical body further disintegrates, and Sethe grapples with her ability to maintain control of the mental capacity to remain in the "real" world of post-slavery. Slavery represents an unreal trauma that she has to work to "keep at bay," and thus the present is haunted by a not-so-distant violent past (ibid.: 135). Yet, remaining in the "real" world is impossible for Sethe, as her historical "rememory" betrays her by taking shape in the sudden surfacing of her dead daughter's figure. Beloved represents a ghostly reinsertion of the historical real for Sethe, in that her physical presence insists on a face-to-face encounter with that which Sethe needs to forget and Denver has to erase. Beloved's reintroduction of the trauma of the slave past and Sethe's desperate act of infanticide to keep her children from being returned to enslavement is represented as a powerful claim on the present. As an example, Beloved wants everything in the house at 124 to remain broken so that her traumatic experience is not successfully repressed by her mother.

As such, Beloved's potential destructiveness represents a rememory for her mother and a non-memory for others: Denver, for instance, is shielded from a tangible knowledge of the slave past because her mother has worked to help her develop without a literal understanding of what the slave past entailed, as Denver was too young to remember it (Sethe was pregnant with her when she escaped with the assistance of her daughter's namesake, Amy Denver). As Denver stands on the porch preparing to get help to rescue Sethe from Beloved's all-consuming presence, she muses at the power of the historical uncanny: "Out there where small things scratched and sometimes touched. Where words could be spoken that would close your ears to shut .... Out there where there were places in which things so bad had happened that when you went near them it would happen again" (ibid.: 135). Here, in tandem with the way that Beloved as ghost child walks "fully dressed out of the water," Denver experiences her own terror at how the past can rear up in your pathway even when a direct knowledge is not available to identify it.

Yet, both forms of coping with the past ultimately fail for Sethe and Denver as rememory—the historical uncanny—imposes its presence on them all. Beloved shows that slavery cannot be successfully repressed for the former or erased for the latter; its impact on the lives of all of the novel's characters exerts a level of control they cannot escape.

Thus, Knittel's theorization of the "historical uncanny" helps to explain how a traumatic event in the past cannot be suppressed even under the most active efforts to obliterate it from view (Morrison 2004, : 243). It moves into one's life when one least expects it, and forces the subject of the event to encounter it even without the necessary specificity of the events it represents. At the Grafeneck killing center, all of the technology of mass murder was destroyed by the occupying Soviet army after the war, and the space is currently being used as "safe housing" for people with severe cognitive disabilities (Knittel 2014: 305). Yet, there is also a Euthanasia Memorial Center on site that tells of the atrocities of the past and thus, as Knittel explains, the present keeps dialogue with the past about atrocity and Nazi state-sponsored efforts to exterminate those like the individuals with developmental disabilities living in the present (ibid.: 717). How, visitors often ask, can a disability community be maintained in the literal space of their historical mass murder? One answer is: the historical uncanny would make visitors and inhabitants do so anyway, despite a lack of access to the particulars of the history that is called forth and discomfort the present.

Like the apparatus of Nazi mass murder in Knittel's history, slavery is effectively gone in Morrison's *Beloved*, and yet its absence allows Sweet Home to present itself as "rolling, rolling, rolling out before her eyes, and although there was not a leaf on that farm that did not want to make her scream, it rolled itself out before her in shameless beauty" (2004: 6). Much as the slave plantation presents itself to Sethe as pastoral beauty, the novel depicts the relationships between the female inhabitants of 124 as shifting and blurring as slavery almost "productively" rearranges hierarchies and caretaking roles in its aftermath of impairment experienced by all of the characters. For instance, all of their familial roles intersect and swap sides for, at times, Denver plays the role of Beloved and Beloved, in turn, plays the role of mother to Sethe, who requires the coddling more commonly associated with childhood (or significantly disabling conditions). This ironic dispersion of caretaking roles also causes Denver to comprehend what actually happened to her mother during slavery: "Denver thought she understood the connection between her mother and Beloved: Sethe was trying to make up for the handsaw; Beloved was making her pay for it" (ibid.: 251). Prior to these insights, Denver does not want to know about slavery, as she feels as if it all took place so long ago and has little to do with her own interests and decisions in the present. Its relevance only surfaces when Denver starts to realize that her life may be endangered during the most commonplace of practices, such as when her mother braids her hair at night as a way to expose her neck for another murder, as she did to her younger sister so many years ago in the woodshed (ibid.: 251), or through the ways in which her brothers Howard and Buglar told Denver "die-witch" stories as a warning if Sethe would ever come after her with destructive intentions (ibid.: 206). In this way, Denver becomes traumatized as well, and her imagination is infiltrated by a slave past that she did not experience directly.

In fact, as the novel draws to its conclusion, the reader is confronted with multiple perspectives that seem to abruptly switch and combine into one merging perspective, as if all of the characters are observers of each other's stories from some ambiguous space on the other side of history. For Beloved to represent slavery through time as not a single occurrence but one that reverberates in multiple directions, her body must not only symbolize the current fractures of the moment, but also the fissures of any future moments in which slavery extends its all-encompassing grip and has to be remembered (i.e. recalled, but also put back together into some semblance of the human). In other words, her disablement underscores the physical toll on human bodies that comes along with enslavement and other horrors, and thus, like the euthanasia mass murders at Grafeneck, *Beloved* also becomes a story to be forgotten. Each time a character in the novel seems to forget a part of her story in slavery Beloved's bodily disruptiveness becomes more visible and her catalogue of impairments multiplies: her bobbling head (ibid.: 19), her decayed "back tooth" (ibid.: 23), her asthmatic-like labored breathing (ibid.: 133), her "drunken" affect (ibid.: 23), the scar "in the kootchy-kootchy-coo place under her chin" (ibid.: 50), and her increasing girth represented by a "basket fat stomach" (ibid.: 239). All of these exterior signs of physical and sensory impairment become akin to the power of a story untold in the intertwining of disability, race, gender, and repressed history of state-sponsored violence in the USA. However, without the speech act of telling, the story does not exist; or rather, as Knittel's theory of the historical uncanny explains it, the story is there exerting its formidable impact, but not fully identifiable by those who encounter it.

In one of the experimental series of first-person chapters that complete section II, Morrison explains this problem through converging perspectives with the employment of ambiguous pronouns in the following way:

> not for her she fills the basket she opens the grass I would help her but the clouds are in the way how can I say things that are pictures I am not separate from her there is no place where I stop her face is my own and I want to be there in the place where her face is and to be looking at it too a hot thing …. (ibid.: 243)

This enigmatic desire that trauma creates into "a hot thing" sears the place of slave history in the novel's disabled present. The verb tense used is the present tense, and the lack of punctuation makes differentiation of time, place, and observers almost indiscernible and inseparable from each other. One is tempted to characterize this outbreak of first-person black female narratives as a form of disabled writing: semiliterate and lacking in the conventions of educated formal expression, yet urgently immediate and emotional, a poetic rawness that the conventional rules of writing cannot fully convey, expression that struggles to emerge as each subject navigates taboo desires for the value of devalued others in their midst: "I am Beloved and she is mine" (ibid.: 105). Slavery becomes an idea equivalent to that of an untellable history or shameful familial hereditary pattern often represented by a disabled family member who is presumably "protected" from the abjection of others by being locked away in a home or institution. The potential for visceral personal harm to one's health is so great that an alternative harm of absolute segregation becomes a viable alternative (ibid.: 210).

Yet, this treatment is harmful to all, as it artificially removes disability from human awareness and segregates disabled people from participation in public. Likewise, slavery is not a story to pass on in the multiple meanings of the ambiguous phrase "to pass": to avoid giving up on knowing about violence (psychiatric mass murder or enslavement) when the temptation is great; to appear to be one thing (white and/or able-bodied) in order to protect oneself from social devaluation due to association with devalued others; to refuse to listen to the story of a violent past because the content is too necessary despite upsetting mainstream historical knowledge (as in the Holocaust or Aktion T4 or the Middle Passage); a pathologized biology (disabled and/or racialized) that requires a decision to police the transfer of bad genes from transmission into the nation's hereditary pool (eugenics and miscegenation); to save oneself (the bearer of tainted genes) and one's children (the carriers of tainted genetics) from a return to radical segregation schemes (institutionalization and/or slavery) because there is "nothing" (in the eyes of the slaveholder) left to enslave (ibid.: 210). This intertwining of the story of race, slavery, class, sexuality, and disability shows how inextricable one mode of being is from the other. The historical uncanny makes encounters with the traumatic past necessary and inevitable, albeit belonging to another's experience—an act of rememory that replays the pain of the original trauma as a further demand on future generations.

This demand on the present and future of the disability past is fully on display in this volume. The chapters seek to bring the disability past to actively bear on the present and the future rather than leave it to languish unattended and neglected by the cultures that foster its abandonment as a result of pathologizing impositions, fashionings of disabled people into perpetual objects of scrutiny, making the means to live in the world with disabilities as resulting in forms of further harm and disability, and the historical erasure of our knowledge of disability as a persistent potential in the Modern Age.

CHAPTER ONE

Atypical Bodies

Queer-feminist and Buddhist Perspectives

BEE SCHERER

1.1. INTRODUCTION: A MULTIVERSE OF ATYPICAL BODIES

Atypical bodies in the Modern Age, as constructed through, for example, gender binarism, ableism, and "sanism" (Birnbaum 1960), are deeply interpolated in Global Northern hegemonic discourses of scientific positivism and capitalism. The cultural discourses and projects of modernity construct corporeal typicality within frameworks of medico-psycho-social normativities, replacing the systemic violence of religio-cultural value judgments as inscribed on individual bodies with equally violent "scientific" societal scripts of centers and margins of corporeality and embodiment. Challenging these re-delineated structures of corporeal normativity, postmodern modes of cultural critique have been increasingly deconstructing, queering, "cripping," and "madding" the oppression of—in (late-/neo-/post-) Marxists terms—the *medico-psychiatric industrial complex*, which, in aid of neoliberal (late) capitalist exploitation, propagates the manageable uni/con-formity-in-isolation of human "production/consumer units" alienated from both their uniqueness and their mutual interconnection. Queer and queering (and, analogously, crip and cripping; McRuer 2006) are terms that point to "critical impulses" (Kemp 2009: 22) empowering embodied subjects to inhabit the very "open mesh of possibilities, gaps, overlaps, dissonances and resonances, lapses and excesses of meaning" (Sedgwick 2004: 8) beyond identitarian reductionism and essentialism.

This chapter explores how atypical bodies and body *performativity*—in the terms of contemporary queer theory, starting with Butler 1990—(can) disrupt the (late) modern nexus of socio-corporeal oppressions. Among the possible venues to showcase the disruption that any contestation of socio-corporeal scripts entails, bodily alterity could have been explored in relation to, for example, twentieth-century fascist eugenics, neurotypical normativities, and the surviving psychiatry & reclaiming madness movements (psychiatric survivor, Mad Studies, etc.). Corporeal othering can be demonstrated through beauty ideals and notions of ugliness and deformation (including fatism, female muscularity and hairiness, and ageism) as inscribed onto the collective psyche by pluto-/medio-cratic capitalist machineries such as mass media and advertising, fueled by and aiding hetero-cis patriarchy. Or one could examine in more detail binary-gendered and religious-cultural body scripts and violence, such as infantile genital cuttings and intersex surgery. The identity performances of consensual/voluntary body modification, tattooing, and body cyber-enhancements could also have been explored, just as could questions of speciesism, non-human rights, and trans-/post-human ethics.

Another possible wide-angle avenue would follow the complex intersections produced by ever-pervasive transnational centers of embodied power, which includes, but is not limited to, *male, heterosexual, cisgender* (identifying with the sex assigned at birth), *procreative/premenopausal, white, possessing a citizen/immigration status privilege, Global Northern, unimpaired/"abled," body-normative, affluent, middle-to-upper class, professional,* and *secular-Christian.*

Beyond ableism, the atypical body in the Modern Age includes most prominently the female body and the queer (including trans*, nonbinary, and intersex) body, but also the religio-culturally othered body (e.g. the Islamic veiled body), the orientalized and colonized body, and the non-human body. In this chapter, I sketch parts of this wider-angle approach while also following intersecting showcase avenues, informed and limited by my own Global Northern white queer Buddhist positionality. In this way, I offer intersectional (queer-/crip-/trans-) feminist cultural-philosophical views on atypical bodies in the Modern Age, infused by Buddhist "theology" (or Buddhist critical-constructive reflection).

1.1.1 Othering and variability

Key to the notion of "normalcy" or "typicality" is *Othering*: the strategic process in psychological (Lacan) and social discourse (Derrida) of identifying an "Other" as excluded from both the notion of a "Self" and from the construction of a stable group identity in relation to power and value productions. The feminist philosopher Simone de Beauvoir identifies alterity (*altérité*) as a foundational principle of consciousness, translating from individual to social identity formation (de Beauvoir [1949] 2010: 26–7). Emmanuel Levinas talked about an otherness that, through the "imperialism of the same," preserves or even reinforces normativities (see Isherwood and Harris 2014: 2). Michel Foucault describes the creation of *altérité* in relation to *folie* (madness) as follows:

> The history of madness would be the history of the Other—of that which for a given culture is at once interior and foreign, therefore to be excluded (so as to exorcize the interior danger) but by being shut away (in order to reduce its otherness); whereas the history of the order imposed on things would be the history of the Same—of that which, for a given culture, is both dispersed and related, therefore to be distinguished by kinds and to be collected together into identities. (Foucault [1966] 2005: xxvi)

Foucault's observations are particularly pertinent in the context of the nascent movement of victims of sanism and survivors of the medico-psychiatric industrial complex who are reclaiming madness in Mad Studies and Mad advocacy (e.g. Cole et al. 2013; Mills 2013; Burstow et al. 2014; Spandler et al. 2015). Abstracting from this particular facet, Lacanian, Derridean, and Foucauldian approaches to alterity are productive when examining (post)modern "atypical bodies," as they can help us to understand the underlying phobias and power interests that drive the creation of centers that always must produce margins, stigmatization, and deviance in order to be effective in their own self-serving discourses. For our purposes, we need to point to the emergence of Critical Disability Studies broadly conceived (see the excellent introduction by Goodly 2017), which challenges the systemic othering of atypical bodies (and minds) implied in the capitalist individualization-cum-alienation of impairment and medical conditions. Such challenges take form through Social Model approaches to "disability" as propagated by key thinkers such as Colin Barnes, Mike Oliver, and Vic Finkelstein (see Goodley 2013: 633); some take poststructuralist (see Corker and Shakespeare 2002: 3), "crip theory" (McRuer 2006), "dismodernist" (Davis 1995a), and "critical realist" approaches (Siebers 2008; Shakespeare 2017) or a "study in ableism" approach (Campbell 2009). Hence:

> Critical disability studies start with disability but never end with it: disability is the space from which to think through a host of political, theoretical and practical issues that are relevant to all. (Goodley 2013: 632)

Relatively unnoticed by the Critical Disability Studies field that thus emerged during the last three decades, the eighteenth-century cultural scholar and queer-cum-impaired activist Chris Mounsey argues for the need to move our attention away from disembodied/ disembodying theory to the focus on concrete embodiment, both paradigmatic and yet unique: Mounsey calls to replace "disability" with a new sign(ifier) "variability": *same, only different* (2014). If we theorize this "variability" further, we can claim that, as a linguistic symbol, it promises to speak to Derridean notions of the impossibility of the absolute Other. Different, here, is not in the sense of Levinas and de Beauvoir reinforcing Self and Same and the norm(ativitie)s they produce. *Same, only different* is subversive of hierarchies, just as in Homi Bhabha's famous notion of "the ambivalence of mimicry (almost the same, but not quite)" (Bhabha [1994] 2012: 123): through variability, all embodiments are taken serious in their nonhierarchical autonomy and non-hegemonized equivalence (see Scherer 2016a). "Atypical bodies" can become *variable bodies*, counteracting both essentialized alterity and systemic erasure of individual embodiment.

The following will focus on variable bodies as actively dis-abled, impaired, and oppressed through the notions of atypicality, normativity, and normalcy in the example of gender/sexuality-related embodiments. Feminist Disability Studies (Garland-Thomson 1997, 2004) and (transhuman) Cyborg Theory (Haraway 1991; see Kafer 2013: ch. 5, 103–28) advance our understanding of corporeal atypicality in its "fleshy" relationality. The queer-/trans-feminist perspective offered in the following sections (1.2 and 1.3) is naturally intersectional, and the focus on gender/sexuality is merely one of several possible routes as identified above, including class and socioeconomic power, as well as race, heritage, and ethnicity. The discussion is widened in section 1.4 by focusing on religious/cultural intersectionalities and tensions. In the final section (1.5), Buddhist philosophical perspectives infuse the discussion in order to propose new avenues to notions of corporeal atypicality.

1.2. DANGEROUS MARGINS: FEMALE BODIES VS. PATRIARCHAL TYPICALITY

The largest marginalized group of atypical bodies recognized in evolving and often reluctant manners during the "Modern Age" (as the time period this volume explicitly focuses on) is female bodies. Beyond "disability" and sexuality (Shildrick 2009), the Othered gendered body is the dangerous margin to patriarchal typicality. As de Beauvoir (1949) argues, femininity is alterity and inferiority; the social Self is man, woman is the Other. The female body is the atypical, alter body *par excellence*, which—if we follow Levinas' view on alterity—stabilizes, solidifies, and reinforces the fragile, labile, and elusive Self (male): "Femininity *inhabits* masculinity, inhabits it as otherness, as its own *disruption*" (Felman 1993: 65, emphasis in original).

Within most premodern systems of governmentality, women's atypicality, otherness, and inferiority were predominantly conceptualized in (socio-)religious terms. When discourses of modernity by and large started to supplant religious discourses and governmentalities with "scientific" (e.g. medical) ones, the equation of the female with alterity became shrouded in seemingly "objective" discourses around female embodiment and the ensuing mainstream medical pathologization of female bodies in the nineteenth century. In fact, this discursive disabling of women (e.g. in the form of the construction of menstrual insanity and hysteria) begins much earlier than the late nineteenth century (e.g. see Kassell 2013 for the Modern Age; see also Cook 2004; Hall 2012). What is new during the Modern Age, with the onset of social liberation movements and feminism, is the full emergence to social consciousness how the sociocultural construction of the female body as atypical and deficient has been utilized in aid of a wider system of oppression. Through the different waves of feminisms (three to four, and counting) in the Global North over the period of the last 120 years, the marginalized atypical bodies demanded equality, agency, and self-determination. In the second half of the twentieth century, second-wave feminism in the Global North set out to dismantle all-pervading patriarchy, in particular the patriarchal oppression of women and the social construction of women (de Beauvoir's famous aphorism from 1949 *on ne naît pas femme: on le deviant*—"a woman is not born but made") in aid of male hegemony. Following on from this, third-wave feminisms broadened emancipatory impulses: liberation from oppression included the deconstruction of gender (from Women's Studies to Gender Studies and Queer Studies to Intersectional Social Justice). Hence, third-wave feminism pays closer attention to different areas of privilege, such as socioeconomic power and whiteness. (Fourth-wave feminism is a recent, somewhat contestable periodization for shifting foci in the 2010s toward persisting sexist violence; arguably, fourth-wave feminism is reprising some fundamental second-wave themes for the twenty-first century). All of these feminist, "dangerous" voices from the seemingly ever-decreasing margins have been—and are—threatening the patriarchal disabling of one half of humanity by the other.

1.3. TRANS/QUEER BODIES AND APHALLOPHOBIA

However, during the post-second-wave process of widening and complicating the emancipatory struggle, a rift appeared around the intersectional widening of the counter-patriarchal fight to include "queer bodies." While rifts in feminist stances in the 1980s centered around sex-positive versus anti-pornography feminists, from the 1990s onward, the most pronounced fissures in feminist communities of practice focused on "the loss of the woman" in feminism. Some self-proclaimed "radical feminists" announced their discomfort with Gender Studies, transgender liberation, and intersectional solidarity, identifying these themes as either distractions or, worse, as harmful "Trojan horses" of patriarchy. Indeed, the fight against patriarchy, they claimed and still claim, has been forgotten in third-wave (and, less so, fourth-wave) feminism.

Yet, in the fight against (hetero/cis-)patriarchy, contemporary queer-feminist resistance, solidarity, and ethics arguably necessarily address sexual and gender identity justice intersectionally in their complex interpellation with the messy wealth of identitarian markers and constructs inscribed onto individual bodies by, among other, reproductive-patriarchal, (neo)colonial, racist, nationalist, classist, ageist, ableist, and other socio-corporeal normative discourses. In contrast, some second-wave "radical feminists" need to answer the question of whether their retention of the binary construction of gender in criticism of queer theory and their trans-exclusivity in opposition to trans-solidarity, as well as their lack of reflection on their Global Northern/white privilege, are not constituting the real Trojan horse in the fight against sexism and patriarchy.

The meta-analysis of recent trans* mental health surveys in the Global North demonstrates an unrivaled and depressingly high prevalence of mental distress, suicidal ideation, experience of harassment, and violence among trans* people due to transphobia (Scherer 2014). I maintain that trans* mental health statistics show the clear symptomatic for the underlying wider system of oppression that so intimately links groups marginalized by patriarchal bio-politics. In the following, I argue that the misogynic-patriarchal "atypicality" construction of the female body is, in fact, the widest expression of a social phobia in aid of this oppression. I maintain that sexism and phobia of queer bodies (homo-, lesbo-, bi-, queer-, trans-, and intersex-phobia) form an inseparable nexus of bio-political oppression around the core mechanisms of patriarchy. I have termed this phobic matrix, with a half-ironic nod to Lacan, *aphallophobia*: the fear of the instability of gender binary power privileges or the fear of losing (straight, cis) male hegemony (*phallus*) as the systemic power broker of hetero/cis-patriarchy (Scherer 2014). To put it simply, patriarchy works in two steps: (1) reducing the human gender lexicon into binaries—male and female; and (2) claiming the superiority of one (male). Hence, any feminism that only opposes Step (2) is intrinsically weakened from the outset and adds credibility to the more fundamental premise of Step (1), aiding patriarchy in the process.

We may want to imagine the aphallophobic matrix as concentric layers of defense mechanisms against the attacks on hegemonic masculinity from its dangerous margins (Figure 1.1).

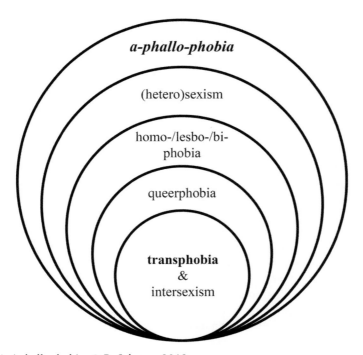

FIGURE 1.1 Aphallophobia. © B. Scherer, 2018.

Normative-oppressive masculinities are ever vulnerable and contested. The claimed superiority of masculinity above femininity means that maleness is in constant need of reasserting (Kimmel 1994), in a state of constant, struggling *becoming* rather than in state of simply relaxing into *Dasein* (being-in-time). Therefore, oppressive masculinities need to reassert themselves in sexism as reinforcing both binary and hierarchy. The link between misogyny/sexism and homophobia has long been established (e.g. see Pharr 1997; Rosky 2003; Anderson 2009): the abjection of atypical masculinities and femininities as blurring the binary distinction in the heart of patriarchy and the abjection of non-normative gender performances become necessary within the same framework of the sexist reinforcement of male hegemony. The blurring of the binarist construct of sex/gender and their pursuing of normativities includes the rejection of intra-gender desire and sexualities as transgressions and undermining binary-stabilizing gender norms and roles (domination/submission, penetration/reception). In its arguably most brutal form, aphallophobia expresses itself in transphobia and intersexism: the occurrence of non-, inter-, and trans-binary individuals with regard to biological sex and cultural gender is perceived as a frontal assault on the validity of the sex/gender binarism that lies at the heart of male privilege. Transition becomes the paradigmatic transgression: "atypical" intersex bodies are regularly surgically violated in infancy in order to achieve (in most case the de-phallic and "inferior"; i.e. female) gender binary status; in the case of trans* people, any "male-to-female" transition must be interpreted within the patriarchal-oppressive script as the abdication of the (superior) *phallus*, while any "female-to-male" affirmation must be interpreted as a usurpation of the *phallus*. Finally, nonbinary, androgynous, genderqueer, gender-fluid, and gender-rejecting identity performances appear as anarchic subversions of the *phallus*. Trans* invades the "ontological security" (Giddens 1991) implicated in cis-hetero-phallic patriarchy and becomes the nucleolic focus of threatened hegemonic masculinity.

Ironically, "TERFs" (so-called trans-exclusionary radical "feminists"—from Mary Daly to Germaine Greer to the emergence of the contemporary vocal minority of "feminists" who oppose trans* rights) employ a similar argument in order to refuse space and voice to transwomen; they claim that transwomen usurp and invade women (or "womyn": female-born women)-only spaces and embodiments. Yet it is not only the inclusion of gender diversities that has divided feminisms. The fundamental binary view on gender comes with dogmatic positions that have successfully filtered into policies and laws. The rise of "carceral feminism" (Bernstein 2010), neo-abolitionism (Wylie 2017), neo-puritan moral panics (Goode and Ben-Yehuda 2009), and "feminist violence" (Zalewski and Sisson Runyan 2013) is, unfortunately, not an imaginary phenomenon: feminist-derived forms of thought-policing, virtue signaling, reductionist moralizing, and, yes, oppression and systemic violence do exist. Harmful dogmatic positions include the "perpetual victimhood of women" in the bio-political and bio-legal systems; the consequences of this particular gender-essentializing political mytheme include, for example, rendering invisible (and even ridiculing) non-(cis-)female victims of intimate-partner and sexual violence. Other dogmata include what I term "homosecularism" and the harmfulness of religion per se (which we will address in the following section), the evils of sex work and sexual cinema ("pornography"), and the necessary oppressiveness of cultural and religious practices such as veiling and arranged marriages.

Against such dogmatic fundamentalism, third-wave feminists have successfully employed, among others, the concepts of "agency" and "privilege" in order to complicate and disrupt the reductionist views on gender and power relations, particularly in the intersectional contexts pointed out earlier. Returning to aphallophobia and to the curious case of TERFs, we may want to note that the very notion of a "trans-exclusionary radical feminism" is absurd within the wider aphallophobic framework. Not only is the term TERF itself a weird euphemism (would one want to term racists "white-only liberation fighters?"); more poignantly, excluding transwomen from womanhood is merely counterproductive, pseudo-feminist transphobia: it has become a rallying cry of dissatisfied, mainly white, middle-class, and socioeconomically privileged people who claim to be feminists and who claim to be fighting against patriarchal oppression. Yet, in fact, TERFs have unwittingly become the fifth column of patriarchy—the very system they claim to fight. Understanding the complex mechanism of heteropatriarchal oppression as conceptualized in aphallophobia, feminist advocacy, and activism must call out, challenge, and aim to eradicate all aphallophobic mechanisms and hence be inherently trans* and intersex inclusive. In line with the well-established power stratagem "*devide et impera*," hegemonic masculinity and patriarchy actively benefit from the compartmentalization of the oppressed in the form of TERF transphobia, as well as from trans-, bi-, and homo-normativities (the latter being the—nonstrategic—complicit, egoistic, and assimilationist adoptions of nuclear cis-heteronorms by lesbian, gay, bisexual, and trans* people).

1.4. ABRAHAM'S LOCKER: CLOSED NOÖSPHERES AND QUEER/CRIP-VERSITY

As indicated earlier, female and queer bodies that form the dangerous margins to the ontologically contested centers of socio-corporeal typicality function in multiple, complex, overlapping, hybrid, and intersecting ways within the multiverse of marginalized and dis-abled embodiments. The resilient reductionism by patriarchy of the human sex/gender lexicon into a binarism is a prime example of a successful ideologeme in the construction kit of closed mind-sets and worldviews. In constant tension with such closed noöspheres, atypical bodies inhabit queer noö- and anthropo-scapes within the constraints of oppressive bio-politics and governmentality. In this section, I would like to widen the focus on intersections between contested bodies and the particular brands of societal scripts that we have grown used to calling "religious," even though no satisfactory definition of "religion" exists (and can exist). Cultural-traditional scripts and systems of symbols we call "religions" often function as such closed noöspheres, reinforcing cis-hetero-patriarchal normativities and oppression in direct or indirect/vestigial (Goldenberg 2015) governmental regimes. Spiritual practices can translate into "spiritual bypassing" (e.g. see Masters 2010) of suffering and victimization as "merited" and/or individual "trials" on the road to spiritual advancement and transformation (such as sainthood or enlightenment). I use the term "Abraham's locker" in order to describe the roles that cultural traditions and systems of symbols play in complicity with or as dominant systems of oppression or vestigial forms of governmentality of variable bodies: the axiomatic and premised ontological and metaphysical certainties espoused in dogmatic true/false claims necessitating a "leap of faith" (in Kierkegaard's terms)—as with Abraham's willingness to sacrifice his son Isaac in *Bərēšīṭ/Genesis* 22 and *Qur'ān* 37, 100–13. Such premodern and modern leaps of faith tend to create closed noöspheres against and at odds with intersectional, postmodern openness.

The term "Abraham's locker" refers to the cultural implication of religious (often, but not limited to, Jewish, Christian, and Islamic elective monotheist) true/false dichotomies and supersessions or suspensions of ethical judgments by faith and metaphysics. The cultural philosopher Jan Assmann (2009) calls this the "Mosaic Distinction," the religious shift from a pure/impure dichotomy to a true/false dichotomy. Critiques of monotheism have claimed that the consequences of such closed religious noöspheres are oppression and violence (Assmann does not claim monotheism to be the sole cause of hatred, violence, and discrimination in the world as other critics of desert monotheism do; e.g. Schwartz 1997). Queer atypical bodies are therefore often constructed as being in natural tension with "religions" as (vestigial) forms of governmentalities, and religious gender/sex/sexuality/body nonconforming people are viewed as suffering from some contemporary version of "Stockholm syndrome." For lesbians, gays, and bisexuals, this can be theorized as "homosecularism"—a compulsory complicity in anti-religious discourses of modernity. In consequence, queer and "crip" sometimes appear to compete in victimhood with atypical religious embodiments expressed in clothes, body modifications (such as genital cuttings/circumcisions, piercings, tattooing, etc.), or dietary rules.

Yet, it is useful to be reminded that victimization does not automatically imply sainthood. Moreover, embodied non-normativity can, in complex ways, include religious non-normative embodiment (e.g. see Amesbury 2016) and can interact with symbolic orders of belonging and yearning; indeed, constructive forms of queer-religious embodiments and identity performances can emerge (e.g. Comstock and Henking 1997; Thumma and Gray 2005; Wilcox 2009; Boisvert and Johnson 2012). Nancy Eiesland's trailblazing Christian Liberation Theology of Disability (Eiesland 1994) shows the potential of religion-based counter-narratives to closed and ableist noöspheres. One danger when theorizing corporeal atypicality in relation to "religion" is the fallacy of accepting the internal premises of Abraham's locker and viewing any and every form of religious agency as beyond the reach of nonreligious ethics and value judgments. Religions as cultural systems of symbols are neither good nor bad: they simply *are (there)* and are morally protean. This means that religiously produced body atypicality can be justifiably judged according to principles such as physical integrity and informed, empowered consent. In consequence, certain cultural-religious practices can be problematized, such as female genital cuttings, but also the Jewish, Islamic, and, in North America, post-religious practice(s) of infant male genital mutilation/circumcision. There are, indeed, harmful embodied "religious" discourses, and there is a need for critical parameters around religious and limited-agentive embodiment—such as informed, empowered consent and physical self-determination (Scherer 2017).

Variable bodies—religious, queer, "crip," etc.—cease their atypicality when the center that creates the margins implodes and the multiversity of messy, intersectional, and complex human identitarian embodiments is accepted as de/post-hegemonic spaces in ways that echo Antke Engel's concept of *queerversity* (2013: 39) and Doris Leibetseder's derived notion of *cripversity*: not only dismantling "hierarchies and structural inequalities," but also recognizing "differences, which elude categorization" (Leibetseder 2016: 142).

1.5. BUDDHIST CROSSROADS: ENLIGHTENED IDIOSYNCRASIES AND PARA-ONTOLOGICAL PATHWAYS

Contemporary Christian theologians have looked at the Buddhist understandings of pain (*duḥkha*) and at Buddhist practices as dialogical engines for the development of a liberatory Christian Practical Theology of "Disability" (Farley 1999; Betcher 2014: ch. 3, 68–106).

Both Christian and Buddhist practices have been explored in their potential for spiritual meaning-making and transformation in relation to the experience of chronic illness and disability (e.g. Schumm and Stoltzfus 2007).

As a scholar of Buddhism and a Buddhist constructive-critical thinker, I see an intriguing kinship between the philosophical dilemmas and tensions produced by Critical Theory and its signifiers/signifying such as "self–other," "center–margin," and "inequality–justice," and core Buddhist philosophical questions around identity and lack. Buddhist philosophy in its fundamental teachings—the Four Ennobling/Noble Truths— starts at the both embodied and systemic experience of "suffering"—unsatisfactoriness (*duḥkha*): pain, change, and contingency. The ultimate cause of this "suffering" is "craving," which, on the most fundamental level, is the attachment to the wrong idea of a stable, independent, inherently existing Self. This tenet of "No-Self" (*anātman*) is a cornerstone of Buddhist thought. Following from this, Buddhist methods are addressing concrete and systemic human experiences of unsatisfactoriness. Such practices include methods of ego-distancing, transcending ego, and transformative experiences of "No-Self" embodiment in action. Trans-egoïc active compassion is trained by means of ethic cultivation and meditation/trance awareness of both the loving interconnectedness and the openness/emptiness (*śūnyatā*) of inherent existence as inseparable. Core Buddhist notions including No-Self, impermanence (*anitya*), and openness/emptiness have invited the comparison with recent and contemporary poststructuralist, postmodern, and Critical Theory thought (e.g. see Wang 2001; Park 2006, 2011; Konik 2009; Boon et al. 2015; Ng 2016; on Buddhism and Queer Theory, see Scherer 2016b). Identity and personhood, in Buddhist thought, can never be statically fixed and essentialized; both the most distressing experience and the most privileged embodiments contain the certainty of change and the opportunity for transformation.

Romance languages such as Spanish and Italian differentiate between static and transitional "being": *ser* vs. *estar* (Spanish) and *essere* vs. *stare* (Italian). From a Buddhist para-ontological point of view, static verbs for "to be" do not make philosophical sense: "being" is always pointing to a "being now" on the way to something else in the future; "to be" points to contingent glimpses of stadia of becoming; there is only *estar/stare*, no *ser/essere*. The constructs and societal scripts that drive marginalization and stigma are in constant flux, in the same way as our delusion of a core self: identities and categories expressed within or against societal scripts are ultimately empty of inherent existence. They are staged within frameworks—*performed* in the terms of Queer Theory. Buddhist texts point in abundance to the ultimate emptiness of categories such as gender, class, and body normativities. Subsequently, Buddhist thought and practice (i.e. "praxis") is invested in extending post-self-ethics by creating the space in any given moment to enact identity performances with a view to overcoming demeritorious ego-clinging and to the training of relaxing into trans-egoïc awareness and transformation—enlightenment (*bodhi*). Unsurprisingly, in global Buddhist modernity, variable-bodied Buddhist practitioners and thinkers have successfully utilized the (para-)ontological openness that Buddhist praxis affords, including Joan Tollifson (1996) in *Bare-Bones Meditation* and Lorenzo Milam (1993) in *CripZen: A Manual for Survival*.

There is, however, an important contingency to Buddhist deconstruction and Buddhism's innately pedagogical (para-)ontology: even in its most deconstructive modes, Buddhist thought is always tightly ethically framed—it deconstructs our notions of static Self and personhood only to enable more space for post-egoïc virtuous activity for the benefit and enlightenment of all. Hence, taking No-Self and openness/emptiness seriously means that, ultimately, the enlightened activities must entail the elimination of any suffering produced by the arbitrary societal scripts of identity essentialisms.

Whatever the given cultural construction of normalcy, typicality, and center, Buddhist thought focuses on the interdependency (*pratītyasamutpāda*): the transient, interconnected and codependently arisen nature of identity concepts and performances. The one center that Buddhist thought appears to produce is practical-ethical: virtue-focused Buddhist philosophies see embodiment as fields of virtuosity—Buddhism constructs "virtuous bodies" (Mrozik 2007). In consequence, the social reality and practice of Buddhist atypical/variable bodies, both in premodern and (post)modern times, is sometimes in tension with Buddhist soteriology, ideal, and thought (Scherer 2016a). Buddhist bodies are physio-morally inscribed, and non-virtuous behavior is often directly connected to detrimental physical variability. For example, a stock phrase in the Pali Buddhist canon combines variable body attributes as groups of karmatic abjection as follows: "ugly/inferior class, unsightly, deformed, diseased, or blind or crooked or lame or paralyzed" (*Vinaya* ii 90, etc.; see Scherer 2016a: 253). However, spiritual progress and transformation are not necessarily affected by dis/variability (ibid.: 256). A different, socially agentive angle on atypical Buddhist embodiments is found in the construction of variable bodies as opportunities for the accumulation of merit (*puṇya-sambhāra*) for the actualization of Buddhist loving-kindness (ibid.: 252–3).

From a critical (and possibly modernist) Buddhist point of view, the decisive impulse in Buddhist philosophy and practice in relation to atypical bodies is that any construction of a linear personal causal genealogy of such (dis)virtuous fields in terms of guilt and sin is decisively interrupted and voided by the understanding of *karma* (cause and effect) as a causal nexus without static essence, Self, or soul: the Buddhist concept of rebirth and re-becoming without a Self is simply *continuity without identity*. (Re)births and human existences express both the weaving together of multiple causes and conditions and the free actualization of potential(itie)s. However, on the popular level of moral governmentality, Buddhist civilizations have approached and often are still approaching dis/variabilities with reductionist simplicities as embodiments of non-virtue. This ignores the important point that the individual experiencers of any variability are simply expressing a complex, non-personal nexus of past potentials: all of our variable present states contain the promise and opportunity for expressing interpersonal virtue and trans-egoïc enlightenment in the future.

Social justice depends on the deconstruction of the typical and, ultimately, on the abandonment of the unobtainable Lakoffian prototype ideal (Lakoff 1987) in favor of the radical acceptance of de/post-hegemonic human variabilities, "*same, only different*":

> varyingly performed embodiment, flowing from time and space and context and situation. Inhabiting such variable anthroposcapes without centre and margin restores the possibility of (biographically fluid or relatively static) individual body-performances without creating oppressive body-normativities. (Scherer 2016a: 262)

Buddhist philosophies around No-Self and interdependency can inspire and enhance contemporary social theories and post-normative utopias of decentralized, rhizomatic landscapes of variability. Embracing and utilizing identitarian insecurity and flux, we *inter(c)are* (to adapt *interbeing*, the concept popularized by the Vietnamese Buddhist master Thich Nhat Hanh). Through interbeing and intercaring, we are able to perform trans-egoïc loving-kindness in non-colonizing and non-domineering solidarity.

CHAPTER TWO

Mobility Impairment

Impairing Mobilities Into the Twenty-first Century

FIONA KUMARI CAMPBELL

Mobility impairment—what the heck does this mean? The phrase appears self-evident, yet upon reflection is somewhat stark and elusive. What does this signifier refer to and draw in? What is emitted or excluded? Are we referring to a description, a categorical imperative, or something else more porous that opens up new explorations about modernity's ethos? As this volume is part of a disability series, a question beckons as to the ways the signifier *Mobility Impairment* frames contemporary disability, ablement,[1] and contestations around space and motility. Is mobility's opposition to presumed impairment co-relational or antagonistic, maybe even oxymoronic? This crude ambivalence toward variable bodies tends only to be released through practices of amelioration, correction, passing, and/or mitigation. A methodological choice is required to either retain this pairing or instead to work within the aporias of splitting and consider the sequestering inheritances of the twentieth century (roughly from 1917 onward) that these markings produce. This chapter opts for the latter—that of *critical disruption*, to act as an encounter that spotlights tensions and lacunae and ultimately provides a clarion call to make mobility a staple component in the renewal of politics in the twenty-first century, a politics that sets aside the endowment of improvability so imperative to ableist relations and the promulgation of the dividing practices of ablement.

Mobility, as an index of social advancement in contrast to income security or labor market participation, does not initially appear to be central to well-being and equality.[2] Like other elusive variables, it is only when drilling down that mobility can be found to be integral to the question of life itself and how equality of opportunity can be facilitated by peripheral peoples (see Langan 2001; Charlton 2010). This chapter will engage in a philosophical dialogue rooted in the etymological branches of certain associated words surrounding "mobility impairment." Each of these branches crisscross other issues pitting the landscape of modernity's conditions and ruptures. Embracing a snowballing of associations, the chapter explores some contemporary sites of culture wars over ablement and the demarcation of disability and peripheral lives. Some issues reveal deep cinctures of uneasiness and the precarious state of mobility ablement and disablement, as not all

---

This chapter is dedicated to Professor Susan Schweik, who would not let distance become a barrier to exercising compassion. I hope to pay her generosity onward.

mobilities are considered equal. For example, on the road, the mobility scooter is seen as a disability apparatus resulting in the vetting of the bodies of riders, in contrast to investments in compulsory walking in the assessment of social security benefits.

2.1. ETYMOLOGICAL RULES AND DESTINATIONS

Do you know where you are going today and how you will get there or whether you have the prerequisite papers[3] to pass through border control? Maybe this is not something that you give a lot of thought, since to be free means that you can exercise a degree of spontaneity, subject to the travails of the weather, traffic, or transportation timetables. This utility of one's heart, mind, and body are captured by the Enlightenment ideal of the primacy of reason, wherein the body acts as a command center, a superlative of *possessive individualism* as denoted by political philosopher C. B. MacPherson (1964):

> [We are] free in as much as he [sic] is proprietor of his person and capacities. *The human essence is freedom from dependence on the will of others, and freedom is a function of possession* …. Society consists of relations of exchange *between proprietors.*

Possessive individualism is a fiction for the multitude and somewhat of a seductive fantasy that suggests atomism is possible or indeed desirable, assaulting the fundamental precepts of coproduction and interdependency while simultaneously denying and defiling the differential experiences of peripheral and subaltern populations, including slaves, indentured laborers, women, disabled people, the colonized, the displaced who roam earthly borders, and those unfortunate enough to be in poverty. Not only is the daily reality for many folks filled with microaggressions and violence; the fantasy of possessive individualism is also inherently violent as a coercive falsehood and extortion, as Weiwei has demonstrated in the documentary film *Human Flow* (2017). A symptom and outcome of ableist processes, possessive individualism exudes a *compulsory ablement* that compels and propels the inauguration of a dynamic promise suggesting ablement is in reach for all—the entitled as well as the abject. Anti-mobility is associated with moral poverty, either individually, typified as the scrounging welfare recipient, or communally, through the assignation of lazy nations that required colonization.

An abled imaginary relies upon the existence of an unacknowledged imagined shared community of able-bodied/minded people, held together by a common ableist homosocial worldview that asserts the *preferability* of the norms of ableism, often asserted by way of political codes of citizenship, including nation building and the idea of the "productivity of the multitude" (Hardt and Negri 2005). Such ableist trajectories erase differences in the ways humans express our emotions, use our thinking, and achieve motility in different cultural spaces and situations. As a practice, ableism, at least in the West, demands and is obsessed (see Davis 2008) with an unbridled form of individualism that is preoccupied with continuous self-improvement and corporeal enhancement (fit, benchmarked, and upgradeable bodies) that struggles with the reality of illness, disability, and contingency. Ableism is married to a sense of permanency, a sense of the unity of the idealized, stabilized, assessed, and ranked human form. Ableism is implicated in racism, sexism, casteism, and practices of humiliation (see Gopal 2011). With the development of enhancement technologies (e.g. cosmetic neurology and surgery), coupled to the wrappings of mobility technologies, the notion of the norm is constantly sliding, perhaps creating a larger pool of "abnormal" persons who, because of "choice" or limited resources, cannot "improve" themselves and hence lapse into deficiency, becoming locked-ins—leaners, sloths, the lazy. Indeed, the sloth is emblematic of the paradox of a cringing slowness and docility, symbolized in Christianity's *seven deadly sins*, yet it is also appealing to dispositions of thoughtfulness and consideration; as Martel notes, "all living things contain a measure of madness that moves them in strange, sometimes inexplicable ways" (Martel 2012: 4). Embracing the sloth, we will move slowly and thoughtfully with panache to explore impairments of mobility.

The inexplicability of mobility impairment is not just a disability issue—there are many faces of abledment, including caste disability resulting in a crushing captivity or containment of movement. In *"I'm Born to Do This": Condemned by Caste, India's Sewer Cleaners Condemned to Death*, Safi (2018) documents the lives of the Valmiki caste whose mobility is restrained by the Hindu caste system to manual scavenging or, put more simply, to manually empty toilets and cleaning septic systems by hand without protection. Paradoxically, there is daily mobility, where "low-caste" women visit multiple houses cleaning waste from deep-hole toilets and moving it to a central disposal site. Ironically, India's rail ministry is the largest employer of manual scavengers.

2.1.1. Boundaries–destinations

Mobility, of course, conjures up movements through environments in a contained way as a bystander or, conversely, mobility within environments co-relationally. Yet we are duped by the idea of a "free world," a kind of Kantian cosmopolitan fantasy wherein exists multiple global worlds with uninhibited exchanges of belonging and intermingling. We are witnessing a particular moment in history when there are great movements and flows of people across the globe struggling to cross nation-state borders to flee persecution and live safe lives. Simultaneously, there is *reterritorialization* by governments bent on securing borders (e.g. Trump's Mexican wall, European fences, the inclinations of Brexit, Australian border control), as well as the reterritorialization of access to benefits and safety nets (UK benefit [re]assessments, the narrowing of disability laws, and Australia's robodebt, to name a few) within nations. There is now *mobility-edutainment* streaming into home television networks sensitizing viewers to regimes of mobility policing. Programs like *Border Patrol* (New Zealand), *UK Border Force*, and *Border Security America's Front Line* regularly show the catching and interrogating of intruders. The UK seems to have a particular obsession with cultivating an incitement to *defensive Othering* in its broadcasting of programs in which people on the margins are trying to live and move in communities, with programs auspiciously titled *The Big Benefit Handout* and *Benefit Street*. The vicious circle of being locked out or restricted in the rental market, whereby women and children become serial movers constantly on the move from place to place without destination, often ending in homelessness, becomes *voyeur-tainment* in shows with emotive titles: *Council House Crackdown*, *The Housing Enforcers*, and *Nightmare Tenants, Slum Landlords*. Such satiations contribute to the territorialization of people's minds and a disassociation from the struggles of others.

The theorization of ableism points to processes that involve *"differentiation, ranking, negation, notification* and *prioritization* of sentient life" (Campbell 2017: 287–8). These five aspects have a bearing on ways that ableist processes are implicated in dividing practices based on the *productivity of the multitude* and the intersectionalities of gender, race, caste, class, and disability, aligned with subject-positions and bodies deemed as normative benchmarks for the building of nation-states and the delineation of "who" is a productive, unencumbered citizen—designating which lives are grievable and which are deemed disposable. Mobility constraints can also impact on rich and poor alike through *notifications* (e.g. legal definitions of sexual behavior) like the global *Pink Line*, which demarcates where LGBTI folk can live and travel, be safe, or be killed. The instrument of *differentiation* is law. Laws, that Lord Chris Smith remarked on as being shameful, having a "continued existence of discrimination, violence and criminalisation in so many Commonwealth countries. [There is a] bitter irony in the fact that the discriminatory laws in these countries were inherited from us [the UK]" (Gevisser 2018). Saudi women who are reduced to the status of a "child" are caught up in a dragnet of a male guardianship surveillance via a phone app called *Absher*, ironically meaning "good tidings," which tracks women's mobility and travel (Bishop 2012). Elsewhere, I have written about *geodisability knowledges* that promote themselves as universal mobile objects for the counting and classification of health and disablement (Campbell 2014). So, all is not as it seems. Mobility is a relation that is interfered with, interrupted, and subjected to interventions that are recalled in truth to power relations within the context of idealized, *able*ment bodies. It is necessary to unimagine and disinherit the canon of pervasive binary thinking of disability/ability that must be thought of as a problem and instead to think about borders and passages, placed as *aporias*, where "there can be no barrier that protects itself or separates itself from something else" (Abeysekara 2011: 24). This is particularly urgent for research in its treatment of social ordering around citizenship, displacement, and productive embodiment, as well as the diminution of relations of societal power. Instead of twofold binary demarcations, it might be more useful to think in terms of tracks, flows, journeys, and boundaries regarding destinations.

Mobility contains an assumption of a destination wherein there is a legitimacy of actions contrasting with those of the wanderer in his/her aimless journey. There is a built-in barometer of *legitimation*, qualifying how time is used and spent. In effect, is mobility and motility *purposive*? What does one "do" at the destination? How does one occupy that space—as onlooker, a flaneur—and are these roles considered as contributory or as burdensome? This is no mere vague assertion. "Matter out of place" does seriously matter, as Keith Halfacree (1996) confirms in *Out of Place in the Country: Travellers and the "Rural Idyll"*, demonstrating that English legislation was used to rein in trespassers on the idyllic countryside. Cast as "folk devils," these travelers cannot merely be allowed to wander and contaminate the exclusivity of the English countryside. The image of nomads as being *space invaders* shows that, far from being seen as intrusions on tranquility, the "outsider" presence reveals the way possessive ableist normativity claims space–time distantiation, relegating others to inferior outsiderness (Kabachnik 2010). There is a danger in casting spatio-human regulation as an old problem or as a new problem—it is more likely to be a continuous problem. A 2017 report in *Fortune Magazine*, "What You Don't Know, But Should, About the Slave Trade Happening in Libya Right Now," narrates the indignation and shock about a report from CNN on migrants stuck in Libya being sold into the slave trade. As shocking as this is, the *African Security Review* published research in 2003 about this trade in an article entitled "Modern-Day Slavery? The Scope of Trafficking in Persons in Africa" (Fitzgibbon 2003), which suggests an epistemological *negation* in the sidelining of a Global South journal in the passing of fourteen years!

Long ago (before 1400), the idea of *destination, destynacyone*,[4] literally meant *destroy*, later being apprehended to denote an *intention*. It was only by around 1787, at the birth of the Industrial Revolution—a time of hope and belief in progress—that *destination* became a "place where a person or thing is *destined.*" *Destiny* allows certain bodies (particularly white, abled, male, propertied classes) to dream—or in the case of disability, signifying the Enlightenment's recidivist element, to *denigrate* (Barnhart 2015: 270). As Giddens (1990: 2) rightly points out, modernity moved from a system based upon the manufacture of goods to an ethos where information became central and generative. This shift had consequences for thinking about mobility and the combustion of a new vitality, an atmosphere captured by Gretton (1913: 11): "[of a] people busy at accumulating and increasing its power, and its capacity for the absorption of material supplies and of ideas … an explosion of energy, an expression of stored force, a revelation of movement."

Modernity ushered in a particularized style of boundary-drawing, although there is less agreement on whether these boundaries are permeable or result in the reconstituting of space with the idea of enclosure and anomaly. Clayton observes that "there are real boundaries to be analyzed, real contrasts to be understood, real walls to be broken down. The deeper answer to the boundaries question is to acknowledge difference— even irreconcilable and permanent difference—yet in such a way that the two halves of the difference being referenced are co-constituted by their relationship with each other" (Clayton 2007: 95). Alas, mobility from on-high-the-eye in the sky allows us to visualize in-depth mobilities of human suffering (the 4.4 million asylum applications that were lodged with forty-four countries during 2013–16) on an interactive map, whereby each point (dot) on the map represents 500 people as they travel from their country of origin to the destination of application (Metrocosm 2017). At the same time, technologies can inoculate against a sense of agency via precision-guided munitions that enable the seeing of even smaller targets for aerial bombings, "mistakes" being reduced to *collateral damage* (Zehfuss 2011).

Still, destinations are not a simple matter of getting from point A to point B as if routes adhere to the symmetries of landscape. Time–space distantiation is conditioned by economies of efficacy and does not necessarily reflect the most direct and quick routes; rather, it is ensconced in the time–space zoning of social life, the abled body, becoming "locales … thoroughly penetrated by and shaped in term of social influences quite distant from them" (Giddens 1990: 19). This chartering through the *haze of the maze* produces apartheid systems of differentiation and ranking associated with bodily differences of class, disability, heteronormativity, and comportment, increasingly operating as enclosures of conviviality. Air travel, and progressively train travel, at least in the UK, is corralled for those who can afford it. Ryanair, a low-cost carrier, now charges extra for guaranteeing that family groups can sit together. Buses become the mode of transport for those on social security benefits, students, and tourists. Whereas the mode of transport remains stable, mobility distantiation is constantly being remade. This has not always been the case—look up the series of posters on the web produced by Greyhound buses from around the 1950s for marketing travel (Figure 2.1). You will find heaps of images of the inside of a greyhound bus with passengers aligned, seated in vertical rows in conversation with others across the bus seating aisles, capsule images of "friends"—but these friends appear to be *mirror images of each other*—of apparently abled, white, heteronormative clusters (possibly wives and husbands) wearing middle-class attire. Yes, there are spaces, seats yet to be filled, but would a person of color, a disabled person or a rough sleeper dare to step on board and upset this friendly ambience? These poster images foreclose diversity of mobility because they are cocooned by invisible captioned borders that make it clear that commonality—homosociality—is the rite of passage onto the bus.

FIGURE 2.1 Relax- as You See- as You Save by Greyhound, 1951

In an era of racial segregation, the mobility of bus travel is a *shared space*—"who" can comingle and sit together on buses has been much contested and resisted (Kohl 1993). Black rights activist Rosa Parks drew attention to this differentiated space, a space that *made* her *mobility impaired*, when on the evening of December 1, 1955, bus driver James Blake ordered her to give up her seat to a white passenger and she refused (Kohl 1993; Theoharis 2015). Blake had previously evicted Parks from buses, but this time he sought her arrest. Parks called out this vehicular apartheid, asking her arresting officers, "Why do you push us around?" One officer answered, "I don't know, but the law is the law and you're under arrest" (Theoharis 2015). Ironically, today in many urban cities it is mainly black or minority ethnic people who ride buses, even Greyhounds! For those with physical disabilities, the sheer activity of getting onto a bus presents an impossibility—technical design based on an *assumed* passenger ablement ensures that disabled people are locked out of entry to this communal automotive space.[5] More often, should that disabled person breach this entrance barrier, they are confronted by the stares and discomfort of other passengers, making this bus not such a friendly place! In fact, even on accessible commercial buses the lift is placed in the back, and wheelchair users are parked and secured behind everyone else. Poet Anna Woodward captured this experience of ambivalence in a research project "Poetry in Motion" that explored the links between mobility and well-being among older people. In her poem "(T)here (i)," Woodward (2018) asks us to imagine a disabled person in a chair or using an assistive *device* who is no longer able to drive. As they walk, they may fall in the street. In getting assistance, they also are faced with intimidating and violating questions about their right to venture outside of their homes. Faced with this inference on the part of the bystander, distressed, the disabled person decides it is best to go home.

On foot, or wheels, or with or without a service animal, destinations—via various ambulations—are far from straightforward; public or private roads, pathways or the lack thereof, cobblestones, physical barriers, and shared spaces can make travel to destiny/nations precarious. In Australia, airlines have an apartheid system of travel, with Jetstar, Virgin, and Tiger airways each having a two wheelchairs rule per flight, meaning that only two wheelchair users can board any one flight and have their chairs stowed in cargo.[6] Destinations, for some, defy the quickest routes on satnav devices, requiring supplementation of these devices with disability mobility access maps (see wheelmap. org), or using Haptomai, customizable tactile maps for blind people (https://vimeo. com/78562730), inaugurating the world of parallel or *alt-spaces* wherein reality is infused with occurrences of taking *the crooked road traveled*: roundabout ways, backways, through kitchens and basements and indirect routes—that is the destiny of achieving so-called accessible destinations. Chances are, you have never visited this particular "our/place."

Homelands of ablement are effectively disembedded and common routes are essentially "lifted out" of social relations from local contexts of interaction (Giddens 1990). With enough interlopers shredding the porous walls to the sounds of "slew the floodgates, breach the dikes," making boundaries and barriers penetrable, we can see transgression, and when mobility access is expanded, such commonplace traveling acts as destinations for multiple crossings (Clayton 2007)—but we have a long way to go for this to become a reality in the majority world. The *prioritization* of ableist relations was challenged recently by Australia's Human Rights Commission, when the Queensland Rail Authority attempted to gain an exemption under the Disability Discrimination Act 1992 during the Commonwealth Games for its new rail stock that has pathways and toilets that are too narrow for wheelchairs. The government had provisioned the previous three years for transportation companies to comply with the legislation and, concerned that the government had procured noncompliant trains, the Commission has refused to grant an exemption under the Act (Caldwell 2018).

Before closing our discussion of destinations, or destiny/nations, I want to pick up on the idea of *destiny*. Destiny is temporal and future bound, invoking "purpose, intent, fate, that which is destined." The idea of destiny, suggested by Niebuhr (1998), is integral to the foundation of Anglo-American relations and the attempt to build democratic, inclusive communities. Destiny appended to notions of virtue and grace (a providence, chosenness, entitlement) recognizes the moral element of power. Marginalized communities may have very different experiences of organizing time in daily life, and ideas of looking beyond the immediate present to a "future" might seem impossible—what Warin et al. (2015) in their discussion of the difficulties of health promotion within deprived communities call "short horizons." A focus on the urgencies of the day today—on getting through the day—often precludes any sense of organizing or imagining tomorrow, or any future. Are disabled people thought of as having destinies or accorded some semblance of futurity? Futurity for disabled people, practically and philosophically, is a vexed question. For disability, imagining *otherwise* is a conflicted zone—there is no future existence, disability positivity is expunged, and the utopian drive is a device of promise (of curability) and quite possibly extinction. So, we are faced with the conundrum of invisibility and a lack of recognition of disability positivity in the present and, at the same time, an erasure or diminished imagination of our anticipated futures (Kafer 2013; Ginsburg and Rapp 2015; Campbell 2017). Disability is the unwelcome guest at the table of liberalism.

Crip theory has attempted to explore futurity. Jose Esteban Muñoz, in speculating about the absence of a queer imagination, elicits a desire to engage in a *queer horizon*: utopian hermeneutics where reimagining futurity requires that "the not quite conscious is the realm of potentiality that must be called upon" (Muñoz 2009: 453). The distance between imagination and potentiality means that "queerness is not quite here." I suggest that holding queerness in a sort of ontologically humble state under a conceptual grid wherein we do not claim to always already know queerness in the world potentially staves off the ossifying effects of neoliberal ideology. Is this the kind of destiny that disabled people can hold on to as well? In later work, Muñoz (2009: 9) speaks in terms of potentiality being a "certain mode of non-being that is eminent, a thing that is present but not actually existing in the present tense." This promise provokes an inquiry—when will the bus or train arrive, and when it does, will we be able to get on? Hence, the characteristics of potentiality are embodied in a *sense of surprise*, not necessarily an expectation or engagement in the processes of reparation. Even when security is assured by way of legislative promises of accessibility targets, international histories have shown us that the security of equalities has been compromised through the winding back of legislative gains on the basis of economic priorities trumping so-called distributive justice.

How does a *crip horizon* come to be dreamed of in the context of having mobile futures? Living in the now and not yet, as outsiders not quite inside, requires a disposition or habit of contemporariness in the pursuit of a destination. At the heart of destination is a bigger existential question about this life and potential afterlives. Dominant in many places is the belief of accepting what life throws at us in the hope that an equality of redemption takes place in the next life, producing a kind of virtuous suffering (Eiesland 1994). Being a rule breaker—because this chapter is meant to be period restricted—I want to put out an alternative view of destiny and destination espoused centuries ago. In the Buddhist narrative of enlightenment, the idea of *samvega* emerges and is useful when thinking about the reception of mobility and destination.

The word *samvega* is used to express the emotions that the young Prince Siddhattha (latter to be recognized as a Buddha) felt on his first exposure to ageing, illness, and death. *Samvega* covers such a complex range of feelings experienced simultaneously: the oppressive sense of shock, dismay, and alienation that come with realizing the futility and meaninglessness of life as it is *normatively understood*, as well as a humbled sense of our own complacency and foolishness in having let ourselves live under such delusions (recalling MacPherson's idea of *possessive individualism*). *Samvega* does not slide into despair because *samvega* is an inclination toward "mindful trepidation" involving agitation, alarm, fear, and a sense of compulsive oppression. What does this story tell us? When the to-be Buddha observed humanity's tendency toward sickness, ageing, and eventually death, these states of being—dynamics of mobility impairment—he correctly observed were not aberrations, but *parts of the cycle of existence*. The impulse into *samvega* confronts the reality of the lie of ableist perfections[7] that denies the existence of *immobility* or has some compensatory measure to get around it, like cosmetic surgery and morphing and enhancement technologies, inclusive of the quest for the elixir of eternal youth. The Buddha's realization of this ignorance is a reminder of the futility of pursuing perfection and an "anxiousness to find a way out of the meaningless cycle" (Thanissaro 1997). The movement to *pasada*—a sense of "clarity and serene confidence"—about the manifestations of ableist practices to resist despair can be a mechanism to realize the unavailability of normative compulsions that, upon realization, begin to be reframed at that moment of realization/awakening. It is important at this point to mention that the Buddha's shock in seeing ageing, illness, and disability did not transmogrify into abhorrence. Rather, his sensing of disability's ubiquity produced a wellspring of compassion regarding the challenges of journeying throughout life.

2.2. VANGUARD MOVEMENTS AND THE RABBLING CROWDS OF MOBILITY

Etymological digs can be fascinating, not just in locating the origins of words and changes to their rendering over time, but also in allowing the academic, who often has to work precisely with materials, to play a little. In other work (Campbell 2017), I engage with the possibilities of the etymology of "rash," as disabled people are often conceived of as being rash, or at least narcissists. There I moved to reappropriate an old 1570 delineation that targeted *savage women* who formed *rash projects*. I like *rash projects*—they feel very subversive and irresponsible! Of course, it is very difficult to conceive of any linkage between rashness and mobility when it comes to disability, as we are normally disciplined by contingency; scarcity denies us in many cases any sense of spontaneity.

Mobilitas designates not just being "moveable," but also the *state or quality* of being mobile, so there is something very phenomenologically textured about it. *Sensescapes* draw attention to disabled people's distinctive sensory experiences of movement, which materialize our social existence, drawing in social relations, emotions, and actions of the body as expressed in the poetry of Anna Woodward and, later on in this chapter, by Nick Nicolls (Gaete-Reyes 2015). Going back in time to 1153, the emphasis of *mobilis* is on being easily moved, a fluidity that is not viscous or firm. Fluidity, however, is suggestive of a vulnerability of being mobile. In the next rendition, *mobilis* asserts that which is "easily influenced, changeable, fickle, readily stirred, and versatile." Similarly, at this time, "mobile" (*mobile vulgus*), at least in 1154, turns to a perception of *threat* on the part of the propertied classes: "the fickle crowd, the mob; the populace [a swill of heaving masses]! [or] … *mobilitate viget*—changeability assumes a fickleness or inconsistency" (Lewis 1991: 511).

All of these different nuances of *mobility* provide rich backgrounds for discerning the underbelly of mobility impairments. I am struck by the shifts in the idea of mobility in the eighteenth century, which births a sensibility with a notion of *personal agency*, the impressing of ability. The conditions of industrialization no doubt provoked impulses and the necessity for factory workers to "get with the flow." *Mobility* denoted the "ability to move or be moved with an ease or freedom of movement, [ensuring that one had the capacity] to change easily or quickly"—to be pliable as an abled body for hire (Brown 1993: 1800). We really have a form of mobility that is transmogrified from its earlier, somewhat transgressive roots to that where active citizenship is constituted by way of relations to objects, subjects, and places, which, in turn, figure citizenship in terms of status and as a set of object relations (Spinney et al. 2015). As Spinney et al. describe, "Different mobility practices, materialities and technologies inform the ways in which movement makes up the subject" (2015: 326). The development of many prosthetic devices was not about mobility per se, but was aimed at getting men back to work and securing normalization after the World Wars of the twentieth century (Ryan 1918; Serlin 2004).

Disability evokes dramatic responses that display a moral sensibility when applied to the context of mobility and the entry into social spaces. In earlier work (Campbell 2009), I describe technologies as *evoking ontologies* because technologies, following the insights of philosopher Martin Heidegger, are essentially *characterological*. The creators or institutional drivers of certain technologies impart in the objects' design or purpose a character reflecting particular time-laden values—technology reveals something about the conditions of society (Heidegger 1977). This characterological nature is described by McGinn:

> Some significant features of the technic are due primarily to the technologist working of his or her will on the constituent ingredients or parts, rather than their all being primarily the result of the operation of chemical ... laws .... In sum, the fabricative character of technology pertains to the nature of the processes in which its issue is brought into being. (1990: 12)

Dis/technologies—those that have the bodies of disabled people in mind—become extensions of oneself. Bodies and prostheses intermingle and *ontologically envelope* in a liberating way or, alternatively, are weaponized in the form of an essentialized reductionism (e.g. disability is all of me, all that you see; or this is what it means to be a "real" woman) by the *ableist right*[8] against us (Campbell 2009).

Envelopment construed as a pitiful state denotes the wheelchair user as fixed/bound to a crate-like device with fixed sides, restrained further by the hazards of the built environment. The hegemony of ableist relations pictures variability as anathema, seeing wheelchairs deployed as "hostage fantasies" of entombment = confinement and bondage. Populist expressions such as "wheelchair-bound" or being "confined to a wheelchair" are mobilized everywhere! This may have been quite accurate in the era of clunky, heavy wheelchairs (up until the late 1980s in many cases). Wheelchairs were designed to push invalids around by residential facility staff or by a caregiver—the user became *in/valid*, having limited power for control of the device. Ludicrous as it may seem—and wasteful in terms of limited resources—an acquaintance recently told me a story that could be "everycrip's story." To get funding for a ramp to access their inaccessible house, a powerchair user was told that they could only get funding if they also had prescribed a manual wheelchair. They complied, despite the fact that they would be unable to propel the prescribed heavy manual chair to access the proposed ramp! The following etymological description suggests that being *bound* is bad news:

Bound, n. [ME] *Bounde, bunne*, abound, limit.

1. A limit, anything that limits the whole of any given object or space, a boundary or confine. (Webster 1959)

Here, the wheelchair enclosing the user acts as a boundary object between themselves and the world.

Bound. (vt)

2. To limit, to terminate; to restrain or confine, as, to bound our wishes. (Webster 1959)

This rendering of boundedness sounds almost terminal, the boundary in this instance concerning restrictions on the mobility of our imagination. Conversely, being bound may actually be a positive affirmation: denoting the making of a covenant, pledging to be obligated to someone or some community. There is something about the containability of a wheelchair, especially a powered wheelchair, being a containment of a different kind from, say, motorized scooters. Generally, the powerchair is characterologically restricted to mobility-impaired *disabled* people, and its aesthetics have not changed much over time. Changes in design have been restricted to size, weight (from steel to titanium), and operational flexibility such as tilt mechanisms, and there has been the introduction of a variety of colors; this is because wheelchairs are a kind of mobility aid that are still characterized as *medical devices* (Watson and Woods 2005; Woods and Watson 2003). The disabled wheelchair user is, in many ways, caught up in a type of Stockholm syndrome where we are compelled to embrace our wheelie love objects and, at the same time, are alienated and inhibited by design features that sometimes cause us grief and immobility (a lack of access). Unlike its scooter counterpart, there has been limited development in personalized customization aside from color choices, whereas scooters emulate the motor car, being promoted as a *lifestyle accessory* with variations like Vespa-mimicking trims, recharge outlets for mobile phone devices and satnavs (Gentleman 2012).

This characterological enslavement of the cripple, doomed to a wheelchaired life, has not always been the representation of this mobility technology, showing that the essence of a device is far more permeable. When coupled with slavery or servants (classism), wheelchairs do not delineate hard work or encumbrance, at least on the part of the incumbent. Shorter (1994: 29) points to the historical existence of the "wealthy invalid" whose lifestyle and money enabled … a cocooned lifestyle of silver napkin rings at breakfast and special quarters in the private nervous clinics for their own servants, with someone always available to accompany and to chaperone their mobility, the important point being that power resided with the rider and not the assisting hands/subaltern bodies. In ancient times and during the era of Western imperialism, there are numerous images of wheelchair carriages denoting expressions of wealth and prestige—where the high-status person is carried around or is being pushed, signifying an immobility-mediated mobility that alluded to class or imperial, dynastic privilege. So, the idea of the wheel/chair carrier device was associated with a this-world perfection, protecting the passenger from polluting contacts with the earth.

2.3. MOBILITY SCOOTERS: THE BOUNDARY POLICING OF A GREENER OPTION

I used to be human once. So I am told. I don't remember it myself, but people who knew me when I was small say I walked on two feet just like a human being. (Sinha 2007: 1)

FIGURE 2.2 A vision of mobility Armageddon? A large group of white, *apparently* able-bodied younger people, some standing, others sitting on or around their six mobility scooters. On this day trip, they are enjoying the sunshine, chatting, and viewing the sea from a parking lookout. Source: Wouter Hagens, photographer, https://commons.wikimedia.org/wiki/File:Adeje_scootmobiel_A.jpg.

In the minds of people and ableist practices wanting to hold a *constitutional demarcation* between abledment and disablement, Figure 2.2 becomes an anathema, a vision of *mobility Armageddon*: the once "human," as Sinha (2007) points out, has become "animal." A seemingly incidental and innocent image of recreational activity is transported into an *unacceptable image of norm-violation* that disturbs the processes of purification into spheres of abled and disabled. The holiday photo acts as a tipping point for confusion over correct social ordering, threatening the idea of disabled people being associated with the trappings of a "distinct insular minority," thereby taking on an existence of *exceptionality* rather than normalcy. In crossing the disability divide akin to a state border, the use of mobility scooters by *apparently* nondisabled people not only transmogrifies this once perceived invalid aid into a mere mobility accessory, it also institutes a crisis of spatial containment that exposes the workings of ableism via differentiation and assignation in spaces of mobility, "where citizenship is claimed and acted out" (Spinney et al. 2015: 353). Instead of acting as an *opportunity*, the *scooter embrace* has instituted a *mobility crisis*, producing a flurry of false questions that aid containment:

> What *sort* of vehicle is this (a characterological assertion requiring a test)?
> How can we ensure that *only* disabled people use scooters?
> What does it *mean to be nondisabled*?

What does the use of mobility scooters by nondisabled people mean for how we understand the nature of that scooter and mobility in general?

> What *kinds of people* (anatomically and character-wise) wish to use a mobility scooter and what is the attraction (are they pretending to "be" disabled or using this kind of transport for mobility)?

An alternative inquiry that asks, "How could this mobility device be used to facilitate greater and cleaner environmental access to a broader population base, thus facilitating social mobility?" drops out of our cognitive framing, becoming erased. The scooter crisis needs to be viewed against the backdrop of wider moves (at least in the West) to rein in legal definitions of disability by adopting reductionist strategies that attempt to rid "disablements" of their leakiness, relationality, and ambiguity. Conundrums about scooters are not about the disabled body per se, but are concerned with the scandal of the belligerent "Other" who, in a sense, *hacks dis/technologies*, repurposing them as fit for another use beyond the boundaries of a medical device. Instead of understanding the crisis of scooter usage as a *moment of opportunity*, ableist relations reframe the debate as a boundary violation and hence a catastrophe. Rooting out possible invaders (those lazy nondisabled potentially feigning disability) is achieved through a rhetoric of hysteria and moral panic. The passion for hysteria is only possible by invoking that imagery of ableist sameness. Such a frenzied reaction is more than a mere dread of falling into the abyss of disability; it is what Laplanche and Pontalis (1973: 194) term a "paroxystic event (e.g. emotional crisis accompanied by theatricality)." A lot is at stake. The crisis is exemplified in a catchcry reminiscent of xenophobia amid perceived waves of immigrants or refugees crashing onto the shore: "If we let *appearingly* non-disabled in, how many more will climb on board? There'll be mayhem on the pavements of the UK!" (adapted from Baker and Campbell 2006). George (Nick) Nicolls (2006), an elderly man, in "Mobility" captures the textures of this *aporia of trepidation*:

> I've bought myself a scooter .... When I first went to use it, I really had some doubt, I thought some might resent me as I trundled about. But then unto my great surprise. This just was not the case. The many folk who passed me had a smile upon their face.

Nicolls expresses earlier in the poem vulnerability and doubts—"I really had some doubt, I thought some might resent me"—about possible microaggressions evoked from "trundling about" on his scooter, exposing the *extent* of percolating stories of distain. Still unsure of public reactions, Nicolls hopes that it is kindness that drives the intentions behind being greeted. Nicolls reflects midway on *transitions around sociality* before and after experiencing scooter usage. Being thankful for pleasant greetings, he nonetheless is aware that as they are "looking down" on him, as he is in a way occupying a different kind of space.

Roughly 350,000 people in the UK use a mobility scooter, although the real number could be significantly higher (Barton et al. 2014). In 2010, the Department for Transport (DfT) undertook a consultation on proposed changes to laws governing mobility scooters and powerchairs (DfT 2010). The recommendations appeared to have lapsed. Unfortunately, the consultation returned only 239 responses, mainly from businesses, medical bodies, and a limited number of third-sector organizations.[9] The legislation that shapes the mobility needs of disabled people is profoundly steeped in arcane language typical of biomedicalism—wheelchairs are referred to as "invalid carriages": "a vehicle, whether mechanically propelled or not, constructed or adapted for use for the carriage of one person, being a person suffering from some physical defect or disability." The twenty-eight-year-old legislation governing this area provides some awful titling: the Chronically Sick and Disabled Persons Act 1970 and the Use of Invalid Carriages on Highways Regulations 1988. Just to reiterate, mobility scooters according to UK law are only meant to be operated by disabled people—how this is assessed and policed is unknown. *Troubles* emerge not just because some users might "not necessarily consider themselves disabled" (DfT 2010: 5), but because users (nondisabled, young people, people with health conditions not "recognized" as disabled) *extend and challenge the boundaries* of not only disablement, but also the character/purpose of mobility scooters—and the idea and conditions of mobility itself! They are usurpers of mobility boundaries; as Baker and Campbell (2006: 324) put it, "the demarcation of the boundary is not overthrown but neither does it stay within the settled territory, so that it is both impossible to pass the border and necessary to cross it."

Referring to an internal review in 2005, the DfT stated "to the best of our knowledge—serious collisions with pedestrians are thankfully rare" (DfT 2010: para. 12), as routine data on incidents are not collected by the police or health services (DfT 2010: para. 56, 21). What the consultation document alludes to but does not explore is the linkage or conflations between *perceptions of risk* and the *increasing* use of scooters (DfT 2010: para. 14, 10). Transport authorities keep sidestepping the issue of profiling scooter users, indicating that many users "would not necessarily consider themselves to be disabled .... [Scooters are] a convenient alternative to public transport .... It is also seen as a replacement for the private car, for shorter distances, when the user no longer feels confident enough to drive" (DfT 2010: para. 23, 12). No mention is made of any possible correlation between usage, affordability, being on a low income, or the possibilities of using these electric transportations for a "greener solution."

Lest you consider I am exaggerating about this hysteria or about ambivalent mobility, consider the provocation of "The Trouble with Mobility Scooters" published in *The Guardian*, a notable UK left-wing media outlet, on May 2, 2012 (Gentleman 2012). Of course, the *trouble* started with the *choice of headline*, a prelude to the ensuing drama about the increasing populist usage of mobility scooters. Percolating away, it had been two years since the DfT consultation, and it appeared to have lapsed from the political agenda; Amelia Gentleman's 2012 piece frames *scooter troubles* in terms of public hostility toward able-bodied users who prefer (secondhand) scooters as cheap alternatives to cars. Trading in moral panic, Gentleman (2012) argues:

> The anti-mobility scooter lobby is confused by the vision of people stepping off their vehicle and walking into a shop. The sense that some people are using them for convenience is stoking the hostility, and legitimate users say the public are vocal in their criticisms. Twitter is full of people complaining that users don't seem to be "disabled enough." "Mobility scooter users are aggressive sociopaths," is a typical tweet.

If we read the expression "trouble" as double entendre, this paroxystic event goes deeper, pointing to ruptures and portals, entries and exits, reminiscent of the idea of sectarian *troubles* in Ireland, which bound, restrained, vilified, and banished aliens and traitors—people who not only crossed demarcation zones, but also those who refused enumeration as they journeyed to their destiny/nations. Proliferations pit the landscape—there are people out of place with 'no place', refugees, rough sleepers, blurred color lines—searching for anomalous zones of sanctuary. I am interested in the "comments section" of the article, as such sections act as barometers of public opinion and provide the interaction of viewpoints. In the twenty-four-hour period after its publication, the article generated 210 detailed reader comments.[10] Reviewing the comments, it became clear that there were five categories of opinion: *judgments*, *environments*, *quality of life*, *microaggressions*, and *regulation*. After conducting a brief thematic analysis, there were a number of converging themes that harnessed discourses of *fat* and *women-shaming* to restrict and rein in mobility devices to the "genuinely" disabled. Overwhelmingly, there were 126 references to *environments* related to the regulation of shared spaces like pavements and roads—drawing attention to social divisions around how society prioritizes space for different users (walkers, cars, bikes, Segways, prams, wheelchairs, scooters). However, with *judgments*, at 125 references, there was a barrage of insults directed toward *fat/obese women who are too lazy to walk/have no self-control/in a frenzy and rash/likely to smoke* (and *watch pornography*), provoking hostility by their *sheer presence*. Mobility of disabled people was exceptionalized—the caveat being that people who need scooters should not face hostility. A minority of critiques linked mobility scooter usage to the idea of scroungers in the broader context of the impacts of austerity measures on many people in the community.

2.3.1. Mobilē vulgus: Threats; mobilitate viget: Rumblings from the fickle crowd

This paroxystic event, determining who is and is not disabled and re-cognizing abledment, reaches its zenith when a politician declares, "At the moment we just don't know who is buying them. It's a real can of worms. The government has to take control." Wow—are we talking about mobility scooter users or illegal drugs? The space invasion of *apparently* nondisabled scooter users becomes a clarion call for the right-wing press (*The Daily Mail* and *The Spectator*) akin to a civil emergency where fear and chaos reign. There has been a spate of inflammatory articles in which the right-wing media aim to orchestrate moral panics, invoking folk devils based on spurious conflated associations. Under the headline "Britain Is Mobility Scooter Capital of Europe: 300,000 on Our Roads and Streets as Obesity and Number of Pensioners Soar," Bentley (2012) adopts a high-alert posture—a nation is under siege. Young people needing cheap transport use scooters to avoid paying insurance and tax are modern-day villains. They become conflated with so-called "obese" folk, selfish people (probably demonic pensioners or scroungers) derided for not walking who are responsible for the rise in *illicit* scooter usage.[11] Adopted is the classic ableist *negation strategy* proposing that able-bodied people make accessing mobility scooters more difficult for people with "genuine disabilities." It is unclear what these difficulties are, as most mobility scooters are self-funded so do not impact the availability of subsidized funding.

The Spectator, a weekly paper, takes this siege mentality further, promoting scooter mobility as an attack on British *nationalism* (Mason 2015). "The Mobility Scooter Plague," authored by Mark Mason,[12] uses a two-pronged attack—inflammatory discourses against people deemed "fat" and the uncontrollability of the risks. Riders become dangerous predators, a conquering militia: "This supersized scooter squadron has conquered Britain," says Mason. The linking of nationalism, disability, and disease with the permeability of open borders is exposed in this piece.[13] These social disrupters who wheeze, have vast backsides, and "pop another Kit Kat into their gob" refuse the "tedious leg business" of walking (Mason 2015). Michael Oliver long ago recognized the walking-at-all-costs argument. In critiquing the description of walking as a mere biological act, Oliver suggested that "walking" acts as symbolic capital associated with normative living. The privileging of walking over other modes of mobility has resulted in large numbers of people submitting themselves to regimes of medical torture—to being surgically modified and resculptured. Oliver (1993: 104) argues, "Walking is rule-following behavior; not walking is rule ignoring, rule-flouting or even rule-threatening behavior. ... Not walking or rejecting nearly-walking as a personal choice is something different however; it threatens the power of professionals, it exposes the ideology of normality and challenges the whole rehabilitation enterprise." Walking becomes the measure of citizenship, from which *no one escapes*, be they pregnant women[14] or fat people, welfare applicants, young people, or people who drink or smoke.

The pavement is something that citizens "brave," a modern-day warzone where hysteria rules: "Shoppers scatter and toddlers are yanked away as the Porker Porches come careering through." When all else fails, there is a return to the ableist strategy of *differentiation* (a problem in achieving clear-cut demarcations between the disabled and outsiders). It becomes imperative that "we" expiate and purge from our midst those infiltrators, horrible mixtures that confuse rather than clarify who belongs to the normal and thus the true citizenry. A story told by a politician is constantly regurgitated in various media pieces: "[The politician] witnessed a woman 'leap out of her mobility vehicle, rush into the shops, come back with heavy bags and spring back into it'" (Bentley 2012; Gentleman 2012; Mason 2015). *And so what? A woman without a car creatively hacks her mobility scooter to shop!* Should the reader still not be convinced that there is a disability-induced mobility crisis, *The Spectator* ramps up this crisis, portraying a mobility Armageddon requiring a call to arms:

> The real danger lies in the future, when the scooter epidemic reaches critical mass (an apt phrase). A couple of generations down the line waits a Britain where nobody ever learns to walk at all. We'll pass straight from baby buggy to mobility scooter with no intervening phase, stair lifts transporting us at home and moving walkways doing the job in public. Shank's pony will have been stabled forever, and as in the plot of some terrifying Will Self novel our legs will atrophy completely, bred out of existence through disuse. Only if we act now can we save the country from this hideous fate. Let us rise up, and make these bogus scooter users rise up. (Mason 2015)

Xenophobic ablement has a provenance, found in the call-to-arms speech of Oregon Republican Senator Mark Hatfield at the Albert Lasker Public Awards of the American Medical Association:

> [We must] ... embark on a disease defense build-up similar to that undertaken in the 1980s to respond to the perceived military threat of the Soviet Union. We must reorder our nation's budget priorities from programs that destroy life to those that will preserve and enhance life. It is ironic that we can defend our country from a foreign foe but we cannot defend our people from disease. ... I will continue to challenge those who believe that our national defense lies solely in our military arsenals. They are missing the point—if we cannot protect our citizens from disease and disability, the true enemy lies within our borders. (Hatfield 1995: 1077)

Placed together, this eugenicist, ableist rhetoric of the New Right is exposed. Otherness is a disease or epidemic, a threat and hence an enemy of nation building. Hatfield (1995) and Mason (2015) see this as a war, a military campaign, where countries need saving and defending through a call to arms. Multiple repetitions and performances of a disability or disability fraudulency crisis, when expressed frequently in the form of "fake news," can establish new realities of social relations and expose broader culture wars of ablement wherein nosologies are harnessed to reduce peripheral populations of nation-states based on appealing to feelings of being overrun by aliens, have-nots coming to our destiny/ nation. As Ian Hacking reminds us: "The census will never be able to use what it finds out about you anyway. The fetishistic collection of overt statistical data about populations has as its motto 'information and control', but it would more truly be 'disinformation and mismanagement'" (Hacking 1983: 280). Make no bones about it, mobility enhancement, in contrast with impaired mobility, is *the* critical challenge of modern times. We are witnessing incursions into the capabilities of human flows, the inequalities of those unable to have "firm plans," who transverse and transgress borders, making new, sketchy, and often uneven paths. In a utopian world, mobility impairment should be nullified. Documentary filmmaker Ai Weiwei (2018), writing in *The Guardian*, evocatively captures this cataclysmic human event:

> In nature there are two approaches to dealing with flooding.
> One is to build a dam to stop the flow.
> The other is to find the right path to allow the flow to continue …
> The nature of water is to flow.
> Human nature too seeks freedom and that human desire is stronger than any natural force.

CHAPTER THREE

Chronic Pain and Illness

States of Privilege and Bodies of Abuse

THEODORA DANYLEVICH

3.1. INTRODUCTION: MODERN TIMES AND CHRONIC SUFFERING

Chronic pain and illness as a medical category describes ongoing experiences of suffering or impairment with periods of remission and relapse. Chronic conditions such as Lyme disease, lupus, or chronic fatigue syndrome will have periods of acute suffering and incapacity that come and go, and yet do not ever go away entirely. Factors that compromise immunity and energy such as stress and discrimination, contracting another illness or infection, exposure to an environment permeated with toxins, or overexertion increase a person's vulnerability, and frequently—though unpredictably—trigger flare-ups.

Chronic conditions frequently have highly complex or unknown causes, are not necessarily terminal, and do not have a cure. Impossibly difficult to contain by discourses of logic and rationality, cause and effect, they may as well be grounds for total epistemological and ontological rupture and reorientation of the ways in which we have been taught to make sense of—and conform to—the social, cultural, and material worlds that we inhabit. Yet, chronic pain and illness is indissociable from the geopolitical, social, and environmental factors peculiar to our historical period. For instance, following the development of vaccines and antibiotics in the nineteenth century, as well as improved sanitation and biomedical advances, epidemics of communicable and often deadly illnesses associated in part with crowded or unhygienic conditions in urban industrialization, such as cholera and tuberculosis, receded into the background. These have come to be replaced by chronic pain and illness as life expectancies rise and as previously deadly conditions

I would like to express my gratitude to all of those whose work (cited in this chapter), advice, and feedback have helped me to fashion this entry. In particular, I would like to thank Alyson Patsvas for taking the time to speak with me at length in the early stages. I am grateful also for timely insights offered by Andrea Lopez, Robert McRuer, David T. Mitchell, Clare Mullaney, Zahari Richter, Sharon L. Snyder, Craig Willse, and Samuel Yates. I am grateful also to Liz Crow and Wangechi Mutu for agreeing to share their work for inclusion in this piece.

have come to be medically managed but not necessarily cured (Wendell 2001; Rosner and Markowitz 2006: Manderson and Smith-Morris 2010).

Experiences of chronic pain and illness take bodies out of time, reach diverse populations, and thwart ableist paradigms of hyperproductivity. As such, chronic pain and illness presents bodies and societies with a paradigmatically modern experience that is at the same time completely incommensurate with the normative time and space of the modern laboring and consuming subject. Chronic pain and illness makes it difficult to work in and move through the spaces and temporalities that are presumed "normal," even if one appears able-bodied. For instance, working an eight-hour workday may be impossible with limited energy.[1] Walking a very short distance or taking a short flight of stairs may pose a barrier or significant challenge to chronically ill but apparently able-bodied persons on certain days. Standing in a long line waiting for social services may also be inaccessible. Having to take frequent breaks to move differently, rest, or seek medical care disrupt expectations of productivity and mobility in a typical work or public space environment.

Chronic pain and illness tends to elude the "crisis" temporality and melodramatic rhetoric of emergency and epidemiology that attended the previous century's infectious epidemics of tuberculosis and cholera, or the early stages of the AIDS crisis. Not conforming to narratives of recovery and rehabilitation, chronic pain and illness presents a deep structural cultural critique that is easier to dismiss than to heed. In a cultural orientation where speed, convenience, and dramatic impact are highly valued, our conceptual impulses and rhetorical tools fall short in the face of what Lauren Berlant (2011) has called "crisis ordinariness" and what Angela Carter, myself, and Alyson Patsavas (2018) have called "states of continuous crisis." The lack of conceptual vocabulary exacerbates the suffering, isolation, and neglect that chronically suffering persons experience.[2]

In addition to such cultural illegibility, the elusive visibility of chronic pain and illness makes those experiencing chronic illness vulnerable to compounding bias and discrimination based on identity such as race and gender. Frequent delegitimation based on race and gender precludes women and people of color from gaining access to care and support (Mollow 2014). Ableism and racism work to neutralize and depoliticize the suffering that disabled people of color experience. Stereotypes of the hysteric, the shirker, laziness, irresponsibility, and so on place blame on the sufferer for their suffering (Erevelles 2011; Geary 2014; Mollow 2014). This social aspect of the experience of chronic illness stratifies incidences and the severity of chronic pain and illness along lines of race, class, gender, and sexuality. Occupationally, politically, and economically created and sustained chronic pain and illnesses compounded with medical bias and delegitimation thus tend to impact underprivileged classes and communities much more than others. Diagnosis, treatment, and legitimation for chronic pain and illness are labor intensive and often costly, making treatment inaccessible to those with fewer resources. Further, austerity cuts to social services and resources in late liberal/late neoliberal policies impact both disabled and racially marginalized communities, which rely on various forms of state and federal welfare programs (Mollow 2014; Aho 2017; McRuer 2018).

As literary scholar and queer theorist Elizabeth Freeman has noted, what occurs in the violence of the bio-political cultural imaginary is a "recalibration of a historically specific aspect of global capitalism into a narrative of individual or demographic degeneration in the face of modernity" (Freeman 2016: 337). That is to say, endemic experiences of suffering become moralized, privatized, and dismissed, and those who are already subject to racism and sexism become moralized and pathologized as "the inevitable waste product of modernity" (ibid.). The field of Disability Studies and the struggle for disability rights has sought to articulate new vocabularies and conceptual paradigms that might allow us to better accommodate bodily difference and impairment. More focused attention to chronic pain and illness as well as to the experiences of multiply marginalized non-white disabled people have led to a more intersectional disability critique that attends to bodyminds, networks of violence and of care, attention to geopolitics, and to the proliferating capacities of incapacity.[3]

3.2. A CONDITION OF PRIVILEGE AND ABUSE

Chronic pain and illness is thus paradigmatic to "modernity" also because of the effects of global capitalist industry, which has generated widespread incidences of illnesses related to toxicity, compounded by an entrenchment of economic inequality that creates access barriers to health care. Along the lines of social status and privilege, geographies of environmental racism emerge nationally and transnationally. As a result, underprivileged communities suffer greater exposures to toxic living conditions. Chronic respiratory illnesses such as asthma are among the most common examples. As manufacturing is increasingly outsourced to the Global South, the transnational rift of what I will be referring to as "states of privilege and bodies of abuse" comes into greater relief. In what follows, I will refer to "states of privilege and bodies of abuse" to describe the relationship between modernity, capitalism, and marginalized sufferers of chronic pain and illness. A whole additional class of "chronics," or "bodies of abuse," has been created by industrial and post-industrial modernity: those impacted by unsafe and unregulated working conditions and those impacted by proximity to toxins released into the environment from manufacturing plants.[4]

In the developed world, suffering from chronic pain and illness can be associated with both positive and negative impacts of "states of privilege." For instance, those from populations with access, education, and economic means might come to chronic pain and illness as a diagnosis or as a condition that is an *effect* of privilege. The privileged experiences of a critical mass of a population having access to research, medication, vaccines, and timely medical intervention have helped to transform deadly illnesses into medically manageable chronic illnesses. These might range from addiction or depression to cancer or HIV/AIDS.[5] On the negative side of "states of privilege," privileged nation-states accumulate capital at the expense of the "bodies of abuse"—disabled and sickened bodies that they simultaneously produce. That is, developed nations and states profit from industry and modes of production that release toxins into the environment, resulting in chronic pain and illness in populations subject to unsafe or harmful working conditions, or whose homes and neighborhoods are exposed to toxins.

Chronic pain and illness in the Modern Age thus comprises a visceral, lived transnational archive—or political geography—of the events and impacts of modernization and capitalist accumulation on bodies, stratified along lines of privilege and abuse; race, class, gender, and sexuality. The category and experience of chronic pain and illness fundamentally challenges—yet is also emblematic of—paradigms through which we understand the long twentieth century, or the "Modern Age." War, gender inequality, medical and environmental racism, and the transnational impact of neoliberal economic policies often dictate which groups or classes of bodies experience greater debilitation and suffering. Prognoses of resulting conditions of chronic pain and illness vary greatly along dividing lines of racial, gendered, and economic privilege. An identity politics that attends to chronic pain and illness asks us to trouble "the conventional divisions of illness, disability, and health; and reflect on how global economic relations shape responses to illness, ailment, and disability" (Manderson and Smith-Morris 2010: 18). I will be focusing this chapter's discussion on these hard truths of chronic pain and illness.

This chapter will show the paradigm-shifting power of chronic pain and illness in the context of and in relation to the long twentieth century in the USA and transnationally. I will introduce and follow a thread of development in Disability Studies and disability activism that begins with the social model of disability and moves into a discussion of more intersectional approaches to disability in recent scholarship and justice work. The paradigmatic shifts that nuanced attention to both embodied and relational experiences of negativity, suffering, and impairment has led to in Disability Studies have also charted a path by which the field is attending to intersectional identities. The second half of my discussion will attend to visceral aesthetics in literature, film, and sculpture. I will read works that articulate and arise out of embodied and relational experiences of the intersecting oppressions that lead to and compound chronic pain, debilitation, and illness, particularly in underprivileged populations.

3.3. RESHAPING DISABILITY STUDIES DISCOURSE: FROM THE SOCIAL MODEL TO INTERSECTIONAL EPISTEMOLOGIES OF IMPAIRMENT

3.3.1. Problematizing the social model of disability

Chronic pain and illness challenges representation and troubles categories, and it has played an immeasurably important role in shifting and complicating conversations and orientations in the field of disability studies. Since at least the 1990s, feminist and anti-racist disability scholars have been pushing disability activism and disability studies to devote serious attention to suffering, pain, and the negative experiences associated with impairment, and to allow such acknowledgment to create a more inclusive and complex definition of disability identity, and thus also of "disability pride."[6]

The field of Disability Studies and the disability rights movement have taken spectacular, visible disabilities, impairments, deformities, and disfigurements as their initial organizing nodes. A distinguishing feature of early disability justice organizing was the conceptualization of the social model of disability as a counter-narrative to the medical model of disability. The medical model has primarily been cast as oppressive and violent, and focuses on treatments, prostheses, and procedures that might bring the body in question toward a greater approximation of normalcy, not just functionally, but visually. The rehabilitative horizon of such curative approaches has been critiqued as being intended for the comfort of those encountering the person in question at the expense of the body's actual lived experiences of well-being (e.g. a prosthetic leg as opposed to crutches or a wheelchair) (Crow 1996: 10). The medical model casts disability as something broken, in need of fixing. As a response, the social model of disability relocates disability as cultural and infrastructural rather than embodied or medicalized (Mitchell and Snyder 2005). Accessible buildings, doorways, ramps, buses, curb cuts, etc., are vital accomplishments by the disability rights movement, aimed at structural elements of the social model of disability, increasing accessibility and inclusion for certain types of disabled bodies.

The social model of disability made important gains for mobility and access, but a wholesale dismissal of medical aspects and considerations of disability is disingenuous and detrimental to the movement. The social model as the only model of disability "reduce[s] attention to those disabled people whose bodies are highly medicalized because of their suffering, their deteriorating health, or the threat of death," wrote Canadian disability scholar Susan Wendell in 2001 (Wendell 2001: 18). The disability pride movement has favored affirmative identity politics, refuting rhetorics of brokenness and almost entirely avoiding the topic of pain, nor viably entertaining any disabled person's desire to be *less* disabled or the relief that medical approaches might desirably offer (Crow 1996; Wendell 2001). "How can we expect anyone to take seriously a 'radical' movement which replicates some of the worst exclusionary aspects of the society it purports to change?" wrote British artist, activist, and scholar Liz Crow in protest of this disavowal of impairment in 1996 (Crow 1996: 5). Indeed, medical treatment can frequently make a great deal of positive difference to the disabled person's quality of life. Merri Lisa Johnson and others have written about the importance of acknowledging the liberatory and world-making potential of receiving a diagnosis by which one can better understand one's experiences and feel *less* isolated (Johnson 2010).

Disability scholar Anna Mollow wrote, pointedly, in 2014, "from disabled people who suffer from our impairments but are discounted as 'hysterical,' *more* medicalization of our conditions, not less, is sometimes desired" (Mollow 2014: 196). Mollow's writings make clear that the problem of sexist and racist delegitimation and lack of credibility dwells within the ableism of the social model as "all" of disability. Repurposing the term "hysteria" into her neologism "criphystemologies," Mollow proposes an epistemology that centers the compounded experience of suffering and invalidation to which those with chronic pain and illness are often subjected. Informed by experiences of chronic pain and illness, disability scholars including Crow, Wendell, Mollow, and others have drawn attention to the field's replication of ableist expectations of political activism (Crow 1996; Wendell 2001; Mollow 2014). If and when we attend and listen to the experience of pain and chronic illness "as the quandary it really is" within the disability justice and pride movements, the need for different epistemologies and rhetorical orientations—and the need to shed the insidious vestiges of ableism (and thereby also sexism and racism) *within* the movement—becomes apparent (Crow 1996: 3). While historically important, empowering, and liberating, the social model as "all" of disability falls short, replicating ableism, sexism, and racism within the movement.

3.3.2. Not private: Complex embodiment and painful networks

Acknowledgment of the negative attributes of impairment and suffering challenges disability scholarship and the disability justice movement to embrace "complex embodiment," such as the late disability theory and aesthetics scholar Tobin Siebers called for about a decade ago (Siebers 2008: 25). Complex embodiment, as Siebers laid it out, accounts for social and medical factors in the experience of disability. It "raises awareness of the effects of disabling environments on people's lived experience of the body, but it emphasizes as well that some factors affecting disability such as chronic pain, secondary health effects, and aging, derive from the body" (Siebers 2008: 25). Complex embodiment offers a better model for valuing disability as *human variation* rather than as defect (Siebers 2008: 25). Further, it moves Disability Studies toward an intersectional view of oppression. Without dismissing concepts of the social model or a sense of disability pride, an ambivalently charged—and even utilitarian—engagement with the medical field and with chronic experiences of pain and impairment allows the field of Disability Studies and the disability rights movement to be more inclusive. Chronic pain and illness encourages Disability Studies to articulate the negativity and suffering attendant to disability experience, and it complicates the politics of disability pride. As feminist disability scholar Susan Wendell puts it, the making visible of pain and suffering within disability experience need not fracture the political agenda of the field and its activists. Rather, it invites us to express a valorization of different ways of being human—fully human. Collectively reckoning with the diminished capacity and energy that accompany chronic pain and illness challenges us to come up with different measures of valuation and inclusion, as well as ways to make participation in the movement more accessible (Wendell 2001: 26).[7]

Pain—unromantic, unglamorous, unheroic, and not tragic—clamors for a more compassionate epistemology, a more capacious analytic, and for politicized modes of representation. As Siebers wrote, "the greatest stake in disability studies at the present moment is to find ways to represent pain and to resist models of the body that blunt the political effectiveness of these representations," citing the pervasive individualizing and privatizing renderings of pain in medical and cultural discourse as a hindrance to realizing the potential of pain to mobilize group identity (Siebers 2008: 61). Far from being singularly contained in the confines of one body, pain radiates out and moves through caretaking and interdependency networks; it is "leaky" (Shildrick 1997; Patsavas 2014). This descriptive representation of pain reflects the actual caretaking relationality that pain both invites and requires. A canonical text in pain and body studies, Elaine Scarry's *The Body in Pain* (1985), has by now been critiqued for reproducing cultural assumptions about the incommunicability of pain, which serves only to reinforce a privatizing and depoliticizing view of pain and suffering (Scarry 1985: 3). Patsavas' discussion, published in a 2014 "cripistemologies"-themed issue of the *Journal of Literary and Cultural Disability Studies*, actively "de-individualizes and de-biologizes the experience of pain" (Patsavas 2014: 209). Weaving together personal experience and analysis of cultural representations, Patsavas articulates instead how "discourses of personal responsibility that are consistently embedded in cultural narratives of pain" contribute greatly to experiences of suffering, and shape representations of pain as so-called tragedy (Patsavas 2014: 209). The power to amplify suffering and create tragedy lies in many ways with the doctor or medical clinic that, for instance, cuts someone off from care or withholds prescriptions (Patsavas 2014).[8] Paying tribute to the feminist and crip methodologies of Margrit Shildrick and Alison Kafer, Patsavas articulates an "interdependence of pain" as something relational as well as material that moves between institutions and bodies, doctors and patients, and through networks of caretaking (Patsavas 2014: 215).

In her charting of an epistemology of pain, Patsavas calls attention to her social positionality as inextricable from her experience of chronic pain, in terms of gender, sexuality, race, and class. Access to legitimation and treatment is *always* contingent on privilege and power, and these are inscribed as cultural geographies that entrench, produce, and perpetuate populations that are more vulnerable to long-term health conditions, be they occupational, environmental, or communicable illnesses. The representational challenges of chronic pain and illness demand intersectional and materialist methodologies. That is to say, they call for an attunement to the compounding multiple axes of oppression and for attention to economic and geographic structurings.

Because of the ways in which chronic pain and illness makes a cartography of social oppression visible, attention to chronic pain and illness—and to the correctives that it demands of the disability rights movement—by necessity ushers the disability rights movement and the field of Disability Studies into a nuanced recognition of the different, *compounded* experiences of disability to which non-white disabled bodyminds are subjected (Price 2015; Schalk 2018). If we follow the "undoing" power of chronic pain and illness upon the discourse of disability studies, we are inevitably led to conceptualize a more expansive politics of inclusion and access and to attend to the diversity of experiences that comprise a lived disability polity.

3.3.3. Critical Disability Studies and crip-of-color critique

At the time of this writing, the field of Disability Studies has recently gained a critical mass of scholars forging connections between critical race theory and disability studies, such that the Spring 2016 and 2017 issues of the journal of the Cultural Studies Association, *Lateral*, hosted a forum on emergent critical analytics in the humanities, which included a cluster on Critical Disability Studies. In this cluster, feminist Disability Studies scholars Julie Avril Minich, Jina B. Kim, and Sami Schalk describe a paradigm shift in Disability Studies as one that moves away from disability as an object of analysis and toward a "Critical Disability Studies" methodology (Minich 2016; Kim 2017; Schalk 2017). This recent turn in Disability Studies has benefited from the methodologies of women of color feminisms, which attend to intersectional, compounding social and economic agents of oppression. Accordingly, in her response, Jina B. Kim describes Critical Disability Studies as a "crip-of-color critique" (Kim 2017).[9] What the methodological and intersectional turn does for Disability Studies is it widens the scope of what scholars take into account in a discussion of disability. As Schalk puts it, these would include "the social norms that define particular attributes as impairments, as well as the *social conditions* that concentrate stigmatized attributes in particular populations" (Schalk 2017, emphasis added). That is to say, together with the networked epistemology of impairment that Patsavas gestures toward, Disability Studies as a field is now developing a specific attunement to social conditions *such as* racism, sexism, economic inequality, and environmental toxicity.[10]

3.3.4. Unvictimizable: Demographic vulnerability and blame

Scholars and social scientists have increasingly been attending to the impacts of social, political, and economic disadvantage as demographic states of vulnerability on illness. Demographic incidences of chronic pain and illness have also allowed us to better understand the "ways in which illness tracks social inequality and vulnerability" (Manderson and Smith-Morris 2010: 3). Chronic and relentless experiences of racist bias in the medical profession, the psychic and physical toll of daily delegitimation, lack of access to equal medical care—all of these work in concert in rendering a certain population more vulnerable.[11] Through the lens of AIDS, fault lines of "states of privilege and bodies of abuse" can be easily discerned along demographic lines: the greater incidence of HIV infection *as well as* the greater incidence of AIDS mortality in black communities transnationally show black bodies to be "bodies of abuse" of chronic and relentless state violence and willful neglect. The advent of PrEP and increasingly effective medical control of HIV, on the other hand, shows *non*-black bodies living with HIV and AIDS as a chronic rather than fatal illness. That is to say, living with chronic illness due to socioeconomic access is a relative "state of privilege" with regard to HIV.

In *State Intimacies: Antiblack Racism and the AIDS Epidemic*—an invaluable contribution to Disability Studies by way of AIDS scholarship, medical humanities, sexuality studies, and black studies—Adam Geary (2014) interrogates the factors contributing to the black community's higher risks and incidences of HIV infection, AIDS illness, and AIDS-related mortality.[12] Examining discourses of intimacy in relation to risk, Geary reformulates the pervasive assumption of a "risky lifestyle," formulating instead the phrases "state-manufactured risk" and "state intimacies" to signify the actual, provable critical factors contributing to the black community's heightened vulnerability to AIDS. With "state intimacies," Geary articulates the health risks and risk factors in the case of HIV and AIDS in the black community in the USA and transnationally as a state-structured and engendered demographic vulnerability. "State intimacies" draws attention to the intimate ways in which the state compromises the health and safety of certain groups, manufacturing conditions of risk that are in fact far more calculable and measurable than, for instance, an *imagined* problem of an endemic behavioral nature, or a "risky lifestyle," which rhetorically and insidiously shifts blame onto already-victimized populations. Such behavioral privatization of communicability—not unlike the imagined incommunicability of pain that Patsavas discusses—deflects attention from the material, structural, and geographical factors that contribute to demographic vulnerability, disavowing any social responsibility on the part of the state.[13]

Anna Mollow's essay in the 2017 *African American Review*'s issue on Blackness and Disability, "Unvictimizable: Toward a Fat Black Disability Studies," introduces the term "unvictimizable" to convey the endemic social disavowal of responsibility in relation to those subject to the compounding identities of race and disability or poverty (Mollow 2017). Mollow connects the concept of "unvictimizable" populations to a "'new racism,' which blames the social disadvantages that black people experience not on biological impairments [as in older forms of racism] but on alleged moral failings such as 'laziness,' and lack of 'personal responsibility'" (Mollow 2017: 105–6). The violence of such disavowal makes it possible, for example, to hold Eric Garner responsible for his own murder by an officer having put him in a chokehold and keeping him there in spite of Garner's repeatedly saying, "I can't breathe" (Mollow 2017: 105). In her essay, Mollow points out the ways in which not only ableism, but also white male privilege are belied by an exclusive adherence to the social model in Disability Studies. I reproduce a long passage in which she details these effects:

> From a feminist and antiracist perspective, the social model's depoliticization of questions about health and illness presents problems. For one thing, chronic illness, pain, and psychiatric disabilities—conditions that disproportionately affect women—do centrally involve suffering. Thus, by disallowing political discussion of suffering, the social model erases many disabled women's lived experiences while valorizing masculinist stoicism .... In addition, uncritical use of the social model shores up constructions of black bodies as unvictimizable. Since African Americans are routinely depicted as incapable of genuine suffering, the social-model-informed disability studies axiom that disability should *not* be understood as "suffering, tragedy, or loss" buttresses the trope of presumed black invulnerability by placing pressure on disabled people of color to downplay any suffering that their impairments occasion. Furthermore, for many people of color, impairments result directly from social injustice. ... In a social context shaped by endemic racialized state violence, disabilities *can* be experienced as unwanted and even tragic. Pretending otherwise risks reinforcing constructions of black bodies as unvictimizable by diminishing the importance of the violence inflicted on them. (Mollow 2017: 113)

The notion that someone is unvictimizable is indeed a deadly form of delegitimation. This "new racism" that Mollow cites is a hyperbolic degree of the moralizing aspect of the privatization of pain that Patsavas and others have described, which has harmfully depoliticized and privatized experiences of chronic pain and illness across populations.

Mollow goes on to align endemic environmental racism with the construction of black bodies as unvictimizable. The disproportionate exposure to toxicity that communities of color experience—from landfills that literally grow around their communities to unremediated or unregulated lead in paint or in the water—reminds us of Elizabeth Freeman's observation that marginalized communities become moralized and pathologized as "the inevitable waste product of modernity" (Freeman 2016: 337; Mollow 2017: 115–16). Not only are they *conceived of* as waste, but they literally live *intermingled among* the waste products of modernity. Environmental racism is just as much anti-black violence as is police brutality, and it has the capacity to be just as deadly.[14]

3.5. BODIES OF ABUSE: REPRESENTING TOXIC ECOLOGIES AND EXPENDABLE BODIES

With increased modernization and the concomitant accumulation of wealth—that is to say, "states of privilege"—many more bodyminds come to experience themselves as "bodies of abuse," subject to conditions of chronic pain and illness that are consequences of, first, industrial conditions of production, and second, delegitimation and discourses of "unvictimizable" bodies and of the global instantiation of "environmental racism" that can be seen in the developing world on a larger scale. The compromising bodily impacts of modern and postmodern industrialization, as exercised, deployed, and perpetuated through structures of power and control, delineate a national and transnational cultural geography of impairment, debilitation, and chronic pain and illness along the lines of race, class, and gender. These are human lives hemmed in by borders, streets, railroad tracks, bodies of water, and prison walls, bearing and not bearing the sociocultural mark of diagnosis, deemed excessive and a financial burden, and monetized or cut off from access to social resources. Given the intermittently visible and cyclical nature of chronic pain and illness, writers and artists have employed aesthetics that both articulate and appeal to visceral sensation and experience as a way of expressing and conveying the deeply cultural—and material—experience of chronic pain and illness in the Modern Age.

3.5.1. Toxic ecologies

In her 1970 novel, *The Bluest Eye*, Toni Morrison's closing description of Pecola, a young black girl whose story shows the psychic impact of anti-black violence, shows the zoning of black communities together with waste products, aligning Pecola's suffering embodiment—viscerally and aesthetically—with "junk":

Picking and plucking her way between the tire rims and the sunflowers, between the Coke bottles and milkweed, among all the waste and beauty of the world—which is what she herself was. All of our waste which we dumped on her and which she absorbed. And all of our beauty which was hers first and which she gave to us. All of us—all who knew her—felt so wholesome after we cleaned ourselves on her. (Morrison 2007: 205)

In this description, Morrison not only places Pecola in proximity to waste products such as Coke bottles and tire rims; she analogizes Pecola to a plot of land that is dumped upon and littered with the waste of a culture whose pleasures of privilege (the novel is set in the 1940s) are emblematized by cars and soft drinks. This final scene of desolation conveys Pecola as part and parcel of a landscape of waste, toxicity, beauty, and injured hope. Not only this, but Pecola's function as a dumping ground seems vital to her community's very sense of wholesomeness: "All of us—all who knew her—felt so wholesome after we cleaned ourselves on her" (Morrison 2007: 205). Morrison's description of Pecola and of the community's affective response of *relief* points to the use value or even profit-yielding function of such "bodies of abuse," for whom Pecola's psychic dishevelment is paradigmatic. The community's need for a "dumping ground" and a scapegoat conveys Morrison's attunement to both the capitalist economic necessities that perpetuate racism and the environmental implications of racism in a daily, lived, material way.

Morrison's rhetorical description of Pecola that presents her as a body of land accumulating postindustrial waste, finds an apt, if rather more dramatic and surreal, visual representation in Kenyan-American mixed media artist Wangechi Mutu's 2013 short film, *The End of Eating Everything*.

Commissioned by the Nasher Gallery of Art at Duke University, Mutu's short film is meant to be viewed as a part of a gallery installation. In a somewhat darkened corner of the gallery, viewers encounter this eight-minute film with a barely audible soundtrack of breaking glass and cawing birds, playing on a repetitive loop, telling the brief story of a haunted and haunting figure making her way across a postapocalyptic skyscape. This film is at once a commentary on environmental pollution, capitalist overconsumption, and anti-black violence. The film (see Figure 3.1) presents in its protagonist and central visual figure a viscerally toxic embodiment that dramatically extends what we are given in Morrison's description of Pecola. Mutu's figure's body is swollen to massive proportions, and, populated with slowly waving arms and slowly spinning and creaking wheels, she is also evocative of the transnational degradation and impact of postindustrial waste and of the indiscriminate abuse and disposal of racialized, gendered, and pathologized bodies.

The figure's surface, shape, and size variously manifest an animate archive of the effects of accumulated waste, evidence of the continuing afterlives of racialized, colonial violence and global and postindustrial capital. Her heterogeneously constituted flesh is suggestive of an island or a landscape contaminated by industrial waste and chemical burns and oil spills. This body and scene on screen that viewers are subjected to is relentlessly played on repeat, in a darkened corner of an art gallery. In a compelling expression of the chronic, interrelated embodied effects of inequality, Mutu creates a viscerally toxic encounter for viewers.

In his ethnographic study, *Vita: Life in a Zone of Social Abandonment*, published in 2005, João Biehl inquires into the social, political, and medical factors leading to total abandonment in the life and death of his ethnographic subject, Catarina, at an encampment that goes by the name of "Vita" (Biehl 2013). Biehl's narrative begins with research into "zones of social abandonment," which are places that resemble hospitals but do not participate in any official system of care. In such zones, bodies and people have been effectively cut off from an already struggling neoliberalized medical care system in Brazil.[15] Through the person of one resident of such a place named Catarina—and through her poetry, to which she refers as her "dictionary"—Biehl begins to trace a creative and

FIGURE 3.1 Still from *The End of Eating Everything* by Wangechi Mutu (2013). This image shows a full "body" view of a large mass with a tiny head on its left side, three plumes of smoke coming from the top and one coming from the rear. The body's shape curves on the bottom, appearing to be hanging down with a heavy belly. The surface of the body is populated with multicolored mottled paint, dark-skinned disembodied arms, and spinning wheels. The body floats in a gray–brown sky, and a flock of birds can be seen on the left side of the still, appearing to fly toward the face of the figure. Image courtesy of the artist and Wangechi Mutu Studio.

detective-like single-informant ethnography of how it is that one ends up in a place such as this—how this exorbitant social zone emerges and is sustained.

As Biehl discovers, Catarina's sickness and suffering are significantly—and ultimately fatally—compounded with and by intimately violent economic and (mis)diagnostic forces. In a deeply impoverished sub-economy of destitute urban workers struggling to survive in conjunction with an impoverished medical system struggling to retain legitimacy, the violence perpetrated against Catarina results in exile from her family and from society at large by betrayal and opportunistic misdiagnosis. While her physical symptoms are in fact indicative of a chronic and degenerative physical condition, Machado–Joseph disease (MJD), Catarina is diagnosed and treated as a psychotic. Once she begins to show symptoms, her husband begins to abuse and cheat on her, and the family seems to collude all together, gaslighting Catarina into a diagnosis of mental illness and unfitness to mother, which leads to a coerced surrendering of her newborn daughter for adoption by a wealthy couple that employed a relative of Catarina's, and then to her exile to Vita. This all comes about because the physical debilitation that she exhibits represents an economic deficit and burden for her family and community.

Thus, Catarina's actual symptoms are physical and wholly separate from mental illness, and they are themselves the clue to the unraveling of her life and story. Her mental illness diagnosis and years of abuse and abandonment (alongside the existing stress and early-onset triggers for MJD) created a hostile social environment and predisposed her to blame for her own condition. The poverty, deprivation (emotional, sensory, sensual, nutritional), and overmedication worked in concert with her abandonment to create a visual and sensory scaffolding around her body and her existing disability in order to bolster the prejudicial approaches of those who would dispose of her in the first place. That is to say, her social and medical context fabricated an unvictimizable status for Catarina via a diagnosis of mental illness and subsequent abandonment. This is the outcome of a setting where a physically debilitated and chronically ill Catarina cannot be defined or accounted for as anything other than an excessive burden due to financial strain. The flailing infrastructure of a national medical system described itself as "more human and humane." However, this rhetoric belied an actual egregious lack of medical oversight, leaving diagnoses to be wholly dependent on socio-economic expedience, which led to an unchecked tendency toward socially constructed and medically induced psychiatric illnesses such as those that determined Catarina's fate. Thinly veiled disposal of sick family members through a machine of medical abandonment creates a site of unimaginable abjection and neglect.[16] Readers come to understand that Catarina's social status and position as a blue-collar poor woman and mother create layers of vulnerability that contribute to her arrival at the terminus of such social abandonment. An excerpt of Catarina's poetry expresses her understanding of her economic positionality:

Expendable Bodies
Dollars
Real
Brazil is bankrupted
I am not to be blamed
Without a future[17]

Catarina is well aware of her status as a "body of abuse." At Biehl's encouragement, she keeps notebooks of poetry, which she called her "dictionary." Biehl used the experiences, facts, and events described in her dictionary to piece together her life and actual illness status. The excerpt that I use in this section neatly articulates her awareness as a "body of abuse" of Brazil's aspirational "state of privilege" in the way in which she has had to suffer from her real and fabricated illnesses *because* of the nation's indebtedness, in a perverse calculus of disposability and fungiblity. Catarina was diagnosed, treated, and disposed of as a "psychotic" because her physical disability presented too much of a potential economic burden.[18] The concession—after years of treating her as a psychotic—that she is in fact perfectly lucid is tragically uneventful in the plot of her life story, as she has already been relegated to the zone of abandonment, and any change of the new status quo would be a logistical and emotional cost deemed too great by the administrators at Vita and her family. In her poem above, her cry for justice—"Brazil is bankrupted / I am not to be blamed / Without a future"—makes a very clear connection to her fatal abandonment as a phenomenon that is beyond her personal life or the private domestic sphere, but rather is induced by geopolitics and economic policy (Biehl 2013: 336).

3.6. CONCLUSION: *FIGURES* OF VISCERAL ENGAGEMENT

Figures, a 2015 mass-sculptural durational performance by British feminist disability scholar, artist, and activist Liz Crow, sought to make visceral the suffering of those who are, in Crow's words, "at the sharp end of austerity" (Crow 2018). In a photograph from the performance, rows of small, oblong, earthen figures look hauntingly and pleadingly

FIGURE 3.2 Photograph of rows of small, hand-sculpted clay figurines in a storage shed (Crow 2015). A grayscale photograph of five stacked rows of small, hand-sculpted clay figurines. The figurines have two small holes on top to represent eyes, and the figures are very simple, with no arms or legs, just a long body and a head. Photograph by Claudio/Roaring Girl Productions. Image courtesy of the artist.

out at the viewer (see Figure 3.2). In a storage shed, on shelves stacked one above the other, the figures have round, hollowed-out eyes, their heads are shaped all slightly differently, and their bodies bear handprints from Crow's hands. As the viewer's eye moves from figure to figure, one gets the impression of a moving crowd that appears, on the one hand—insofar as it is of hardened earth—already dead and memorialized, but on the other hand—insofar as each figure resembles a small, living being looking right at you—tugs at one's emotions in its semblance to a cute, bird-like, fragile, innocent life. *Figures*, as is Crow's intention, speaks directly and bears material witness to the suffering and mortality of those who are impacted by austerity measures in her country, which had been cutting the social services and welfare upon which disabled and impoverished people rely for daily lives.

A cold, calculated interpretation of the human lives and experiences of people with disabilities in terms of cost and burden, such as that to which Catarina was so clearly subjected, is something that Crow carefully and quietly worked to both represent and dislodge in her 2015 durational sculptural performance. As Robert McRuer has detailed in his discussion of British austerity measures in *Crip Times: Disability, Globalization, and Resistance*, disabilities that were not immediately apparent or that did not, for instance, impede one's ability to stand up (which, of course, would describe so many sufferers of chronic pain and illness) often resulted in loss of the benefits that people relied on, with devastating individual and community-wide effects (McRuer 2018)—all of this being due to the government's efforts to improve financial appearances.[19]

Figures gives material bodies to and begins to convey the lived experiences that something like a statistic or a large number—"figure"—quite simply destroys. Making a visceral impact is also the work of a very visceral performance, requiring endurance on the part of the artist. After having excavated and rendered the mud and prepared it for sculpting, in April of 2015, over a period of twelve consecutive days and nights, while seated on the foreshore of the River Thames in London, Crow sculpted 650 small figures out of mud to represent the 650 seats in British parliament. A wheelchair user, Crow had her attendants carry her for each sculpting session down to the foreshore. The sculpting period was socially interactive, as curious passersby from all walks of life would stop and chat. In a later stage of the performance, when the figures were fired, Crow read aloud the stories of a total of 650 disabled individuals whose lives were severely impacted or lost as a result of austerity measures. Crow describes these as individuals "at the sharp end of austerity," as a memorial gesture, during the process of baking the river mud into hardened clay. Then Crow and her team took the figures to be ground up, and scattered the dust from the sculpted, fired, and ground up earthen figures in the ocean. Throughout work on the project, which coincided with the campaign period leading up to British parliamentary elections, 650 stories of individuals "at the sharp end of austerity" were tweeted out.

The temporality of this project, requiring many hours to complete and connected to the manufactured endemic suffering that was policy-created, speaks to the temporality of chronic pain and illness as long-term, endemic, and worsened by social and political delegitimation. Crow characterizes this work as covertly political, contending that in our activism we sometimes need to shift to a practice that is beyond immediate response, geared toward the long term. In her keynote speech at The George Washington University's biennial "Composing Disability" conference in March of 2018, she spoke of "going undercover to do more" (Crow 2018). While, as Crow describes it, *Figures* is "covertly" politicized, the project sought to engage people from all walks of life who may have been affected to far lesser and far greater degrees compared to one another to impact them on a personal, visceral level, which might become politicized within a given individual. Above all, this work is about "a dry statistic made visceral" and breaking down a sense of otherness (Crow 2018). In her discussion, Crow described her performance's approach to politics as "a sideways approach," one that does not leave questions fully answered (Crow 2018). Rather, I would venture that she wants it to *haunt*, as her figures very much do, once you have spent some time looking at them. Durational, quietly contemplative, viscerally evocative art articulates and capacitates a different kind of protest, one that has the potential to be continuous and endemic.

CHAPTER FOUR

Blindness

A Cultural History of Blindness

ROD MICHALKO AND TANYA TITCHKOSKY

4.1. INTRODUCTION

In Anishinaabemowin, says Maya Chacaby,[1] "*Aatisokan*," or traditional story, is rooted in the word "*tis*" (or "*dis*"), meaning umbilical connection to the source of existence, as well as in "*kan*," meaning an artificial construct made for a certain purpose. A relation to this Indigenous meaning of a story as "a device created for the purpose of connecting us to the source of existence" is what orients our telling of this cultural history of blindness. By collecting and addressing some Western ways of depicting the significance of blindness since around World War I, this chapter will focus on how these depictions connect to modern forms of knowing the existence of blindness. We do so, however, by assuming that blindness—a historical presence that always signals human potentiality—is itself an umbilical connection to the source of existence whose meaning might exceed any modernist perception of it. Treating blindness as an occasion to reveal modern commitments grounding ordinary descriptions and representations ironically provides us with a method of inquiry that can put readers in touch with the workings of the cultural history of perception itself.

This chapter explores how life with blindness has been described in order to examine modern ways of "seeing" people, including those who do not see. James Baldwin (quoted in Brim 2014: 1) suggests, "What one can and cannot see says something about you." Consider, for example, the following encyclopedia entry regarding blindness—how does it see and not see blindness, what does this say about modern existence, and how does it connect us with what is essential to a modernist understanding of blindness?

> The history of the blind is difficult to chart. There are few examples before the 19th-century of sustained organized efforts by the blind to act in concert to achieve collective goals …. What is left to the historian is a collection of biographies of "extraordinary" individuals, from … Helen Keller, Louis Braille to Jorge Luis Borges, which provides little in the way of a narrative thread that one can pull together to create a tapestry of blind history … in large part blindness was assumed to be a ticket to misery, a curse, or a sentence to second-class status.

Maddy De Welles provided insightful editorial comments, for which we are grateful.

The blind, in truth, occupy no greater or lesser a place in history commensurate to their numbers in the general population. (Miller 2015: n.p.)

Narrating the history of blindness is a difficult one, this entry suggests that this is so because "it" is no greater or lesser than any other thing that occurs within a population. Nonetheless, blindness is framed as a difference, a quantifiable condition located in individuals that might not make much of a difference beyond the numbers of people that it effects. Rod Michalko (2002a: 148) suggests that this particular modern story of disability as a difference that should not make a difference connects people to the Western enlightened commitment to undo mystery or, failing that, to keep at bay uncertainty and the unknown. Blindness, narrated as connecting us only to the sense that some minority of people are more effected by conditions than are others, is part of the biomedical orientation that empowers modern practices such as counting the number of people with "it"—253 million people among the 7.6 billion people of the world, says the World Health Organization (WHO) (2017).[2] Knowing that these millions have "it" and that it is not a good thing requires no other understanding than that blindness results in negative effects for both individuals and populations.

A modern conception of blindness, one that proclaims that it is void of myth and mystery, depicts blindness as a negative condition effecting a more or less known number of people in a population, some of whom manage to stand out as exemplary. By way of contrast, consider traditional Anishinaabemowin stories—some animals or people go blind for a little while, narrating the danger of putting eyes above all else—in which a reliance only on sighted eyes is depicted as a way to lose touch with others and with one's world (Chacaby 2011). Whereas such stories suggest blindness is part of the action of our essential relatedness to ourselves and to others, the encyclopedia entry cited above suggests blindness is more like a thing that happens to some people—a condition that can be enumerated but is not itself animated. Blindness, from a modernist point of view, is a more or less static condition of a few people, and a negative one at that. Thus, within the modernist purview, prevention of blindness programs might be the most prevalent and highly resourced form of cultural engagement with blindness (WHO 2017). Moreover, the encyclopedia entry suggests that it is difficult to produce a history of blindness since there are few examples of organized efforts to achieve collective political goals on the part of blind people. In this way, neither the medicalization of blindness nor the life of blind people is connected to a sense of politics. What is left, then, is only a more atomistic rendering of extraordinary individuals who represent an "Enlightened" adaptation to blindness where its meaning is reduced to the impairment of "not seeing."

Even though we are said to live in a time when visual culture is paramount, blindness is understood neither as a form of action nor as a form of political engagement. Blindness *is* typically understood as a condition and thereby is not often read for its perceptive prowess, narrative thrust, or complexity. Situated between modernity's enchantment with visual culture and the medicalization of all things, including its normative order of capacities, appearances, and functionalities, modern renderings of blindness can strip it of any essential distinction, or difference. This sets the putative sighted modern reader up to believe that the development of braille by Louis Braille in 1821 is one of the few defining features of the history of the blind and "the most important advancement in blind education" (Miller 2015: n.p.).

But notice that modernity "sees" technology, such as braille, as lively, active, political, and progressive, but does not see blindness in these ways. In the midst of visual culture and its constantly proliferating visual products and edifices, the sense that blind people "occupy no greater or lesser place in history commensurate to their numbers in the general population" might yet have much to reveal about the sources of existence that fit under the banner of Western modernity. This chapter pursues a cultural history of blindness that addresses representations of blindness that base themselves on the modern understanding of possessing a condition that reflects a reduced capacity to which an individual may, more or less, adjust. We turn to such representations—that is, conventional stories of blindness—so as to work toward revealing the version of existence that this modernist take on blindness puts us in touch with.

4.2. THE MODERNIST TRADITION OF BLINDNESS

Sightlessness is an unnatural condition, a minority condition, thus it is largely up to the sightless to adjust themselves to the rest of the world and not the contrary. It was in those things that I had allowed myself to react spontaneously but without understanding. Another phenomenon is that blindness inevitably renders its vessels away from externals and back to what seems like a somewhat childlike state, which becomes a form of compensation. Blindness isolates a man; he never sees ugliness at very close range. Contacts are usually limited to those who modulate information for his benefit. His isolation from externals—the hardening surface of society—is much more complete than the sighted imagine. Strip a man of that and he will return to fundamentals, as a child does. He seeks normalcy in simplicity, abandoning all the adult refinements. (John Howard Griffin 2004: 154)

John Howard Griffin is better known for his monograph *Black Like Me*, in which he documents his experience passing as black in the deep south of the USA in 1959, than he is for the monograph *Scattered Shadows*, from which the above excerpt is taken. Griffin documents his experience of becoming blind in 1945 as a result of a World War II injury. In 1957, he became sighted again. This particular quotation, from our perspective, very neatly encapsulates a—if not *the*—dominant representation of blindness in Western culture of the Modern Age. Inasmuch as this is the case, it must share some salient features with other representations of blindness in the West, and so we continue.

The representation of blindness by Griffin encapsulates the understanding of blindness as sightlessness and its mainly negative consequences. From the outset, Griffin represents blindness as a "condition," one that is "unnatural" and a "minority." Sight, in contrast, is depicted as the non-condition of the "natural" human, a nature that everyone has with the exception of those few that have an "eye condition." Blindness is thus represented as the unnatural and minority condition of sightlessness, a condition that, because it is unnatural, bears the burden of negative consequences. These consequences are both numerous and far-reaching. Griffin's experience of his blindness leads him to represent blind people as required to "adjust themselves to the rest of the world and not the contrary." Griffin says that it is to this that he allowed himself to "react spontaneously but without understanding." This spontaneity is the reaction of anyone whose culture represents, and thus understands, sight to be a natural phenomenon, one that does not generate thought or reflection unless something goes wrong. Sight—looking and seeing a world external to the self that is there for anyone who is sighted to see—has been a taken-for-granted aspect of human life since at least the Enlightenment. Understanding sight is an activity usually left to those such as medical doctors, who choose to understand the workings of sight, and to those such as philosophers, who choose to contemplate the nature of knowing and knowledge. Reacting spontaneously to blindness understood as an unnatural and minority condition is narrated to be as natural as sight itself. This connects us to the modern sense that it is seemingly natural to fail to see blindness as an occasion to understand the cultural character of sight.[3]

Griffin builds upon this representation of blindness by suggesting that "blindness inevitably renders its vessels away from externals and back to what seems like a somewhat child-like state." Blindness is depicted as a condition that requires a "vessel," something to carry it; it requires embodiment. Blindness comes alive only in an individual life; the individual becomes the host—the vessel—for blindness. It (we) give life to blindness—we do so by representing and thus making sense of that which has entered us, and the representation we give blindness is that it is an unnatural and minority condition rendering the individual helpless, dependent, unknowing, as somewhat like a child. It is just such a rendering of blindness that some rehabilitation programs react against. Cathy Kudlick (2005: 1589–90), for example, writes about her experience in an intensive training program run by blind people for blind people in the USA at the National Federation of the Blind (NFB). This program is committed to "independence, confidence, assertiveness," and was where she learned, among other skills, to travel with the long white cane. Kudlick narrates how "a macho cane environment spawned an interesting culture that ran counter to everything most sighted Americans have thought about blind people and blindness." Whether counter to and/or in line with the conception of blindness represented by Griffin, blind people are situated, as David Mitchell (2002: 15) says about disabled people in general, "in a profoundly ambivalent relation to the cultures and stories they inhabit." That is, whether experienced as an isolating barrier or as a mere inconvenience, a profound ambivalence remains in that blindness is framed as little more than an "obstacle" to which one must adjust, even as blindness is lived as something more or other than an obstacle. The cultural character of blindness as an essential form of existence remains downplayed and disconnected from most rehabilitative attempts to deal with it, including that of the NFB. Thus, we return to reflect on the meaning of blindness enacted within Griffin's account.

The logic of representing blindness as a removal from the external world leads, almost naturally, to "isolation," as Griffin puts it. A blind person "never sees ugliness," according to Griffin, at least not "at very close range." Presumably, blind people do not see beauty either, although Griffin has nothing to say about this. After all, the representation of blindness as childlike does require a sense of innocence, and not seeing ugliness does the trick. Contacts with and to the world "are usually limited to those who modulate information for his benefit." For this representation, Griffin relies on an ocular-centric version of knowing that takes for granted: first, that there is an external world to know; second, that eyesight is a key apparatus for doing so; and third, that those without eyesight know very little of the world and must rely on sighted others for whatever they do know. This empiricist representation of knowledge suggests that whatever aspects of the external world blind people receive from their other senses and the memories from when they were once sighted, if they were so, must be "modulated" by sighted others in order to give blind people at least a partial understanding of the external world. Lack of "information," as Griffin puts it, leading to the lack of knowledge about the world marks the fundamental ground upon which notions of dependence as an essential characterization of blind people are built. Blind people's contact with the world is dependent upon sighted others and, moreover, this dependence is for the "benefit," as Griffin puts it, of blind people.

It is no wonder that Griffin's representation of blindness requires blind people to "adjust to the rest of the world," and that it is not up to sighted people to adjust to blindness, since that would be "contrary," as Griffin says. This adjustment orientation can be witnessed in sighted culture's general interest not only in braille, but in guide dogs, white canes, and the acquisition of skills of daily living. This interest also asserts itself in unquestioned media attention today to any new technological advancement (whether efficacious or not), such as bionic eyes, blind beacons, sensor canes, sonar glasses, etc. Given that blindness is normally narrated as both an unnatural and a minority condition, it is only reasonable that blind people engage in adjustment. Moreover, given that blindness yields very little information regarding the world, there is really no point for sighted people to adjust to blindness, since blindness has nothing to offer to anyone, including blind people, except distortion and misinformation, and within a eugenic orientation blind people are rendered "feebleminded." Blindness is *contrary* to both knowing and knowledge production, which are understood to be central to modern times. It is to this contrariness and to the "natural" and "majority" version of knowledge given by sight that blind people must adjust. They must "see" themselves as vessels of blindness and as bereft of valid and reliable information regarding the world. The "unnatural" and "minority" condition of blindness thus renders blind people as vessels not empty, but as vessels filled with distortion, inaccuracies, and flawed knowledge. This orientation generates the twentieth-century demand—one that has entered *this* century—for blind people and other disabled people to speak the insufferability of "their" conditions, which marks the experiential base of "their" lives.[4]

Griffin says that blind people are isolated "from externals," from the "hardening surface of society." He says, too, that this isolation "is much more complete than the sighted imagine." The "hard surface of society," the real world, reality—these are not available to blind people; these are what blind people lack; these are what are missing when eyesight is missing, according to the modernist tradition. And who can imagine a world without reality, an unreal one, one whose surfaces, hard or soft, are missing? Completeness of living in this sort of world, if it can be called a world, is unimaginable. It is difficult, if not impossible, for "the sighted" to imagine a world being complete without sight. Therefore, imagining "living blind" is tantamount to trying to imagine living a life of incompleteness. The only life "the sighted" can imagine that is stripped of completeness is a life that returns to "fundamentals," the life of a child. This marks the final step in modernity's project of infantilizing the incompleteness embodied in such lives as those of the blind.

The modern story of blindness is, then, one that connects us to a version of the human that generates a sense of difference as incompleteness. In this sense, a cultural history of blindness is, at the same time, a history of its representation; culture may be understood as the social process of interpretation and representation, and this process marks the analytic category for a cultural history of blindness. Almost every culture understands blindness within some version of "sightlessness." Blindness, in this sense, becomes an obstacle to seeing; it not only prevents us from seeing the world, it prevents us, too, from seeing ideas, points of view, opinions, facts, and the like. The thin conventional sense of representing blindness as sightlessness may be conceived of as simply negative. The notion of sightlessness gives blindness its meaning of the negative consequences of being without sight and what that way of being prevents. Blindness, represented as sightlessness, receives its sensibility from an ocular-centric conception not only of knowing, but also of functioning "normally" in the world where lack of normalcy is understood as an incomplete way of being human. This restricts blindness to something that can only happen to sight, and this is how many modern ways of attending to blindness connect people more to the existence and power of sight than to anything else. More complex and even seemingly paradoxical understandings of blindness remain submerged behind the glare of sighted ways, as is hinted at, for example, when blind theorist Georgina Kleege (1999: 1) writes, "Writing this book made me blind," or when Rod Michalko (1999: 2) writes of "going blind over and over again," or when David Bolt (2016: 2) "gate crashes classes in psychology, sociology, and creative writing" rather than becoming a piano tuner.

What is in store for blindness represented not as a way of life, but instead as a barrier to life, as an obstacle, as incompleteness? How does this cultural story connect us to some of the essential interests of modernity? What is in store—the very thing to which blindness connects us—is the power of "normalcy," but only of the "simplest" kind, Griffin says. "He [blind people] seeks normalcy in simplicity," where simple entails a memetic relation. From this perspective, blind people do what children do: they pretend. They pretend to be adults. And they do so since, like children, they know they are not. They can only pretend. They can only pretend to be normal in the simplest of ways. They can look toward the voice of the person with whom they are speaking, use braille to read, and use guide dogs, white canes, or sighted others to move about, but this is "seen" to do nothing other than feign normalcy. Blind people can only act like adults; they can never *be* adult. As Griffin says, "blindness leads to … abandoning all the adult refinements." Like children, blind people are not refined. Unlike children, though, blind people do not have the potential for adult refinement, since the life of blindness is an incomplete one, one bereft of even the potential of the refinements of normalcy.

As important as it is to explicate Griffin's representation of blindness, it is even more important to understand that his representation is not his alone. Griffin's narrative not only connects us to his essential proclivities toward blindness; this story also connects us to the cultural ways of being conscious of blindness, a consciousness inherited from modernity and destined for its reproduction (Merleau-Ponty [1945] 1958: xii, xx). This means that blindness can be read as a kind of umbilical connection to what is regarded as essential to modern ways of being, thinking, and knowing. Our experience is mediated by culture and its meaning is culturally derivative. The cultural meaning of blindness exists long before any one of us becomes blind or comes to engage a blind person. Any experiential engagement with blindness, whether our own or that of others, is a cultural experience; blindness finds its embodiment in culture. Blindness, like the sight used to see it, is cultural through and through.

It is within this cultural act of depiction, ironically enough, that influence and creativity can also be found. Even though Griffin's experience of blindness is a derivative of culture, his life and depiction of blindness become part of the cultural script. We, blind people and others, do not simply and strictly follow the cultural script of blindness. We often improvise. The tradition of the blind black blues singer is testimony to this improvisational possibility, as researched and documented by Terry Rowden. This remains even if Rowden, with his modernist orientation, aims to explain away any mystery of living blind within the "economy of sight" that takes itself as the "most reliable" and "straightforward feedback mechanism" necessary for full communication, action, and citizenship (Rowden 2009: 36–40). Blindness finds its life not in the monologue of culture, but in the dialogue of living a life in culture. This dialectic inserts phenomena such as power, knowledge, and voice into the cultural conversation that is blindness. We now turn to some of the ways in which the modern story of blindness reflects the power and voice of medicine within the cultural history of blindness.

4.3. BLINDNESS AND THE CULTURE OF MEDICINE

As we said earlier, nearly every modern culture "views" blindness as sightlessness. The problem then becomes one of finding a way to represent this view. Ordinary representations of sightlessness, and thus blindness, include, as we have demonstrated, a variety of manifestations not only of dependence, but also of social isolation. Understood as an unnatural and minority condition, blindness leads to dependence and isolation that, as Griffin illustrates, takes the blind person "away from externals." The only region remaining when externality is removed is, of course, the internal. And, given that individuals are "vessels" of blindness, or are imagined, as Michalko (2002a: 63) shows us, as "sighted people with the sight missing," the notion of the internal is represented by interiority, by a reality experienced almost solely from within.

The danger of blindness from within the structure of this representation is the one presented by extreme isolation, by a retreat to interiority understood as solipsistic and even as narcissistic (Siebers 2002: 40). It is this understanding of blindness that has grounded the possibility of much contemporary psychological and neurobiological interest in blindness. Thus, finding what they already know blindness to be leads researchers to say:

Numerous studies have examined the emotional impact exerted by vision loss. ... There are three types of responses to sight loss: acceptance, denial and depression/anxiety. (Moschos 2014: 87)

Interestingly enough, the conclusion of this limited narrative may, in fact, also be its starting point, something the researchers already knew before embarking on their research, namely:

Seeing the surrounding world is undoubtedly a wonderful experience. Throughout history, deprivation of eyesight has been perceived as the most severe form of punishment, second only to loss of life. (Moschos 2014: 89)

Such an understanding provokes our interest in examining how there can be any possibility of creativity for those perceived as suffering from this profound form of psychological deprivation.

It is such deprivation that leads to life being experienced privately, as an isolating interiority that marks the fear understood as residing in blindness. Fear of sightlessness (blindness), then, is the fear of being taken away from the external world and placed squarely in the isolating terror of interiority. The prevention and removal of such terror is the basis for remedial responses to blindness, such as those found in Western conceptions of healing. This medical understanding of blindness is one of the most dominant representations of it in the Modern and Postmodern Age. The cultural conversation that is blindness almost always begins with the dominant voice of medicine. Medicine positions itself not as a representation of blindness, but as both its mouthpiece and solution. Given that blindness is sightlessness and that sightlessness is the virtual removal of "external reality," it follows that the isolating condition of privacy leads to the prime reality of interiority understood not as reality, but as its distortion. Thus, the fear of blindness becomes the fear of living in and with the "unreal." It is to this problem that medicine positions itself as a solution.

This solution is no longer restricted to the West; because of such organizations as the WHO, the medical representation of blindness is now global (e.g. Hubley and Gilbert 2006). This transcultural version of blindness transcends whatever other cultural differences there are in both the social relations to it and the "actual experience" of blindness. Indeed, alongside its technical, medical definition of blindness, the WHO (2015) defines blindness as "the inability to see," and it measures its impact in terms of loss of productive years of life though such activities as disability-adjusted life-year counts, depicting blindness as part of the calculus of the global burden of disease.

This "inability" to see from the point of "view" of the WHO requires, first and foremost, the response of prevention and cure. The WHO's first concern is that "75%" of blindness worldwide can be prevented or cured. This concern with ridding the world of blindness follows directly from a Griffinesque—that is, modernist—representation of it. Isolation from the external world, a sense of the world modulated by sighted others—these are not characteristics of a life worthy of living. Prevention, cure, and rehabilitation are the only "reasonable" narrative themes within the confines of this dominant traditional story, putting people in touch with the technological prowess of modernity while downplaying the vessel that has transported this story into our midst.

Blindness defined as the "inability to see" says more about an attitude or understanding regarding blindness than it does about the WHO's technical/medical representation of it. Still, the WHO defines blindness as distinct from "low vision," which is also defined in technical terms and in relation to sight. The overriding concern of the WHO, though, is not blindness, but sight. Its 2017 action plan is titled: "Vision 20/20: The Right to Sight Action Plan." The WHO defines this plan as a "global initiative for the elimination of avoidable blindness." The quintessential interest and concern of the WHO is embedded in both its name and in the name of its action plan—"Health" and "20/20"—a medical expression of "normal" eyesight is its conception of healthy eyes. Blind eyes, in contrast, are clearly unhealthy, and this should be avoided as a means to the end of elimination. The cultural consequence of not only developing a form of vision that can see others through the cultural orientation of lack, limit, and loss, but also believes that this is a true way of perceiving and ought to dominate is not often part of this modernist vision quest (see also Titchkosky et al., 2019).

The WHO represents sight as a "right." The human is imagined in this representation as sighted and, as such, they have a right to sight, and when "they" is understood as human, this right becomes a "human right." Since the WHO calculates avoidable blindness as comprising 75% of blindness globally, particularly in the Global South, people have a "right" to have their avoidable blindness cured—or better, prevented—thus restoring their human right to sight. The WHO has nothing to say of the relationship between "unavoidable" blindness and the human. Presumably, those of us who are unavoidably blind relinquish our human right to sight.[5]

It is necessary to reflect upon the WHO's choice of rhetoric. It is a right to *sight* that concerns the WHO, and not the right to *see*. Understanding seeing as a human right would require a much different representation of blindness than the Griffinesque one employed by the WHO. Following Baldwin (quoted in Brim 2014: 1), we add that what the WHO "sees" and "does not see" says something about it. Sight is conceived of as a right in that the human comes furnished with a "human biology," and a healthy one at that, and this means, in part, healthy eyes—20/20. No other representation of sight is offered by the WHO.

Seeing, in contrast, is an altogether different matter. Unlike sight, the phenomenon of seeing raises the question of meaning, including that of sight represented as biology and as a right. Closely aligned with the interpretive category of seeing is that of blindness. It takes on a multilayered representational scene when paired with seeing rather than sight as an experiential phenomenon—"turning a blind eye," "blind to the facts," "color-blind," "are you blind, ref?" and the list goes on. In these ways, both seeing and blindness emerge from their biological restrictions and move into the realm of human experience. It is crucial to realize, though, that linguistic expressions of seeing and blindness in Western culture and, for the most part, globally rely for their sensibility on the epistemological position of ocular-centrism. Without this, these expressions lose their potency and plausibility. Moreover, along with an ocular-centric "viewpoint" comes ocular normativism. It is to these phenomena that we now turn.

4.4. OCULAR-CENTRISM AND OCULAR NORMATIVISM

The expression "ocular-centric" tries to capture the understanding that eyesight is a fundamental phenomenon; it suggests that an entire way of perceiving is centered on the ability to see. Representing sight as the central and fundamental aspect of perception is what is intended in the expression "ocular-centrism." Griffin's account of blindness relies for its possibility on this version of sight. Ocular-centrism suggests that, without sight, perception is extremely limited, and when blindness gets represented as sightlessness, what blind people perceive is understood as distortion at best and unreality at worst. What ocular-centrism represents, then, is sight as completeness and blindness as its opposite: incompleteness.

David Michael Levin (1997: 398) says that "the history of Western culture is a history of ocular-centrism and that, in the modern age, this ocular-centrism has taken on a quite distinctive character—and equally distinctive sociocultural functions." David Bolt brings blindness into the discussion of ocular-centrism, generating a sense of ocular normativism. He says:

> If ocular centrism is thought of as the baseline of assumptions, the very foundation of the meta-narrative of blindness perhaps, then this neologism ocular normativism denotes the effect: the perpetuation of the conclusion that the supreme means of perception is necessarily visual. (Bolt 2016: 14)

As is suggested by both of these authors, ocular-centrism is not a methodological call to focus on the ocular as a biological function. Instead, as Levin says, ocular-centrism has a history, and that history is tied to the history of Western culture. Moreover, ocular-centrism, he says, is a set of sociocultural functions. Levin thus removes ocularity from the realm of the biological and places it directly in the realm of the social. Sight is then as much a culturally interpretive act as it is a biological phenomenon; indeed, the latter representation relies upon the former for its possibility.

Conceived of as the "baseline of assumptions," Bolt suggests that perhaps ocular-centrism represents "the very foundation of the meta-narrative of blindness." Our assumptions in relation to the physical and social world presuppose an ocular-centric "viewpoint," and do so in a meta-narrative that necessarily creates its opposite: blindness. Knowing and even understanding the world relies upon the prerequisite of sight, at least if the world is to be known and understood to the "best of our ability" and, of course, the best ability there is in relation to perceiving the world is sight.

Ocular-centrism, Bolt says, generates this "best ability" of sight as its effect. He goes on to say that the neologism "ocular normativism" denotes this effect; namely, "that the supreme means of perception is necessarily visual." The assumption here is that there is an objective world "out there" for anyone to "see"; for anyone, that is, who possesses the supreme means of perception and thus, recalling the WHO, the right to be human.

The "out there" character of the world is thus open to those with sight, and only open to blind people in a very limited way. Their blindness takes them away from the external world, and they must rely on their remaining senses and on sighted others to modulate the world for them. This marks the world of blindness as it is created by ocular normativism, and there is nothing about this world that recommends itself. Given its limited and thus distorted character, no one is imagined as interested in what is produced by blindness, represented as an "inferior means of perception."

But what interest in blindness does Western culture, expressed in the history of ocular-centrism, recommend? Clearly, this cultural history has no interest in what it can learn from blindness, since there is nothing to learn. Blindness represented as sightlessness, with its concomitant restricted and distorted perception of the world, has nothing to offer any quest for knowledge. Indeed, the putative distortive character of blindness impedes any such quest. An interest in blindness, therefore, does not lie in any value placed on our desire to understand reality as it is put together by blindness understood as a legitimate mode of perception.

The interest in blindness that remains from the legacy of ocular-centrism and its effect, ocular normativism, is cultural, represented as epistemology. In relation to blindness, this interest is twofold: first, there is an interest in what "it" (culture) needs to know in order to "help" blind people adjust to the "sighted world"; and second, there is an interest in what can culture learn about itself and its own epistemology from blindness. It is to these interests that we now turn.

4.5. BLINDNESS AND EPISTEMOLOGY

The overarching interest and concern that blindness has generated in the West have centered on and have been oriented by episteme. This epistemological interest in blindness has become more deeply ingrained since World War II and has become so not only in the West but, through globalization, around the world as well. Such an interest did not, of course, emerge on its own; instead, it grew from an age-old sense of blindness as mysterious, fraught with intrigue, and tinged with a sense of wonder at how blind people—or anyone, for that matter—could possibly get along without sight.[6] Moshe Barasch (2001: 7) puts it this way: "So far as our knowledge and imagination can reach back into past ages, we find that there was probably no time and no society in which the blind were not tinged with some mystery."

In modern and even in postmodern times, "mystery" has been not only thought of, but also experienced as a riddle or a puzzle requiring resolution. The positivistic and scientific orientations to the "nature" of life have seen to this. Mysteries—of whatever type—are now sites of methodic contemplation aimed at unraveling the mysteries of life. Indeed, and in a tongue-in-cheek way, we might characterize the contemporary age as that which is committed to unraveling the meaning of life, one mystery at a time.

But what do we make of blindness understood—and at times even experienced—as mysterious? And, as a corollary, how do we approach the phenomenon of blindness with the singular aim of unraveling its mystery? We might begin to address these questions with the understanding that the idea of "mystery" is already a partial resolution, albeit an implicit one, to the riddle of blindness. It is also necessary in addressing these questions to historically contextualize blindness understood as a mystery or as a riddle. Let us return to the work of Moshe Barasch and his discussion of the premodern conception of blindness. He says:

> Once again, then, a certain ambiguity or ambivalence characterizes the image of the blind. On the one hand, he is the unfortunate creature, deprived of what is often considered man's most precious gift, the ability to see the world and to find his way without the help of others. On the other hand, he is endowed, however vaguely, with an ability given to no other human being—to be in direct communication with a deity. He dwells in two worlds or hovers between them. The undefined, intuitive impressions suggest how complex people's understanding of the blind person was in premodern times. Blindness was a riddle. Throughout the centuries, with the memory of it remained the sense of mystery, the feeling of anxiety that accompanies it, but also the entreating fascination of the song's rhythm and rhyme. (Barasch 2001: 3)

When deprived of the "precious gift" of sight, of the "ability to see the world" and to make our way in it without any help, what else remains for us than the status of "unfortunate creature"? This cultural story of blindness reduces the blind person not only to a creature, but to an unfortunate one as well. Sight is often imagined not merely as a gift, but as a "precious gift." It is a gift that opens the world to us with all of its beauty and ugliness, its glory and shame, its mystery and certitude, its possibility and limitation, its open horizons and closed borders; it is this world that is the precious gift, the gift that is given to us when we are presented with the gift of sight. But the precious character of sight does not end here. Not only does sight open the world to us, it also gives us freedom of the most precious sort: the freedom of movement without the burdensome necessity of "help" and without the equally burdensome necessity of need in the form of interdependence understood as dependence. There is no equality between forms of perception; only in techniques of accessibility. Deprived of the "precious gift," it is ambiguity or ambivalence that truly becomes the gateway to the world for those of us who are blind.

Even though Barasch characterizes ambiguity and ambivalence vis-à-vis blindness as residing in the contrast between "unfortunate creature" and the ability to "be in direct communication with a deity," there is more to the story than that. Ambiguity and ambivalence are imagined, first of all, as properties of blindness and not of sight. There is nothing ambiguous or even ambivalent about the clarity of sight, the clarity that opens up an equally unambiguous world to those who are given the precious gift. A world fraught with ambiguity and ambivalence, in contrast, is the world that opens up to those without the precious gift. It is in this way that ambiguity and ambivalence become dialectically united with one another. The cultural story of blindness imagined as "ambiguous eyes" forges nothing other than an "ambiguous world."

Living in the quagmire of ambiguity and ambivalence, what else remains for blind people other than direct communication with a deity? There can be no direct communication with other humans since, as Griffin has told us, sighted others are united with blind people only by the thin thread of those who "modulate" the world for those without the precious gift. A relationship of modulation is never a direct one. It is always a relationship between the gifted and the "unfortunate creature" dispossessed of the gift that would open up the clarity of the world if only the gift had been bestowed upon the creature.

Deity represents a different sort of creature altogether, if a creature at all. Unlike the world of clarity that opens up before those with the precious gift, the deity is clarity itself. For the premodern blind person, according to Barasch, while finding nothing but ambiguity and ambivalence when they "look" at the world, a direct communication with a deity provides an otherworldly clarity, one that no other human being has. And yet, it is a clarity, as Barasch suggests, that offers its own ambiguity and ambivalence; that comes, as he says, with dwelling between two worlds or to anyone who "hovers between them." This betweenness is characterized by the ambiguous life of modulated communication with sighted others and the otherworldly life of direct communication with a deity. Not only do sighted people experience ambiguity and ambivalence toward blind people within the framework of this image of blindness, so too do blind people. What other than ambiguity and ambivalence can emerge from an image of oneself as communicating directly with clarity on the one side and living with this clarity in the ambiguity of the other side? Hovering between the two may be the only social location open to blind people in modern times.

And yet, it is not as though the Modern Age "saw" an end to ambiguity and ambivalence in relation to blindness. Nor has the Modern Age ushered in a clarity regarding blindness and a removal of its mystery. "Blindness was a riddle" during premodern times, and perhaps it remains so. As Barasch says, "a sense of mystery" and a "feeling of anxiety" remain integral parts of the image of blindness "throughout the ages." A fascination with blindness, with its "rhythm and rhyme," also remains securely within contemporary images of blindness (Healey, 2019).

Alicia Meseguer (2012) takes exception to Barasch's claim that "blindness was a riddle" and remains so. She emphasizes "was" and says, "Blindness *was* a riddle. *Was.*" She emphasizes the past; the Modern Age solved the riddle that *"was"* blindness. This logic, of course, aligns with modernity's invocation and privileging of "reason" as the quintessential human faculty. Nature, including the human type with its behavior and action, is governed by laws. The unraveling of any mystery and the resolution of any riddle are the results and by-products of the "discovery" of the laws of nature and of human behavior and action.

Within a modern scientific paradigm, blindness is framed as a phenomenon of nature and thus as subject to its laws. Paradoxically, this paradigm conceives of blindness as both natural and unnatural; natural insofar as it is a biological phenomenon and unnatural in that blindness is understood as "biology gone wrong" (Michalko 2002a: 91). Either way, nature takes its course, and blindness is a deviation from the course that sight naturally takes. Modernity frames nature not as a riddle, since the solution to the riddle of nature is that it is law-governed, leaving it to modernity through its methodic theory and practice of science to uncover the laws of nature. Thus, the riddle of blindness *was*, but no longer *is*. What remains a riddle is now on a "waiting list," a list of phenomena awaiting society's contribution of resources (largely time and money) to science so that it may discover the "cause" and thus the origin of any riddle.

The premodern cultural conception that blindness is the inability to see the world and to move independently in it is a conception that the modern world has inherited. The cultural conception that blind people have direct communication with a deity is another matter altogether. "Direct communication with a deity" may be read as an explanation—if not a solution—to the riddle that *was* blindness. That the Modern Age has solved the riddle that was blindness by offering the solution that blindness is governed by the laws of nature eliminates any need for communication, whether direct or indirect, between blind people and a deity. Whether or not such communication, especially that of the indirect kind, has come to an end is another matter and requires further exploration.

4.6. TWISTING THE CONNECTION BETWEEN EPISTEMOLOGY AND BLINDNESS

Meseguer suggests that modernity has restructured the mystery of blindness. She says:

> The uncanny also shifts from an appendage of religion to a homelessness in which it becomes itself. This detachment exiles the uncanny from the sanctuary of its veiled place, making it newly visible. The change can be thought of as a "triumph" of the "age of reason", a result of the secularization of society, but let us not forget that it is also a story. (Meseguer 2012: 200)

Meseguer says that modernity shifts the uncanny sense of blindness from an "appendage of religion" to a "homelessness in which it becomes itself." The uncanny character of blindness moves with it from premodern times to modern times, according to Meseguer. This part of the mystery of blindness remains.

There is something uncanny about blindness in terms of how its appearance in the world is culturally conceived of and understood. To be dispossessed of the ability to see the world as well as the ability to move freely in it while at the same time having direct communication with a deity forms the background of the uncanny character of blindness during premodern times. It is uncanny that communication with a deity is bestowed "freely" on those who are understood as essentially not free. The uncanny character of blindness, according to Meseguer, shifts from this premodern orientation to the modern sense as a result of secularization, of the uncanny character of blindness as no longer an "appendage of religion," but a "homelessness," one "in which it becomes itself."

At home with itself while at the same time homeless in the "sighted world" is the way in which blindness makes an appearance in modern times. "Becoming itself in homelessness" may be read as a distinctly modern "story," since Meseguer reminds us that modernity is itself a story of the connection between episteme and blindness. Even though blindness retains a sense of the uncanny in the Modern Age, the premodern version of the connection between the uncanny and blindness is detached, exiling, as Meseguer points out, the uncanny from a place of sanctuary and making it "newly visible." This "new visibility" may be read, Meseguer suggests, as a "triumph of modernity," a triumph understood as an aspect of the story of modernity.

The "new visibility" of the uncanny in relation to blindness, according to Meseguer, is a form of exile—the uncanny is exiled to the place of its new visibility as an attempt on the part of the Modern Age to detach blindness from the uncanny. The premodern image of blind people as those deprived of the ability to see the world and thus of the capacity to move independently in it while at the same time being in direct communication with a deity requires an uncanny sense of blindness. The familiarity of the futile attempt of blind people to move independently in a sighted world is fraught with the uncanny connection between futility and the divine. There is something "special" in witnessing blind people participating in the mundane act of moving in the world of everyday life; in witnessing an act of sheer futility and incompetence and of supreme dependence; in witnessing these acts as they appear in "direct communication with a deity": this, truly, is uncanny.

But what of the detachment of the uncanny of blindness in the Modern Age? What do we make of this triumph of the Age of Reason? The uncanny, says Meseguer, is exiled "from the sanctuary of its veiled place," and this is what makes it "newly visible." Whatever sanctuary the uncanny enjoyed during premodern times has evaporated and has become newly visible in modern times. The dependent movement of blind people is no longer witnessed through the veil of the communication of the deity. This detachment has certainly detached the uncanny, as Meseguer says, and exiled it into a new visibility. The connection between the uncanny and blindness is undoubtedly a secular one since modernity and is now newly visible in the secular image of blindness.

Modernity has ushered in a different kind of connection between the uncanny and blindness, twisting the connection between blindness and episteme, between blindness and knowledge of the world. Since this knowledge is no longer given over to "direct communication with a deity," the uncanny becomes visible in the tenuous connection between blindness and knowledge, with its concomitant relation with the act of knowing. The site of sight has always been connected implicitly with knowledge. The deprivation of sight has been and continues to be understood as the simultaneous deprivation of knowledge together with the means of knowing. Within this perspective, blind people are understood as moving in the world without direct communication with sight. There are just the remaining senses and the modulation of sighted others to give blind people knowledge, and a second-order kind at that. And yet blind people do move through the world, at times dependently, at other times independently, and at still other times—and for the most part as do sighted others—interdependently. This movement demonstrates knowledge as well as some understanding of the world, and it does so in the midst of blindness; this is uncanny, and this is what marks a new twist in the connection between blindness and episteme.

Modernity's interest in blindness differs from that of premodern times. The latter's interest focused on the pathetic character of blindness and on the unknown and unknowable relation that it had with the divine. Despite its pathos, it communicated with a deity, and this was not only uncanny, but unsettling as well. Modernity, in contrast, no longer interested in the divine in relation to blindness, began to focus more on episteme: What did blind people know and how did they know what they knew? This became a source of wonder for modernity. This sense of wonder was wrapped in the question of what a blind person could know if they gained sight.

4.7. A TWISTED EPISTEMOLOGY

Modernity's interest in blindness was, at bottom, an interest in sight. Since sight is understood—at least in modernity and in the West—as the predominant way of knowing the world, blindness becomes antithetical to this way of knowing. What do blind people know without the precious gift, and what would they know if they had this gift? These were questions that preoccupied modernist thinkers. This preoccupation, of course, was and still is not restricted to the intellectual pursuits of philosophers and scientists. There is a fascination with how blind people perceive the world and with what the world is through "blind eyes," especially for those who are congenitally totally blind.

This fascination is more about sight and the "sighted world" than it is about blindness and a "blind world." Perhaps the most well-known example of this fascination is to be found in what has come to be known as the "Molyneux Problem." Einat Adar quotes Molyneux from a letter he sent to John Locke in 1688 in which he poses a hypothetical question. He introduces an equally hypothetical blind man[7] and suggests to Locke that this man, born blind and now an adult, had learned, through touch, to distinguish between a cube and a sphere. Molyneux continues:

> Suppose then the cube and the sphere placed on a table and the blind man to be made to see. Quaere whether by his sight, before he touched them, he could now distinguish and tell which is the globe, which the cube. (De Beer 1979: 651, original spelling retained)

Interestingly enough, Berkeley says that "the blind man will not even understand the question" (quoted in Adar 2017: 3).

There is no question that, for Molyneux, Berkeley, and anyone else for that matter, sighted people can distinguish without difficulty between a globe and a cube, even through touch. This ability, Molyneux presupposes, stems from learning this distinction not from touch, but from sight. It is a visual distinction. Those without the precious gift learn this distinction *only* through touch. Touch, though, marks the acquisition of a second-order kind of knowledge, and its primacy can be tested only through the imposition of sight. Molyneux's "hypothetical blind man" can distinguish between a globe and a cube by touching the two, and this distinction represents knowledge that, while as effective as that of sight, is nonetheless inferior to it.

Molyneux's interest is in knowledge transference, and his implicit question might read: Can the knowledge gained through touch (blindness) be transferred to that gained by sight? Berkeley is not convinced, and he is not even convinced that the hypothetical blind man will even understand Molyneux's question. Neither are interested or even curious about knowledge transference the other way round. And this understanding of the relationship between blindness and knowledge is the paradigmatic conception of blindness bestowed upon us by modernity. This relationship between blindness and episteme provides for the possibility of Molyneux's hypothetical experiment. He begins with the premise that blindness is epistemologically inferior to sight. This is why Molyneux does not conduct his experiment the other way round. He does not explicitly posit a "hypothetical sighted man" who has learned to distinguish a sphere from a cube only through sight. Nor is he interested—or even curious about—whether if the sighted man were made to be blind he could distinguish the sphere from the cube through touch. This experiment would be superfluous, since knowledge gained through sight is knowledge that is transferrable to the other senses. This is not the case for blindness, since knowledge gained through it lacks the completeness and certitude inherent in knowledge gained through sight.

Given that blindness is understood as sightlessness, what blindness becomes is the opposite of sight, and this means the opposite of the ability to "see" the world, to move freely in it, and to know it. Except for what is gained through senses other than sight and that sense of the world provided by the modulations of sighted others, blindness acquires the status of distortion. From this conception, the "view" that blind people have of the world is unequivocally a distorted one, and what sort of an interest is an interest in a twisted view, in distortion?

There is, first of all, the commonsense interest in distortion framed in the experience of intrigue. How blind people experience the world and what they know of it is often a source of intrigue for sighted others. What is intriguing, of course, is how a sense of the world is possible without seeing (a reconfirmation of the myth that sighted people have a complete sense of the world, one affirmed by an interest in blindness). From this, the interest in blindness is reduced to one in discovering how much of the world blind people know. Whatever may have been intriguing about blindness usually ends here, and the interest changes into one of discovering how to "replace" as much of the knowledge of the world that blind people are missing as is possible. This interest may be read as the basis for rehabilitation. Blind people cannot know everything, according to this interest, but they can be given as much as possible in order to "fit into" a sighted world. Any interest in blindness—its intrigue, its mode of perception, what it can teach—is cast to the side as a twisted interest in distortion, and is replaced by a process of determining what blind people know and need to know in order to be as "normal" as possible, to be folded in, made to fit in like everyone else (Stiker 1999: 133, 136–7), to become the "abled-disabled" (Titchkosky 2003: 517, 520).

It is this mundane interest in blindness that provoked Diderot's blind man to say, "I've been the object of your wonder so often that I have a very low opinion of the things that amaze you" (as translated by Tunstall 2011: 199). Diderot's blind man is amazed that he continues to be the object of wonder for sighted people. There is nothing intriguing about blindness for Diderot's "blind man," and he is amazed that people wonder about him. A blind man could be a source of intrigue unless this "man" was like every other "man," and there is nothing intriguing about this. If this orientation to blindness is what Diderot's blind man adopted, then there is no wonder that he is amazed. This lack of intrigue regarding blindness, together with its everyday orientation toward it, may be read as a precursor to the contemporary understanding that blind people are just like sighted people with the sight missing who happen to do things differently.

4.8. THE INTRIGUE OF A CULTURAL HISTORY OF BLINDNESS

The intrigue of blindness is exiled from its home in mystery through the history of modernity and is placed into the realm of the banality of doing things differently represented as the essential difference of blindness. Intriguing, too, is that while blind people are conceived of as lacking freedom of movement, their blindness moves freely through this cultural history. This movement includes echoes of the cultural meanings of blindness, meanings that move freely from one historical moment to another. Recall that the WHO (2017) suggests that blind people "by definition, cannot walk about unaided." This is an echo of Barasch's (2001: 3) characterization of the premodern conception of blindness as the inability of a person "to find his way without the help of others." Neither interrogate the sort of freedom of movement that may come from walking aided or from moving with others. After all, sight is a constant and continuous traveling companion of blindness, and the one never moves through a cultural history without the touch of the other. This sort of movement may represent a freedom that is far richer than the one found in the banality of moving or doing things differently. Blindness may be conceived of as a movement that is itself distinct and not merely different.

Returning to the sense of *Aatisokan* with which we began this chapter, perhaps the umbilical connection toward which the existence of blindness gestures is the narrative of the necessity of our essential need to move with others. But this is a story that modernity has ignored; by twisting blindness into dependency and lack, modernity has made blindness interesting only insofar as it reflects sight as an independent power of knowing. Nonetheless, blindness and sight remain connected, and in the movement of that connection we can reveal something of the meaning of modernity. Perhaps, we can follow the umbilical of blindness and embark on a journey toward the source of the freedom of movement as connection with others.

It is clear that a modern cultural history of blindness is a cultural history of sight. What has emerged is that if blindness had a history, it would necessarily have to be a cultural history of its movement throughout time and space with sight. This movement demonstrates that sight has overestimated its disconnection with blindness and has "viewed" blindness merely as its opposite and thus as a detriment not only to moving freely, but also to the acquisition of knowledge and knowing. Blindness is not the only limitation in this formulation, since sight has also limited its own acquisition of self-understanding. Sight may learn much from blindness, and when blindness is removed from the limiting conception of the oppositional, it too may learn much from sight. Recall James Baldwin (quoted in Brim 2014: 1), who suggests, "What one can and cannot see says something about you." When sight sees and does not see blindness, it says something about how sight looks and what it sees. The potentiality of perceiving what sight might not is the perceptual space from which blind people may offer a creativity and a conversation that says more than how sighted culture sees and knows.

CHAPTER FIVE

Deafness

Screening Signs in Contemporary Cinema

SAMUEL YATES

Audiology booths have always caused me anxiety. Sitting alone in the large soundproof box, gazing at stickers of Donald Duck and Mickey Mouse sparsely tacked up in an attempt to enliven the space while a pair of too-tight headphones supposedly blasted beeps into my ears was an annual exercise in failure during my childhood. *No, I don't hear the beep, the buzz, the high-frequency squeal, or the siren through the static*, I would remind my audiologists emphatically. Without mouth shapes to "read," all of the sounds mushed together. A series of ever-retreating phonetics during the speech recognition portion faded into static, like trying to watch a movie on cable through television noise: chalk (*or is it walk, maybe?*), baseball, hotdog, burn (*or learn, perhaps?*), snowflake, and so on, until my examiner could satisfactorily confirm my hearing to be unchanged or dramatically altered. Raised in a speaking household with parents unlearned in American Sign Language (ASL), I adapted to living with my cross-aid hearing aids, reading lips, finding the advantageous positions for maximal acoustics in a given space, and watching television with the closed captioning on (or, if my protesting brothers watched with me, with the volume blasting on high). Growing up without a noticeable Deaf community in West Virginia[1] and with parents firmly set against any notion of having a "disabled child," my first and only encounters with ASL and Deaf culture were watching Mrs. Nelson translate Sunday mass to her son in the front pews at church and a pair of films: *The Miracle Worker* (1962) and *Children of a Lesser God* (1986).[2]

In this chapter, I consider Deafness performances in commercial film during the twentieth and twenty-first centuries and how modern cinema frames d/Deaf–hearing relationships. By "performance," I do not mean the relationships generated from the daily performance of everyday life (Goffman 1959), but art-framed events explicitly aestheticized, improvised, scripted, and intended for a spectator (Kuppers 2014). Complicated and diverging relationships to one's status as hearing or d/Deaf emerge in the everyday, but these are far more difficult to track. Today, a young, hearing–speaking boy of seven might have a very different relationship to a Deaf–signing playmate in the park if he lives in the Trinidad neighborhood, which sits beside Gallaudet University in Washington, D.C., than a girl in Omaha, Nebraska, where the Nebraska School for the Deaf shuttered in 1998. Where Deaf communities flourish, d/Deaf and hearing persons live alongside each other with Deaf persons modeling different ways of being in the world to persons taught "[ours] is a hearing world" (Harmon 2010: 32–3). In the absence of a visible Deaf community, most people (deaf, hearing, or somewhere in between) first encounter d/Deafness onscreen.

In the sections that follow, this chapter takes up film, and commercial cinema in particular, as a technological development of the modern era unique in its impact on the d/Deaf community. Film, as a medium, has been described as the "printing press of the Deaf community" for its ability to capture and disseminate sign performances (Krentz 2016: 52).[3] Deaf and disability scholar Brenda Jo Brueggemann, highlighting ASL's performative aspects, asks, "What happens to a language like ASL in the wake of digital and video technologies that can now enable sign-language literature to be 'published' and shared across distance, time, and space?" (2009: 34). Her query begets other questions and investigations into how signed languages evolve as signs and styles are transmitted across time, space, and national borders; how accessibility may encourage new users (d/Deaf, Hard of Hearing (HoH), and hearing alike) to learn sign language and, in turn, shape its development; and how to preserve global d/Deaf languages and cultures beyond the ephemerality of an embodied language. These significant questions get at the impact of the mechanical reproduction and proliferation of ASL in community, academic, and creative spaces, although they do not form the center of this chapter.[4] Instead, I focus on cinematic engagements with d/Deafness to frame contemporary cinema as a d/Deaf–hearing contact zone with the potential to template "best practices" for filmic access technologies for the deaf/HoH; provide ethical representations of d/Deaf persons in popular entertainment; and facilitate cross-cultural conversations.

Film may seem like a surprising place to begin a consideration of d/Deafness in the modern era, but it seems apropos for discussing deafness in a volume on the cultural history of disability given how deafness itself is a kind of "betweenity," as Brueggemann writes in *Deaf Subjects: Between Identities and Places* (2009). Many Deaf persons do not consider themselves disabled, and Deaf Studies has a rich history outside of and predating Disability Studies. Working from a cultural model of disability perspective, I think of disability as a constellation of medical, sociohistorical, and environmental framings of the non-normative body. Whether one identifies as disabled or not, one can still be hailed as such by a family member at home, a stranger on the street, a co-worker, or a peer in the classroom. Despite many d/Deaf people balking at the application of a "disabled" label or association, Brueggemann reminds us how "they *are* often labeled as such and that these labels—in all cases—are not always accurate, though they may be, as it were, with consequences" (2009: 12).

In framing d/Deafness as a disability in this volume, I turn to the cultural model of disability, emphasizing what Patrick J. Devlieger (2005: 8) argues is "the potential of disability as a state of being," or what H-Dirksen L. Bauman and Joseph M. Murray (2009: 3) call "Deaf Gain": "a reframing of 'deaf' as a form of sensory and cognitive diversity that has the potential to contribute to the greater good of humanity." My use of "d/Deafness"—a toggling between the lower-case "deaf," a medically oriented identity position separate from the capitalized "Deaf" subject identifying with the sociocultural belonging of a wider Deaf community—has its lineage in James Woodward's *How You Gonna Get to Heaven If You Can't Talk to Jesus: On Depathologizing Deafness* (1982). Woodward argues that the "handicapped classification" of Deaf people is detrimental to Deaf and Hearing alike; it narrates the Deaf as "inferior" and allows hearing people to "reject Deaf culture, Deaf values, and the self-worth of Deaf people" (1982: 76).[5] He continues, charging both Deaf and hearing communities with the "impetus for attitudinal changes towards Deaf individuals" (1982: 77). As a deaf writer who is contextually hailed as deaf, Deaf, and hearing, I live in Brueggemann's betweenity, a slippery landscape in which I am frequently called upon to relay information, solve miscommunications, and bridge cultural divides. I find film is a helpful tool in this work.

I will first differentiate between a Cinema *of* the Deaf and Deaf Cinema, or Cinema *for* the Deaf. The former cites the d/Deaf experience but is produced by predominantly hearing individuals with little access to or experience within Deaf culture; the latter is created by and for individuals within Deaf culture. As will be made clear, these two traditions organize themselves—to considerably different effect—around d/Deaf communication experiences, social expectations, physical sensations, and cultural concerns. Commercial cinema and television featuring deaf protagonists or secondary characters are abundant, but they often fail basic accessibility needs for the very audiences these projects claim to represent. Movie theaters, television, and streaming services unevenly offer accessibility tools in the USA, despite the Twenty-First Century Communications and Video Accessibility Act of 2010, signed by President Barack Obama in October 2010. This two-pronged law addresses communications access and video programming, including a mandate for the redistribution of television broadcasts on the internet to have closed captioning.[6] Internationally, open captioning is an industry norm for cinemas catering to multilingual spectators, but access issues persist elsewhere. I will then discuss a set of films blurring the lines between "Deaf-worlds" and "hearing worlds": *Signage* (2007), *Words* (2010), *Sign* (2016), and *A Quiet Place* (2018). Mixed-hearing casts and creative teams produced each film and, anticipating mixed-hearing viewers, incorporated or played with visucentric[7] access in their respective finished productions.

5.1. SCREENING SIGNS

Although film memorializes singular moments in time, it is a highly portable entertainment medium. A film can move between communities, beyond national borders, be screened in public spaces, or viewed on personal digital devices, provoking new responses with every (re)iteration. By naming the subtitle of this chapter "Screening Signs," I am purposefully leaning on Paul Longmore's influential disability film essay, "Screening Stereotypes: Images of Disabled People in Television and Motion Pictures" (2003). Longmore asks why viewers "screen" out their encounters with disability on film, and he posits that this practice reflects how most able-bodied people act when they encounter disability in their daily lives:

> Disability happens around us more often than we generally recognize or care to notice, and we harbor unspoken anxieties about the possibility of disablement, to us or to someone close to us. What we fear, we often stigmatize and shun and sometimes seek to destroy. Popular entertainment depicting disabled characters allude to these fears and prejudices, or address them obliquely or fragmentarily, seeking to reassure us about ourselves. (Longmore 2003: 132)

If the impetus to stigmatize, shun, and destroy disability is predicated on a viewer's explicit acknowledgment of disability as a threat to impossible bodily integrity instead of a tactic of avoidance, then able-bodied, normate audiences must take up the task of noticing, recognizing, and engaging with disability in a productive way that is not solely about their own anxieties. This type of engagement is a reformulation of Woodward's argument about Deaf and hearing communities. Able-bodied film producers must similarly challenge themselves to create work that does not leave the burden of representation of (and education about) disabilities to the disabled. In answer to Longmore's dictum to uncover the "hidden history" of disabled people while challenging "unconscious images" in the media, and to "liberate disabled people from the paternalistic prejudice expressed in those images and to forge a new social identity," I turn to contemporary cinema as a generative contact zone between abled bodies and disabled bodies. What happens when we push Deaf culture to the fore – when signed languages are the primary mode of communication? A hearing viewer cannot "screen" Deafness out because a Deaf perspective is necessary to make sense of the world; in referencing screening signs, then, viewers are immersed in a visucentric mode of storytelling and communication.

In 2017, for example, *The Silent Child* (dir. Chris Overton) won the Oscar for Best Live Action Short Film. The short, about a deaf girl born into a hearing family and living without access to sign language, highlights the hold oralism still has on deaf education and the toxicity of audism in a familial environment. When Rachel Shelton, an actor in the film and its writer, accepted the award in British Sign Language (BSL), she stated: "Deafness is a silent disability. You can't see it, and it's not life threatening, so I want to say the biggest of thank-yous to the Academy for allowing us to put this in front of a mainstream audience." Shelton's signed acceptance speech powerfully fulfilled her promise to Deaf child actor Maisie Sly (the film's titular "silent child") to accept the award in BSL and created a direct link to Marlee Matlin's signed 1987 Oscar acceptance speech for *Children of a Lesser God*. Deaf people remain, as Lennard Davis explains, "a linguistic minority" (1995b: 3). Her prime-time television representation of sign language, used to communicate achievement on an equal playing field in cinema, combats harmful stereotypes of Deafness and enables non-signers to see the complexity and beauty of sign language in two spaces they might not have imagined it to exist: at a high-profile global film awards ceremony celebrating artistic excellence and on primetime television.

5.1.1. Cinema of the Deaf and Deaf Cinema

A "Cinema of the Deaf" is rhetorically different from Deaf Cinema chiefly in its being *about* d/Deafness rather than being from the perspective of—or for—members of the Deaf community. Following Jane Norman, I distinguish a Cinema *of* the Deaf as typically produced by and for hearing audiences despite its reliance on deafness as a narrative device or metaphor. Such deployments of d/Deafness are usually in service of an audist narrative or to champion oralism, however well-intentioned the creative process may be. Feature-length films such as *Hear Me* (dir. Fen-fen Cheng 2009) and *Listen To Your Heart* (dir. Matt Thompson 2010) position deaf female characters as central in the narrative, but the plot hinges on their integration into the hearing world; both films depict a deaf girl as the creative inspiration and love interest for a hearing suitor.[8] In *Hollywood Speaks*, John Schuchman asserts that cinema, "more than any other medium ... [has] popularized simple-minded views of deafness" (1988: 99). Depictions of passive Deafies waiting to be loved or saved or awakened to the sound world from which they are excluded are precisely the harmful stereotypes Schuchman argues Hollywood perpetuates. A key element of a Cinema of the Deaf is cultural isolation. Isolation allows the singular Deaf person to be viewed as disabled and for a pathological framing of Deafness because there is no cultural context of comparison. Schuchman writes: "The deaf community does not exist in film or television, only deafness and deaf individuals do. The reason for this is clear. Hollywood cannot or will not deal with the issue of language in the deaf community" (1988: 101). Or, as Harlan Lane argues, "The loss of choices is largely the result of the social construction of what it means to be *deaf*—the result of audism—rather than any sensory limitation that deaf people have" (2002: 364).

Schuchman and Patti Durr (2016) note how silent films during the first quarter of the twentieth century employed Deaf actors. Silent film was a broadly accessible entertainment form for d/Deaf, HoH, and hearing actors and patrons because intertitles displayed narrative information beyond body gesture and action. Deaf performances in—and patronage of—commercial cinema fell away as the film industry transitioned to "talkies" with integrated sound allowing for spoken-language dialogue. Following official recognition of sign language in the 1960s, manual languages began to be incorporated into mainstream film for hearing audiences—a Cinema *of* the Deaf—but so too were Deaf-authored and -produced films, such as the Peter Wolf-directed films *Deafula* (1975) and *I Love You, But* (1998). These Deaf Cinema (or Cinema *for* the Deaf) films, by and for the Deaf community, radically reorient toward a visucentric performance. *Deafula*, for example, is performed entirely in ASL, although a voiceover track in spoken English does play for non-ASL-fluent audiences (this attention to access not only for hearing spectators, but also for audiences who might rely on auditory instead of visual modes of storytelling, is striking).

In an entry on "Deaf Cinema" for *The SAGE Deaf Studies Encyclopedia*, Durr charts the explosion of Deaf Cinema in the early 2000s, giving a concise reference list of Deaf film festivals and filmmaking companies, so I will not replicate that information here (2016: 157–8). The rise of Deaf Cinema artists and venues, however, does highlight an increasingly sharp juxtaposition between films capitalizing on deafness as a narrative vehicle and projects investing in Deaf subjectivities. Today, the barrier of Deaf entry into mainstream entertainment is arguably the lowest it has been since the beginning of cinematic entertainment, where intertitles allowed for the widest range of hearing and d/Deaf participants (blind persons remain the most excluded even with today's audio description). This change is partly due to an increased sense of responsibility on the part of filmmakers creating new art in an age of internet callout culture (producers and directors can no longer use the standard excuse, "We could not find a Deaf actor" in a hyper-connected digital age) and the increased visibility of the Deaf community that social media brings. Articulations of Deaf perspectives as valuable, even preferable to hearing, have also aided this shift. In "Reframing Deafness," Bauman and Murray explain how the concept of "Deaf Gain" inverts the spoken English phrase "hearing loss," although it has no direct translation into ASL. Instead, ASL glosses "Deaf Gain" as "DEAF INCREASE," "DEAF BENEFIT," and "DEAF CONTRIBUTE" (2009: 3). The interplay of "increasing" deafness rather than describing it as a lack, articulating Deafness as a "beneficial" experience, and acknowledging its "contributions" offer Deaf and Disability Studies inroads to generatively associate Deafness alongside a diverse array of fields and cultural products, most especially media and film. ASL's visual–spatial elements and storytelling structure are, as Bauman and Murray argue, "comparable to that of film language" (2009: 8).[9]

5.1.2. Television

In 1988, John Schuchman noted how television is where d/Deaf access, cultural representation, talent, and viewership have most advanced in the film industry. The same is still true nearly thirty years later. Although there are more movies featuring d/Deaf characters, television offers an engagement with deafness as a staple of the return of serialization from the nineteenth-century novel beyond the confines of the feature-length film. Diverse revenue streams have democratized television production, and while content is undeniably a driving factor of a show's popularity, video-streaming services such as

Netflix and Hulu have broadened a production's reach through suggestive algorithms and full-season availability allowing for "binge-watching." Thus, "plotted" and reality television series are accessible to a broader degree of variously embodied audiences in a way unlike the limited distribution of Deaf cinema, and their comparatively short production schedules allow for shows to engage in more of-the-moment Deaf–hearing issues such as cochlear implants or inefficient sign language training for law enforcement personnel.[10]

Fictional television series have embraced long-form storytelling beyond the sitcom model, a move allowing for lengthier and more nuanced story arcs as well as the narrative time for a show to cultivate specific audiences. *Switched at Birth* (ABC Family/Freeform, 2011–17), for example, was produced with particular attention to its Deaf viewers, but its strong performances and intelligent writing about topical interests have generated a hearing fandom, too. The series dramatizes the culture clash between Deaf and hearing communities through two girls (one hearing, one Deaf) who were accidentally switched at birth. *Switched at Birth* debuted with 3.3 million viewers, a strong number for basic cable viewership and the highest rating in ABC Family history (Barney 2011). The production regularly employed Deaf and HoH talent alongside its hearing actors and attempted to bridge cultural and communication gaps throughout the show's five seasons, with particular attention being paid to the audism prevalent in hearing communities, complications from deaf students mainstreaming into hearing schools, and how "mixed" d/Deaf–hearing relationships work. Even if *Switched at Birth* is evidence of the mainstream appeal of Deaf culture in popular entertainment, its means of production were not a watershed moment for the Deaf community. Katie Leclerc, the actor playing the central Deaf character, Daphne, has met criticism for being an actor raised in hearing culture. Although Leclerc has Ménière's disease, a symptom of which is fluctuating and progressive hearing loss, she simulates a "Deaf accent" or speech patterns in her portrayal of the cochlear-using Daphne. The show infrequently used medium frames to ensure ASL is afforded equal communicative space to spoken English, although several scenes throughout the five-season run are entirely in ASL. Over-the-shoulder shots or cross-cuts prioritizing facial reactions in dialogue often obscure signs, and the ASL is sometimes "SimCommed," leading to non-grammatical or incomprehensible ASL.[11]

Reality television competitions offer ostensibly unscripted seasons with every(wo)man contestants from diverse backgrounds. Contestants for these shows are often anything but "every(wo)men," given their extraordinary talents, but producers select casts with a wide demographic angle in mind. In reality competitions such as *Project Runway*, *America's Next Top Model*, *The Amazing Race*, and *Chopped*, Deaf fashion designers, models, development associates, and chefs have won or ranked in hearing/oral-dominated environments, challenging preconceptions about the talents and abilities of Deaf persons. These shows are not designed to showcase or advance specific agendas, but in the vast majority of iterations, Deaf contestants have used the platform to promote Deaf culture and dispel common myths about being Deaf.[12]

Deaf reality contestants have helped popularize signed languages a cultural contact point for hearing spectators that may partly explain the 432% increase in university ASL enrollments between 1998 and 2009 (Brueggemann 2009: 31). Justin Leblanc, for example, has been outspoken about the benefits of ASL following his appearance on *Project Runway* season 12 and season 4 of *Project Runway All Stars*, arguing, "[B]ody gestures speak louder than words …. With verbal language it's hard to convey the emotion. ASL is performance in a way. All of us could benefit from using more gestural communication" (Donahue 2013). Nyle DiMarco has used his visibility following back-to-back wins on *America's Next Top Model* and *Dancing with the Stars*, as well as recognizability from print campaigns and *Switched at Birth*, to be an activist for the Deaf community. DiMarco, an alumnus of the Maryland School for the Deaf and Gallaudet University, uses video platforms on phone apps and social media to teach hearing fans basic ASL signs and phrases in short dictionary-style clips. Leveraging his cultural cachet to help endorse Deaf stories, DiMarco produced the first Broadway revival of Medoff's *Children of a Lesser God* in spring 2018. Deaf actress Lauren Ridloff played the role of Sarah, for which Phyllis Frelich and Marlee Matlin won Best Actress accolades in the original stage and screen versions.[13]

Whether a hearing audience encounters ASL in scripted scenes or impromptu dialogue, the encounter alters the still-common perception of "Deaf and Dumb," usually through acknowledgment of ASL's linguistic complexity. Following DiMarco's performance on *Dancing with the Stars*, *Access Hollywood* writer Carrie Ann Inaba echoed a version of Leblanc's description of ASL's performative nature:

> Nyle DiMarco ... [has] such beautiful expression .... I was thinking about how incredible he is as I was drinking my coffee this morning, and realized that sign language is a kind of a dance—it is a movement that expresses. So in a way, he's been dancing with his hands his whole life. I think this is part of why his performances are so deeply moving. (2016)

Inaba, traversing between sign and dance, articulates ASL's embodied and visual nature for her readers as a kind of Deaf gain emanating from Deaf epistemologies. This orientation toward the poetics and performance of body language and gestural expression native to ASL conveys critical aspects of Rebecca Sanchez's position in *Deafening Modernism* (2015) to non-academic audiences. Throughout rich readings of Hart Crane's poetry, Gertrude Stein's *Tender Buttons*, and Faulkner's Benjy Compson, Sanchez demonstrates how modernism's fixation on image and temporality are more richly understood by ASL's visual, embodied structure.[14] Thinking through a Deaf epistemology in spaces where Deaf and disability representation is missing or nonapparent, Sanchez argues, broadens engagement with Deaf critical insight and reshapes assumptions about Deaf perspectives.

5.2. FILM AS A DEAF–HEARING POINT OF CONTACT

At the end of *Children of a Lesser God*, Sarah and James confront each other about his strident oralism and her refusal to speak on his terms. Reconciling, James asks, "Do you think there's someplace where we can meet that's not in silence and not in sound?" This space outside of silence and sound, between d/Deaf and hearing, anticipates Brueggemann's description of "between space [as] one of longing, yet also one of belonging, and one, too, of limits" (2009: 2). As a disability scholar with profound sensorineural deafness raised in an oralist tradition, I sometimes feel I live in this in-between: not hearing, but not quite Deaf either. For Sarah and James the invention of an in-between is a practical solution, although its utility extends beyond their relationship. Sarah and James are hardly metonyms for all Deaf and hearing individuals, nor should they be, but the question of how to find a way toward another's bodymind when you are acculturated to prioritize different sensory stimuli transcends the particularities of their relationship. What might we feel or "hear" in a space outside silence and sound? How might that "someplace" look? Must we abdicate from silence and sound to connect, or can we combine them in ways that acknowledge the hearing person's auditory reception while still foregrounding a visucentric world? Cinema is a medium that allows us to experiment with these questions before "audiences" composed of both d/Deaf, HoH, and hearing persons.

For the remainder of this chapter, I want to explore how contemporary cinema is beginning to collapse the divide between Deaf and hearing spectators, even as it reinforces and values the particularity of perspectival difference. *Children of a Lesser God*'s critical and commercial success marks an obvious beginning point in the lineage of cinema as a Deaf–hearing contact space. The film's director, Randa Haines, describes deafness as a "metaphor for the things in each person which separate us from other people, the barriers that we have built up around us, the way in which none of us can ever really experience the way in which another person hears or sees the world. All of us are, in a sense, deaf to what's inside other people's heads" (quoted in Summerfield and Lee 2006: 155). Haines' articulation and deployment of deafness is consistent with what David Mitchell and Sharon Snyder name "narrative prosthesis," a treatment of disability as a narrative device that reveals how "disability is foundational to both cultural definition and to the literary narratives that challenge normalizing prescriptive ideals" (2000: 51). The normalcy Haines affirms is that of the viewer, who presumably sees Sarah and James' miscommunications as a universal experience. But, of course, Sarah is not abstracted from the Deaf community, alone in a hearing world. The paradigm Schuchman describes of the isolated Deaf individual is reversed in the adaptation of Medoff's play; James, the hearing instructor, is entering into a vibrant community at a school for the Deaf and HoH.

Moreover, Medoff developed the stage play and its film adaptation with Deaf talent, so Deaf perspectives are central to the work. Thus, the film becomes a point of contact between Deaf and hearing persons (onscreen and off) that productively revel in the "betweenity" of classification; *Children of a Lesser God*, and the films I describe hereafter, are "[s]ituations of contact … [that] make at least three things clear: disability is about lives; there is an art to living and showing disability; and disability is political" (Crutchfield and Epstein 2000: 7). d/Deaf characters are no longer figured as "disabled folks [who] are mere nonselves waiting to become selves," as Crutchfield and Epstein remark on the status quo of many disability identity constructions in the arts, but rather they are fully "round" characters who challenge conceptions of selfhood that able-bodied, hearing audiences might hold (2000: 9).

5.2.1. Sign, Signage, *and* Words: *Mixed-hearing relationships in short film*

Sign (dir. Andrew Keenan-Bolger 2017) explicitly addresses the beauty and the communication issues in Deaf–hearing relationships. Unlike *Switched at Birth*, which plots Deaf–hearing relationships with attention to the politics of dating outside of the Deaf culture, *Sign* portrays a relationship burgeoning naively. The independent short film follows Aaron (John McGinty), a Deaf man, and Ben (Preston Sadleir), who is hearing, as they begin dating after repeatedly meeting on their neighborhood subway platform. Billed as "a silent film," *Sign*'s narrative is delivered in a mixture of gesture and ASL, as well as a few insert shots of phone text conversations. Co-writer Adam Wachter also composed an original score for the film, which serves the dual purpose of augmenting the action for hearing audiences and covering over any diegetic noise (such as voices, traffic, phone rings, etc.). This effect is suggestive of a Deaf World experience for spectators who have to watch the action with greater acuity to follow the plot—no subtitles are offered for any spoken or signed dialogue. Additionally, *Sign* was developed with Alexandra Wailes, an actor who frequently works with the Los Angeles-based Deaf West Theatre, as the Director of ASL and Culture. Advisor roles for ASL and Deaf Culture are increasingly common in television and film productions with mixed-hearing creatives and crews.[15] In front of the camera and behind the scenes, *Sign* challenges d/Deaf–hearing interactions in productive ways.

Cross-language heteronormative romances are a well-worn trope on stage and screen. Expectations that love will conquer all and find expression even in the direst of circumstances frequently play on the eroticism of the ontologically "silent" partner—who may speak, but is linguistically unknown, an Other—but this plot device is complicated when the divide is between spoken and signed languages. Signed languages intertwine deeply with Deaf cultural identity and politics—the recognition of sign languages as legitimate forms of communication is a defining cultural battle for Deaf communities throughout the twentieth century. In the USA, for example, ASL is still not recognized as an official language native to American society by the federal government; sign language is categorized as a "foreign" or "instructional" language. When a hearing–speaking partner engages in a love plot onscreen, the question is not simply who will compromise on language acquisition. The question is, will the hearing partner understand d/Deafness as a valuable—or even preferable—way of being in the world instead of as a loss or lack?

Sign's plot shares similar elements of earlier short films about Deaf–hearing relationships. *Signage* (2007), directed by Rick Hammerly, follows Lex (played by Hammerly), a hearing gay man in his early forties who struggles to feel desirable, as he heads to a local bar during "shirtless night." There, he helps Jonathan (Jason Wittig) and his friends—all of whom are Deaf and students at Gallaudet—order from the bartender, who does not understand ASL. Lex and Jonathan strike up a flirtatious conversation before Jonathan ultimately rejects Lex's advances, citing unease at being in a relationship with a hearing man despite Lex's proficiencies in ASL. *Words* (2010), directed by Anup Bhandari and starring Deaf actor Russell Harvard, uses a similar Deaf–hearing flirtation to comment on audism.[16] In *Words*, a hearing photographer named Juliet (Miriam Ganz) begins to court Owen (Harvard) after a chance encounter by the Bethesda Fountain in Central Park. Over a series of days, Juliet makes rapid progress in ASL, demonstrating a romantic interest in Owen, but the relationship abruptly ends following her declaration, "Yes, I am interested in you. Interested in talking to you, interested in listening to you. I can be the words that you want to speak." Juliet fails to understand how her statement is ingrained with the logics of audism and oralism during the moment of articulation, but the final scene implies she realizes her error as she reviews video of Owen signing his reply: "Silence is best described without words."

Given these films' cultural proximity to the spring 2006 "Unity for Gallaudet" protests demanding the Gallaudet University Board of Trustees rescind its appointment of incoming President Dr. Jane Fernandez, both shorts offer a pulse on Deaf–hearing relations.[17] *Signage*'s Gallaudet students communicate an explicitly antagonistic relationship to hearing people, insinuating Jonathan fetishizes hearing men; *Words*' Owen twice suggests he is romantically invested in Juliet, but realizes they have fundamentally different approaches to sound, language, and culture that would follow her explanations of how music sounds and enhance his understanding of her offer to be his "spoken words." The segregation of Deaf and hearing patrons in a Washington, D.C. gay bar gives *Signage* a verisimilitude beyond its 2007 moment—on Friday nights, groups of d/Deaf men and ASL users are still visibly set apart on the dance floor in D.C.'s LGBTQ establishments. Owen's openness to courting a hearing girl in *Words* over a series of days is a vastly different mind-set toward mixed-hearing relationships than that of the background character Russell Harvard plays in *Signage*. The change is incremental but significant, and the viewer cannot help but wonder if a relationship might still be possible between Owen and Juliet after she realizes her complicity in audism.

Sign advances these shorts' theses about mixed-hearing relationships in two key ways: time and cultural context. Whereas *Signage* takes place during a single night and *Words* over a succession of days, *Sign* shows the long arc of Aaron and Ben's relationship through successive jump cuts. This technique takes the viewer from first dates, meeting parents and moving in together, to microaggressions, fights, and their eventual breakup. *Sign*'s ability to move through a broader stretch of time goes past the foreclosure of possibilities in *Signage* and *Words*, a move that lets its spectators navigate Aaron and Ben's relationship much like the characters do—as a progressive series of negotiations, compromises, and challenges. This longer temporal arc takes the viewer into Deaf and hearing cultural spaces; we see Ben fumble through faux pas during an all-Deaf gathering, and Aaron feel ignored during a hearing event at a bar when Ben does not translate the conversation. It is here that *Sign* gently educates its hearing viewer about the expectation that making mixed-hearing relationships "work" is as simple as learning a new language. Yes, Ben is learning a new language, but his apperception is still entirely aural. When Ben assumes Aaron can follow a conversation in a loud bar by reading lips or answers a ringing phone without acknowledging the sound of his partner, he demonstrates a fundamental misunderstanding of how their varying hearing statuses yield different communication expectations. The film knowingly plays on this by inverting conventional associations of "deaf and dumb." In the nineteenth century, nonspeaking deaf persons were often identified as "deaf-mute" or "deaf and dumb." Whether through an inability or lack of desire to speak, deaf persons without access to sign language experienced greater challenges within hearing cultures. English speakers carried "dumb" into the twentieth and twenty-first centuries, where its twin etymologies signifying feeblemindedness or muteness combined in the eugenics movement's response to deafness—a condition and community Alexander Graham Bell infamously remarked posed a threat to social order.[18] During a language-acquisition montage in which Ben begins learning how to communicate with Aaron using ASL, Ben is seen in a park practicing handshapes of basic signs like "tomorrow" from a book, *Signing for Dummies* (Figure 5.1). A hearing spectator outside of Deaf culture might easily miss the visual pun, but the book's brief presence depicts ASL as a complex language and playfully suggests anyone with insufficient signing skills must be a "dummy."

Despite *Sign*'s apparent disability aesthetic and Deaf orientation, the short was primarily received as an LGBTQ film in its first two years of screening. Of *Sign*'s ten major awards following a fifty-festival competition circuit from 2016 to 2017, seven explicitly recognized it as an LGBTQ film compared to the one disability film award (at the Bluenose Ability Film Festival). Anecdotally, advertisements for and clips from the film circulated on several social media pages belonging to Deaf colleagues at Gallaudet, in D.C., and elsewhere, often with a commendation on the realistic portrayal of Deaf–hearing relationships. The sexuality of the central couple was a secondary concern in these posts, if mentioned at all. The reading of the film as queer cinema instead of Deaf cinema underscores how deafness can easily be co-opted as a broader "universal" metaphor for communication differences in any relationship and, contradictorily, suggests that its narrative appeal is rooted in a valuation of the particularities of this cripqueer and

FIGURE 5.1 Video still from *Sign*. Photograph by Andrew Keenan-Boger, 2016, courtesy of Adam Wachter.

mixed-hearing couple's experiences rather than being understood in spite of them. As a piece of independent disability film, *Sign* is unique among the productions I discuss in this chapter because a crowdfunded Indiegogo campaign financed the film. Marketed to potential backers as a "silent film about the relationship between a hearing man and a Deaf man," *Sign* raised US$12,625 from 185 backers, surpassing its goal of US$5,000 by 253% (Keenan-Bolger 2016).[19] *Sign*'s early financial backing, critical success, and participation from well-known d/Deaf actors in the New York community articulate a hunger for more cinema addressing how all hearing and Deaf people live their lives: in occasionally conflictual yet proximate contact with each other.

5.2.2. Collapsing the Deaf–hearing divide in A Quiet Place

The 2018 thriller *A Quiet Place* (dir. John Krasinski) offers an unexpectedly sensitive commercial mediation on contemporary issues in the Deaf community. *A Quiet Place* is ambiguously set eighty-nine days following some "event," after which creatures who have invaded Earth have decimated human civilization. Tight close-ups of bare feet tiptoeing across the tile floor of an abandoned pharmacy during the opening sequence quickly establish the stakes: this is a world in which any noise is a death knell. Marketed as a horror film, *A Quiet Place*'s premise is having to stay silent or risk death-by-alien-monster. Krasinski's film, however, is less a conventional take on what constitutes "horror" as such (the monsters, while terrifying, are hardly ever-present) and more an experiment in pushing the boundaries of the horror genre. Given how little the viewer comes into contact with the alien antagonists and the rapidity of death following any noise-making, the actual horror element is sound—and those precious few moments before death when the too-loud subject realizes their error. Put another way, "Silence is Survival"—the tagline for the film—is a shorthand for how the film upends hearing culture's reliance on auditory cues for flourishing.

Moreover, its centering of a Deaf character (Reagan Abbott, played by Deaf actor Millicent Simmonds) in the plot of *A Quiet Place* also offers examples of Deaf gain and the valuation of ASL as a linguistic minority, oralism (distinct in this film from audism, although the two are historically linked), and the culture clash between d/Deaf and hearing persons regarding surgically implanted "bionic ears" like cochlear implants and bone-anchored hearing aids. Thus, *A Quiet Place* offers a progressive depiction of d/Deafness that positions the movie as a commercially successful Deaf Cinema project despite being co-written and directed by the hearing Krasinski. By understanding how the film values d/Deaf talent and Deaf culture rather than recycling tired tropes of deafness as "grist for its mercantile mill," *A Quiet Place* demonstrates how Cinema can play to Deaf and hearing spectators without compromising its commitments to either group (Norman 2003).

Lennard Davis, in a review of the film, observes how "*A Quiet Place* puts us in the position of listening very carefully," itself an acknowledgment of sound's centrality to the film's design and plot (Davis 2018). The film follows the Abbotts—Lee, Evelyn, Reagan, Marcus, and Beau (played by Krasinski, Emily Blunt, Simmonds, Noah Jupe, and Cade Woodward, respectively)—as they navigate daily life on a farm in upstate New York following the invasion. Reagan, the eldest Abbott child, is congenitally deaf and, although she has a cochlear implant, primarily communicates using ASL. While it is never explicitly stated, the viewer is made to assume that the family's fluency in ASL has been key to their survival. Much of the film is composed of medium shots that offer the spectator an unimpeded view of a character's signing space, and nearly all of the ASL in the film is subtitled. Despite the valuation of ASL, *A Quiet Place* assumes a predominantly hearing audience (rather than d/Deaf spectators), so there are surprising access issues regarding the sound. Characters converse primarily in ASL with subtitles at the bottom of the screen translating for non-ASL-fluent spectators, but the film does not caption the few spoken lines of dialogue for d/Deaf and HoH spectators. Tellingly, Lee, the family patriarch who secretly welds new cochlear implants for his daughter, is in both spoken-English scenes. The lack of open captions on these interactions between Lee and his hearing son and wife reiterate the character's oralism.

The sound design toggles between two diegetic soundscapes during key moments: the first is a "hearing soundscape" replete with whistling wind, water, the rustling leaves of corn, and the echolocation-like clicking of the aliens; the second is a "deaf soundscape" characterized by a muted hum and the intermittent screeching of Reagan's broken sound processor. The second soundscape brings hearing viewers into Reagan's "Deaf-World," but with the privilege of a scope of vision beyond the young woman. Reagan repeatedly comes into contact with the monsters, whose proximity incites her implant's feedback loop at high intervals: whatever frequency the aliens communicate with is received and amplified by the sound processor, creating a high squeal that drives off the aliens and saves Reagan from an untimely death.

In a fair critique of the film, Deaf literature scholar Pamela J. Kincheloe (2018) contends that Reagan's cochlear implant is the "hero," not Reagan herself. Her eventual realization of how the technology debilitates the aliens leads to her amplifying the sound further, a move that gives her mother Evelyn enough time to kill the intruding creature. While Kincheloe's thesis that the presence of the cochlear is heroic is persuasive, as a viewer with a failed bone-anchored hearing aid, I read the ending with an eye and ear attuned to the effect on the alien itself. Reagan and Lee's argument about her refusal to wear the cochlear implant, presumably because she finds her father's insistence on the device to impose unnecessary physical and emotional pain on her, dramatizes an argument that is all too familiar for deaf and HoH children of hearing parents. But just as the use of the cochlear dramatizes physical pain for Reagan, so too is this pain experienced by the aliens as they enter proximity to the defensive feedback played by the cochlear device. If the film argues that Reagan's deafness as a disability, then the alien's hypersensitivity to sound is the obverse side of the equation; the film exploits the alien's capacity to hear a wide range of nuanced sounds as a physical weakness in a profoundly hearing world.

Given that Reagan and the alien both feel pain when the sound processor's transmissions are amplified, *A Quiet Place*'s use of the cochlear implant to paralyze and kill the alien invaders can be read as the ultimate refusal of bionic ear technology. As Lennard Davis argues, "If we look carefully, we can see that the aural/oral method of communicating, itself seen as totally natural, like all signifying practices, is not natural but based on sets of assumptions about the body, about reality, and of course about power" (1995b: 16). Or put another way, the conceit of *A Quiet Place* demonstrates the assumption of oral communication/aural reception as the "natural" or most effective form of discourse; in another, it rejects intervention technologies (even at the risk of "alienating" Deafness to do so).

5.3. CONCLUSION

While Deaf storytelling may be approaching a "tipping point" with regard to achieving mainstream recognition, as Naveen Kumar (2018) suggests, a comparatively small group of Deaf talent cycles through most productions: *Sign*'s McGinty and Wailes performed in the DiMarco-produced Broadway revival of *Children of a Lesser God*; Douglas Ridloff, the ASL coach for *A Quiet Place*, is married to *Children of a Lesser God*'s star, Lauren Ridloff; *Wonderstruck*'s Millicent Simmonds plays a central character in *A Quiet Place*; Marlee Matlin, who famously worked in the film adaptation of Medoff's play, was on *Switched at Birth* alongside DiMarco before his reality TV fame or Broadway production. This small sampling of works demonstrates the intricate connections of the Deaf community, but also the room for growth. The Gallaudet Research Institute estimates that "anywhere from 9 to 22 out of every 1,000 people in the United States have a severe hearing impairment or are deaf," and that range increases to 37–140 out of every 1,000 if one uses the broader category "hearing loss" (Mitchell 2005). While roughly 13% of the population in the USA alone identifies as d/Deaf or HoH, d/Deafness is on par with other minority populations—yet the amount of Deaf representation onscreen is still comparatively small, even in spite of the rich performance traditions in Deaf culture. Beyond the limited number of known-quantity actors, other stage performers, ASL poets, and community storytellers are not cast in roles even where Deaf experience or a native facility with a sign language is compulsory to the narrative. If we considered global numbers of d/Deaf and HoH-identifying persons and the accurate available cultural representations of d/Deafness in their respective cultures, the numbers would be even more unequal. In other words, the opportunities and recognition afforded Deaf artists in film throughout the twentieth and early twenty-first centuries are disproportionate to the size of the population they represent. Until there is at least a more proportional Deaf presence onscreen, hailing the 2015–18 trend towards Deaf-inclusive casting and Deaf storytelling as a "tipping point" is premature.

Yet, as I have argued, modern and contemporary film offers more contact points between d/Deaf and hearing cultures than ever before. Commercial cinema and television regularly combat the stigma of "deaf and dumb" that permeated the late nineteenth and early twentieth centuries, normalize Deafness, advance access to signed languages, and acquaint viewers with Deaf culture in ways unprecedented just decades before. The increasing collapse between cinema about the Deaf and Deaf Cinema facilitates cross-cultural interactions between d/Deaf and hearing communities; it offers hearing spectators footholds into Deaf-world-making by reorganizing value away from aural perception and giving Deaf spectators a space to see their own experiences more complexly reflected in entertainment media. Most significantly, the increased proximity to the d/Deaf or hearing Other will inform the Deaf community's sense of self, and reshape perceptions of deafness in hearing culture throughout the coming century.

FILMOGRAPHY

This filmography offers contextual information on the film and television projects mentioned throughout this chapter. A few additional projects featuring referenced Deaf talent are also included. It is not an exhaustive update of the filmography of Deaf and disability films offered in John Schuchman's *Hollywood Speaks* (1988), the timeline including ASL videos in *Signing the Body Poetic* (Bauman et al. 2006), or the films discussed in the *Cultures of Representation: Disability in World Cinema Contexts* (Fraser 2016), but this list does provide a snapshot of late twentieth/early twenty-first-century projects portraying d/Deaf persons, culture, and experiences. Other films can be found under the entry "Film: Deaf Characters" in *The SAGE Deaf Studies Encyclopedia* (Lerner and Sayers 2016). I have listed each project's languages to highlight transnational valuations of regional Deaf talent, language, and culture; where appropriate, languages are ordered by prevalence within the project.

TV episodes, series, and movies

Breaking Through, Dir. Fred Gerber, 1996 Lifetime TV [English, American Sign Language]
Jericho, CBS 2006–8 [English, American Sign Language]
"Kessler Epstein Foundation," *Difficult People*, Season 2, Episode 2, Dir. Jeffrey Walker, Hulu
  [English, American Sign Language]
Orenji deizu (*Orange Days*), TBS 2011, 11 episodes [Japanese, Japanese Sign Language]
"New York, I Love You," *Master of None*, Season 2, Episode 6, Dir. Alan Yang, 2017, Netflix
  [English, French, American Sign Language, Kinyarwanda]
The Magicians. Season 2-present. (Sy–Fy, 2015—) [English, American Sign Language]
The Stand, Dir. Mick Garris, 1994, ABC [English, American Sign Language]
Sweet Nothing in My Ear, Dir. Joseph Sachs, 2008, CBS [English, American Sign Language]
Switched at Birth, ABC Family/Freeform 2011–17 [English, American Sign Language, Spanish]
This Close, Sundance Now, 2018– present [English, American Sign Language]

Short film

The Silent Child, Dir. Chris Overton, 2017 [English, British Sign Language]
Sign, Dir. Andrew Keenan-Bolger, 2016 [American Sign Language]
Signage, Dir. Rick Hammerly, 2007 [English, American Sign Language]
This Is Normal, Dir. Justin Giddings and Ryan Welsh, 2013 [English, American Sign Language]
Words, Dir. Anup Bhandari, 2010 [American Sign Language]

Feature-length

A Quiet Place, Dir. John Krasinski, 2018 [English, American Sign Language]

Babel, Dir. Alejandro G. Iñárritu, 2006 [Arabic, Berber Languages, English, French, Japanese, Japanese Sign Language, Russian, Spanish]

Baby Driver, Dir. Edgar Wright, 2017 [English, American Sign Language]

Claustrophobia, Dir. Harlan Schneider, 2011 [English, American Sign Language]

Children of a Lesser God, Dir. Randa Haines, 1986 [English, American Sign Language]

Deafula, Dir. Peter Wolf (as Peter Wechsberg), 1975 [American Sign Language]

The Hammer, Dir. Orin Kaplan, 2010 [English, American Sign Language]

Hear Me, Dir. Fen-fen Cheng, 2009 [Mandarin, Mixed Sign Languages]

I Love You, But, Dir. Peter Wolf, 1998 [English, American Sign Language]

Jenseits der Stille (*Beyond Silence*), Dir. Caroline Link, 1996 [German, German Sign Language, English, Spanish]

La vida secreta de las palabras (*The Secret Life of Words*), Dir. Isabel Coixet, 2005 [English]

Listen To Your Heart, Dir. Matt Thompson, 2010 [English, American Sign Language]

No Ordinary Hero: The SuperDeafy Movie, Dir. Troy Kotsur, 2013 [English, American Sign Language]

Piano, Dir. Jane Campion, 1993 [English, British Sign Language, Maori]

Plemya (*The Tribe*), Dir. Myroslav Slaboshpytskyi, 2014 [Ukranian Sign Language, No Subtitles]

Sign Gene, Dir. Emilio Insolera, 2017 [English, Japanese, Italian, American Sign Language, Japanese Sign Language, Italian Sign Language]

The Shape of Water, Dir. Guillermo del Toro, 2017 [English, American Sign Language]

Versa Effect, Dir. Mark Wood, 2011 [American Sign Language]

Wonderstruck, Dir. Todd Haynes, 2017 [English, American Sign Language]

CHAPTER SIX

Speech: Speech Disability's Awkward Late Modernity

A Multimodal Historical Approach

ZAHARI RICHTER

To consider "speech disability," one must consider speech in its complexity. Is speech just an oral equivalent of text? Is speech merely mechanistic? Is speech primarily cultural? Is speech the product of psychological processes? Is speech historical? Is speech intention? Is speech political? Is speech sensory? The answer is that speech cannot be known strictly within any one of these categories. This chapter will seek to better understand the anomalousness of "speech disability" to complement an anti-structuralist critical reading of the gaps in Disability Studies itself and the gaps in the dominant Western imperialist accounting for speech disability by way of the three explanatory devices of intellectualism, empiricism, and psychoanalysis.

I draw on Maurice Merleau-Ponty's *Phenomenology of Perception* to demystify speech as neither defined by mechanistic elements, desire, development, or semiotics. Merleau-Ponty's account of speech is immensely useful due to its anti-essentialist mode that manages to refuse both scientific and humanistic accounts, while prioritizing a vision of speech as part of gestural and stylistic intersubjectivity or holistic interrelationality. Yet, speech also exists between worlds, for Merleau-Ponty, as the verbal image, which is described as a reflection of the subjective accounting of the local discursive–material–organizational world. Furthermore, I use Merleau-Ponty from a grounded perspective as a speech-disabled person for the specific reason of my own experiential realization of the inaccuracies of empiricist speech language pathology, psychoanalysis, and sign-oriented approaches to what is referred to as the communication disorder component of my disability.

In intervening with the claim that speech is neither mechanistic, desiring, developmental, nor semiotic, I do not actually hope to claim that the above modes of explanation are false; instead, I am deriding the failure of explainers of speech via nature and culture to synthesize their findings with the findings of other thinkers and scholars as well as scientists in the academy. My approach is to recognize speech itself as multimodal. Gunther Kress theorized multimodality as having "assume[d] that all modes of representation are in principle of equal significance in representation and communication" (2009: 104). To take Kress's multimodality model seriously, it may be possible to draw also upon Volosinov's *Marxism and The Philosophy of Language* (1973) for its concept of multi-accentuality, which may be treated as a parallel concept to multimodality. Volosinov notes that "existence reflected in signs is not merely reflected but refracted ... thus various classes use one language ... as a result differently oriented accents intersect in each sign ... this social multi-accentuality ... is very crucial" (1973: 23). With Kress's multimodality and Volosinov's multi-accentuality, this chapter finds embodied modes or accents as well as structural linguistic modes or accents to be formative.

Multimodality and multi-accentuality as concepts are invoked for the purpose of capturing the breadth of experience. Multimodality speaks to the multiplicity of sensory modes through which experience occurs, such as the visuality, gesturality, and auditory qualities, and even the tactility of speaking with another person and hearing, seeing, as well as feeling through the reverberations of their body movements upon the ground, air, and possible extra spittle. Multi-accentuality arrives to show how words and expressions differ based on one's class orientation. Calm, quiet, and polite speech may be the baseline in refined or wealthier settings, whereas for those coming from a background of poverty, the same language is experienced as halted and delayed and thus inauthentic. These concepts of multiplicity in speech are used to approach the complexity of real-life experience in greater nuance than representations of speech and language that turn away from both class experience of habitus and multisensorial details.

From my own experience of being speech disabled, I am knowledgeable only about stuttering. As a stutterer, I have encountered rhetorical teachers who were convinced that I would not stutter if I simply slowed down and calmed down; I have encountered speech language pathologists who attempted to teach me a slow sing-song-like way of speaking that was impractical as a way of hiding my stutter as early as elementary school; and I have also encountered both bullies and potential lovers who became convinced of a pseudo-psychoanalytic reading of my life wherein my stutter was evidence of my fearfulness, anxiety, cowardice, femininity, or other character flaws. While I am aware that psychoanalysis reaches greater depths of complexity than that employed by schoolyard bullies, I do find reflected in my own peremptory review of the scholarly literature that the speech language pathologists I met did adopt positions similar to others who have published much—and that is mainly an empirical motor-mechanical view of speech disability; similarly, the debate and communication instructors I have encountered do not seem to have strayed greatly from that corrective, normalizing field born in post-Enlightenment Britain known as "elocution." Based on my experience and on Maurice Merleau-Ponty's sly negotiation between three extremes of determinism, the unit of analysis in terms of speech disability that is to be narrowed in upon and apprehended for this chapter is "the gestural."

Phenomenologist Maurice Merleau-Ponty is used as a key theorist for this chapter in part due to his pragmatic philosophical approach that does not abnegate positivist scientific empiricism or philosophical nominalism. Merleau-Ponty's strategy as a thinker located between psychology and continental philosophy is one that refuses the tendency to move toward either representationalism that hinges purely on the constructedness of language or positivism that treats reality as scientifically knowable through systematic observation. The sensory as a field of being is neither encapsulated by language, as language cannot name subtler sensory experience, nor by observation, which moves past the ambiguity of sense data toward an assuredness of the quality of the observable and the mathematically quantifiable or measurable that can verify what is observed. Gesture occupies the sensory realm because body gesture is not representable in textual form but merely accompanies spoken language and is not representable as scientifically observed fact because gesture is too wide and subtle a field to be able to be quantified universally.

In *Phenomenology of Perception*, Maurice Merleau-Ponty points to the debate between the scientific positivist strand that views speech disability as motor-driven and its opposition—which he deems "the intellectualist"—that understands speech disability strictly in terms of symbols:

> What establishes its inherence in the body is the fact that linguistic deficiencies cannot be reduced to a unity and that the primary disturbances affect sometimes the body of the word, the material instrument of verbal expression—sometimes the word's physiognomy, the verbal intention, the kind of group image on the basis of what we succeed in saying or writing down a word exactly—sometimes the immediate meaning of the word ... and sometimes the structure of the whole experience. Speech then rests upon a stratification of powers relatively capable of being isolated. (227)

In discounting the previous theories that would locate speech disability in one of two poles, Merleau-Ponty opens up the task of carrying anti-essentialist speech disability research forward through tracing speech disability's anti-essentialist modality that defies both physical and symbolic causes. In actualizing this explanation, Merleau-Ponty provides for speech to be a force that "presents ... the subject taking up of a position in his world of meanings," whereas language is understood as having "an inner content," but is (in contrast to Derrida's position) "not a self-subsistent self-conscious thought." Merleau-Ponty elaborates on how language has a representative meaning when he writes, "[T]he phonetic gesture brings about ... a structural coordination." Thus, for Merleau-Ponty, against the Derridean anti-doctrine demanding that all language is arbitrary, language comes into being through speech already coordinated with a realm he describes earlier known as "the gestural." Nonverbal gesture for Merleau-Ponty occurs automatically and imminently and with the additional element of style suggesting a form of semi-intentional cohesion between all speaking human subjects, but one that is in the "anthropos," or in the local human community.

Merleau-Ponty and Derrida are put in dialogue in this chapter because of their presence in the French intellectual world during the same period of the late twentieth century and because, as noted previously, their theories are close to one another due to their questioning of the absolute certainty of previous structuralisms (whether linguistic structuralism or empirical structuralism). The debate between the two figures is illustrative for this chapter because it helps to reveal the difference between language-centered approaches and sense-oriented perspectives.

It is appropriate to recognize Derrida and Merleau-Ponty as contemporaries of a post-holocaust genre that takes criticism of scientific positivism as its basis, but where Merleau-Ponty cautioned against getting too caught up in language, Derrida reveled in it perversely. Thus, Merleau-Ponty returns to the materiality of the word just as Derrida finds words to be reducible to grammatical structures. The opposition between Merleau-Ponty and Derrida comes from two different approaches to opposing bio-political domination. Derrida challenges the bio-politics of the postmodern era through deconstructing it or diagnosing it as a linguist or psychoanalyst would diagram a sentence; Merleau-Ponty questions the bio-political power of the state through resorting to oppositional gestures and memory practices held in Merleau-Ponty's own affirmation of dance and freedom.

Instead of accepting either a bio-determinist or a linguistic determinist approach to speech disability, this chapter affirms a multidimensional approach to speech where speech itself is composed preconsciously of gesture, which is not reducible to biology or culture but mediates between biology and culture. Accompanying gesture, the notion of style also serves a mediating role in-between biological and social reality, but unlike gesture, which is most often preconsciously performed, style arrives through consciousness. In any case, this chapter takes a "both–and" comprehensive approach to speech disability through arguing with metaphor for the uneven and disjointed character of speech disability itself. Instead of speech-disabled people being socially awkward, the broad global understanding of speech disability is itself awkward and uneven, and we must be able to mediate between contradictory sensory and descriptive worlds to fully encounter the epistemological and ontological awkwardness of speech disability.

The intention in using Merleau-Ponty to break down dominant narratives about speech disability might fall into oppressive patterns of assumption that predetermine engagement with racial, sexual, gendered, disabled, and nonhuman others. Phenomenological sociologists such as Clifford Geertz use the concept of "bracketing" to suggest how phenomenology allows its users to apprehend parts of experience outside of the dominance of normative judgment. In this sense, the cultural history of speech disability may be read as a series of gaps between judgment and fulfillment: on the one hand, we may locate the invisibility of speech disability accessibility from disability rights discourse and history. On the other hand, we may locate a series of gaps in the history of the science of speech language pathology where the possible agency of speech disability is literally restrained by an assumption of torturous need of cure. But to arrive at those two histories, it will first be necessary to reflect on speech language pathology's beginnings as it relates to colonialism.

Once the "phonetic gesture" is embraced as a key deconstructive refashioning of speech such that it cannot be delimited by empirics or linguistic determinacy and language is known as present in the unconscious (but more autonomous from desire than Lacanian accounts would give credit), it becomes possible to genealogize physicalist speech disability explanations, psychoanalytic speech disability explanations, and exceptionalizing poststructuralist explanations in their historical backgrounds in connection to the rise of nationalism in the mercantilist age just prior to the main subject of this chapter's analysis: the twentieth century.

Relying on historian Eric Hobsbawm's account of the requirements for nationhood aspired to by the British Empire, the refinement of national language and national literature was the final step in the certification of the British Empire's pursuit of likeness to its forebear, the Roman Empire. Linguistic anthropologists such as Lesley Milroy offer an account of how the diagnosis of speech disabilities as well as language complaints within the English language only began in the 1700s, after Britain had established colonies in locales across the globe. Also influential as a factor that places the rise of speech disability diagnoses in English to the 1700s is Walter Ong's (2005) commentary on the invention of the printing press in 1440, spurring nearly 300 years of influence of Petrus Ramus, who held that speech and dialectic were ultimately bound to physics and physical causality, a position that is carried forward by the contemporary era discipline of speech language pathology.

It will be the argument of this chapter that the splitting of speech-normalizing forces across diametrically opposed poles of illocution and medicine represents the cultural reverberation of the brutality of settler–colonial regimes just prior to the Enlightenment. Further, late modern Taylorist and Fordist disciplinary measures reflected optimizations of disciplinary power that had formerly been used on racialized and colonized bodies. My hope is to draw on Mbembe's theory of "necropower" to suggest that the practices of seizure of space and seizure of objects were only perfected in industrial capitalism through emulating its original, more violent iteration in the colonial and racializing situation. That the arrival of disciplinary power upon the voice only starting in 1700 reflects the ways in which Enlightenment rationality moved from a stricture only used by mercantilist nobles upon nonhumans and dehumanized populations to becoming a general methodology for operationalizing social existence.

On such a basis, it will be key to reread the annals of linguistic anthropology for key moments during which discipline is extended upon the voice as part of such efforts to stabilize a given language largely for imperialist purpose. In the following section of this chapter, early modern attempts at stabilizing the English language by both medical practitioners concerned with speech and by rhetoricians in the same period will be reviewed, starting with Jonathan Swift's "A Proposal for Correcting and Ascertaining the English Tongue" and moving to the taxonomization of speech impairment by French medical doctor Francois Boissier de Sauvages de Lacroix.

6.1. THE ACADEMIC/SCIENTIFIC BACKGROUND OF THE LATE ENLIGHTENMENT: THE FIRST LANGUAGE-USE COMPLAINT AND THE FIRST TAXONOMY OF SPEECH IMPEDIMENT

Since this chapter has embraced the understanding of speech as inherently gestural, we may have cause to reread Jonathan Swift's "A Proposal for Correcting and Ascertaining the English Tongue" (cited in Milroy and Milroy 2002), which somehow manages to parallel both Petrus Ramus and Derrida by railing against the idea "that we ought to spell exactly as we speak," while making a more general commentary on the degradation of language. Milroy and Milroy's citation of Swift in this capacity for a linguistic anthropological reading is most upset by Swift's desire to stratify language, but one may also take offense from the Merleau-Pontyan stance against symbolic determinacy at the claim that written language should predetermine speech. What is described by classicist John Miles Foley as the "ideology of the text" is also present here.

Parallel to Swift's origin of language-use correction, a corollary advance in medicine in the 1700s presented the taxonomic definition of insanity in the same period noted in Foucault's *History of Madness* via Pinel and Linnaeus. Speech pathology historian Judy Duchan relies on French professor of medicine Francois Boissier de Sauvages de Lacroix for the definition of eleven distinct speech disabilities, who is referenced in James Hunt's 1870 scholarship:

> psellismus ischnophonia, or stuttering: difficulty of moving the velum, the uvula and the root of the tongue.
> psellismus rhotacismus: problem with the r sound
> psellismus lambdacismus: problem with l sound
> psellismus traulotes: indistinctness, (lisping?)
> psellismus balbuties: problem with labials
> psellismus mogilalia: problem with labials (another kind?)

psellismus metallicus: a speech problem caused by metallic poisons
psellismus iotacismus: a problem with guttural sounds
psellismus nastas: nasality
psellismus lagostomatum: cleft lip and palate
psellismus a ranula: a speech problem caused by tumors.

Drawing from this portrait of speech regulation in the post-Enlightenment and pre-twentieth-century periods, it is clear that between the mechanistic portrayals offered originally by early medical scientists like Boissier de Sauvages de Lacroix and the early illocutionist correction measures, the two institutional seeds of speech disability definition had been sown, one more directly infused with nationalism and empire by way of its concern for the canon of Western empire, and the other content with what would be appropriately recognized as a bio-reductionism of stuttering as a purely pneumatic phenomenon. In the passage out of the Enlightenment, a third explanation for speech difference would come into being in the form of the start of Freudian psychoanalysis in the nineteenth century. However, prior to the Freudian emergence, it is important to understand speech impairment as primarily a dialectic between linguists loyal to ancient academic texts and scientists loyal to the objectivity of physical and material explanation. Between the scholastic academic analysis and the scientific observation, all forms of speech disability were first known in this epoch as a flight from normal functioning, either by the scholastic sin of misenunciation or by mechanical violations of uniformity in the pronunciations of specific phonemes.

6.2. THE FREUDIAN INTELLECTUALIST REVIVAL AND THE BROCA/WERNICKE LOCALIZATION

One hundred years after Boissier De Sauvages de Lacroix's mechanical theory is brought to seed, it is to be specified by early neurologists Broca and Wernicke's localization of speech areas of the brain just which physiological locations cause speech dysfunction, and simultaneously Freud's psychoanalysis would revive the importance of Swift's usage error and in doing so give it an important psychoanalytic meaning by way of books like *On Aphasia* (1953). A proper understanding of Freud's intervention into language is that his is an interpersonalist expansion of Swift in suggesting that symbol errors are connected to emotional–interpersonal histories or what would be called more abstractly the realm of "the psyche" or "the psychic." Also, in Freud is found a mentalist account of speech, which is his principle similarity to Swift's injunction, as indeed both theorists of language see language literacy as an inherently unreliable process as it must rely on the psychic history and the intentions of the reader. Conversely, Paul Pierre Broca's 1861 discovery of the localization of speech (a scientific achievement not greatly detached from his bio-reductionist, sexist, anatomical, anthropological views) and Carl Wernicke's discovery of jargon aphasia caused by brain injuries to the left posterior area of the brain offered two localizations of speech to specific areas of the brain but could not articulate the discoveries of such locations in terms of how they specifically effect symbolic comprehension or expression, or even perception.

In engaging both Freud and Broca as major progenitors of modern twentieth-century American debates around speech, it may be necessary to engage with the polemics against them, offered by Stephen Jay Gould on Broca and by Adolf Grunbaum on Freud. In reading refutations of both Freud and Broca, we may understand how neither figure attained permanent influence, but only managed to shift debates concerning human expression and pull or push in either extreme of mentalism or bio-determinism. It may also be crucial to understand how Freud and Broca's works each became iconoclastic for academic disciplines of psychology and for disciplines of psychiatry.

Gould's critique of Broca in *The Mismeasure of Man* (1996) centers on how Broca used statistics to justify conclusions already supplied about the racial superiority of whiteness and the sex supremacy of cisgender men. Other major figures such as Carl Sagan praise Broca for locating speech in the brain. It will not be difficult to offer two perspectives on Broca: Broca has generated entire swaths of contemporary science via his studies of brains, but he has also fathered the most expansive eugenic ideologies used for the most despicable of practices—namely, eugenics against disabled people and racial minorities by European countries during the twentieth and twenty-first centuries, and also throughout colonialist history.

Freud's corpus offers the opposite problem: his brush is too wide to apply to the many instances of speech disability that are caused by issues in the body and are not hysterical symptoms, as Freud would have them. Freud's thesis that speech disability represents a refusal to speak out of a madness that effects the will or unreason itself is a very inconvenient one for any speech-disabled person that seeks political redress, as the government repairs problems caused against oneself only with containment. Additionally, reading Grunbaum (1984), Freud's attempt at naturalism in terms of representing the communicative performance of his patients as symptomatic is contradicted by psychoanalysis's extremely interpretive methodology.

The debate between symbolic interactionist understandings of speech disability such as that of Freud and more bio-deterministic treatments such as those provided by Broca (and critiqued by Gould) would never be complete. However, the bio-determinist justification would have greater success in the American political scene because of its high standard of evidence. Nevertheless, the same debate would play out specifically within the American political scene through Chomsky's upset of Skinner not even eighty years later. These newer debates, however, are more proof of the irresolution of the conversation between Freud and Broca, only in the later repetition, behaviorism would take up the determinist view and cognitivism would take up the more social scientifically enabled view.

Furthermore, the incommensurability of Freudian and Broca-influenced views of speech is a major aspect of why this chapter argues that speech-disabled people could never be added very easily to the psychiatric disability or to the physical disability worlds. The far-reaching arguments between major figures in opposing academic disciplines meant that many of those involved in debating the nature of speech impairments like aphasia felt that their disagreement was paradigmatic and could not be resolved—thus, outside of phenomenology, there has been almost no attempt to find a pragmatic view of speech disability between Freudian and Broca-influenced sides. Psychologists and speech therapists likely did become well read in both Broca and Freud, but those that did became host to aspects of both thinkers that this chapter finds to be worth criticizing— incoherently naturalistic qualitative descriptions and incoherently simplistic uses of data to support predesigned conclusions instead of to test hypotheses. Psychologists who view speech disability as neurodevelopmental, for instance, have often done work replete with the worst habits of both thinkers—using psychology as an intellectualist tautology to be justified instead of disproven with data.

6.3. BETWEEN MENTALISM AND MECHANISM

In positioning the Freudian intellectualist account that is biased toward mentalist symbol management and mechanist psychology that is biased toward a disease model together, it becomes necessary to draw upon a theory of mediation that can connect between symbolic—or, as Merleau-Ponty calls them, "intellectualist"—approaches and overly mechanistic approaches. Actor network theories, most popularly advanced by Bruno Latour, as well as new materialisms, such as work by Karen Barad, and neurophenomenological work using Merleau-Ponty but also drawing on later disciples such as Hubert Dreyfus, Francisco Varela, and Walter Freeman III offer a series of ways of mediating between symbolic and material worlds, often by way of conceptualizations of either "action," "practice," or "intention" as a force that moves between such realms. Many such scholars call back to theorists such as Thomas Aquinas, whose faith is placed in intention or Hegelian dialecticians that use mediation. Additionally, at the heart of some actor network theories, as well as new ideologies such as object-oriented ontologies, is a critique of anthropocentrism that does not give human subjectivity enough reflection. At the heart of theories of materiality that posit inert actants is the suggestion that materiality is itself a convergence between multiple worlds of influence. Such a suggestion is also consistent with Young Hegelian and Hegelian–Marxist dialectics that recognize categories of being such as the ideal and the raw coming into conversation by conflict or debate and producing the future by way of synthesis.

Understanding the unresolved quality of the debate between mechanistic and symbolic understandings of speech that dates back to a series of Enlightenment and then Late Modern theorists supports the striking conclusion of Bruno Latour in *We Have Never Been Modern* (2012). Accordingly, this cultural history's account of the mechanism-symbolism debate around speech disability as it extends into the twentieth and twenty-first centuries highlights how the resolution of speech's signification or materiality was adjusted in different global regions on differing terms. In the heart of the American Empire of the twentieth century, however, we must regard the Broca/Wernicke interpretation as scientifically victorious. In continental Europe, where the emergence of such poststructuralist luminaries to the intellectualist symbolic tradition as Derrida and Lacan arose, more symbolic accountings of speech disability were successful. Thus, speech disability's mechanical reduction within the American sciences sets the condition for its emergence as a part of the Disability Rights movement in the 1970s by way of the Stuttering Self-Help movement. Only when speech disability could have had one-hundred years of materialization within physical science could it begin to have a life of class struggle in which the patients opposed the hierarchies of the clinic, similar to moments of class struggle attached to other disability categories. It will be important that my account of the twentieth and twenty-first centuries of speech disability cultural history hinges on two major sites of rupture: international and American portrayals of speech disability culture in the twentieth and twenty-first centuries and their attachment to either mechanical or emotive theories of stuttering and points of coalition and isolation, and the similarities and conflicts between the twentieth- and twenty-first-century Stuttering Self-Help movement and the Disability Rights movement.

In the move from the Freud–Broca debate toward the advent of anti-theoretical behaviorism and its corollary of deeply theoretically entwined cognitivism, major thinkers in the development of medical and social science no longer originate in continental Europe, but are instead found in the American academy. The move toward the American metropole is constituent with the American imperialist victory during the First and Second World Wars and the ravaging of France and Germany as major centers of intellectual thought by the same events. In the American academy, the uniquely American ideology of pragmatist psychology founded by none other than William James causes the Freudian thread of focus on childhood development to be pulled into a highly scientific positivist fold. B. F. Skinner and his disciples agree with Freud on the susceptibility of childhood speech to influence, but not upon the sexuality of the psyche and not upon abstract notions of degeneracy, psychosis, or schizophrenia. Similarly, cognitivists agree with elocutionists about the function of the body as a tool for expression, but refute the ability of teachers to correct such verbal action. As will be shown in the following section, the behaviorist and cognitivist schools reflect a pragmatist reconsideration of the guarantees of repairing or fixing speech disability, with Skinnerian behaviorists skeptically regarding anything but reward and punishment-based operant conditioning and Chomskyan cognitivists skeptically questioning the affixation of a universal development timeline.

6.4. B. F. SKINNER'S VERBAL BEHAVIOR AND CHOMSKY'S REVIEW: POST-HUMAN PSYCHOLOGY'S MATERIALIST ROOTS

Until 1959, Harvard psychologist B. F. Skinner's behaviorist theory of learning was the most prominent perspective of learning and skill acquisition of any kind. Outside the realm of language and speech, Skinner was immensely successful in proving experimentally that conditioning based on reward and punishment could be used to train first animals and eventually children to adopt a multitude of improved skills and outcomes based on careful use of such training methods. Skinner's work on a behaviorist theory of speech was, however, entirely theoretical and not based in experiment. As such, his 1957 book, *Verbal Behavior*, endured only a two-year tenure before being shredded by notable cognitive linguist Noam Chomsky.

In the twentieth century, the most major change in the science of speech can be found in linguist Noam Chomsky's rebuke to B. F. Skinner's book, *Verbal Behavior*, on the basis that language, learning, and speech acquisition occur independent of the training given to children. Chomsky's well-documented rebuke would later be said to be the birthing event for what is currently known as cognitive psychology, but besides Chomsky's conversation with scientists, he is also quite conversant with major social critics via his public stance in favor of a materialist anarchism and through debates with major literary critics like Michel Foucault and Slavoj Žižek. Parallel to Chomsky's founding of the cognitive psychological account of speech learning, one may find a disciple of Merleau-Ponty, Hubert Dreyfus, refuting the computational model of consciousness on similar terms to his mentor in *What Computers Cannot Do*.

However, unlike the extremely influential debate between Freud and Broca, speech pathology historians do not mention Chomsky, and instead tend to adopt a version of cognitive thought that is disciplined by behaviorist values as demonstrated by the twentieth-century application of cognitive–behavioral therapy to speech disabilities. This reformed behaviorism, now described as "new behaviorism," purports to use insights from computer models to better train the body. Opposed to the "new behaviorism" labeled "cognitive–behavioral therapy" is the much more sensorily based eye movement desensitization and reprocessing (EMDR) that seemingly applies Merleau-Pontyan-inspired insights about eye movement and intentionality. However, EMDR is attacked by the therapeutic establishment for defying the post-Freudian focus on interpersonal performance for perceptual association, and also for not maintaining the same standards of evidence as its more empirical cousins.

The history of speech disability as a scientific puzzle caused either by mechanical accident or mental maldevelopment is placed next to the explicitly political history of Disability Rights as well as Stutterer Self-Help with a turn toward the factors that cause speech disability to defy location within either the major psychiatric disability or physical disability camps of the Disability Rights movement. The scientific history of speech disability is invoked strategically to position the scientific debates around speech disability as unresolved and to posit that such scientific irresolution and lack of consensus marks speech disability outside of the traditional binaries and categories that most disability discourse rests upon. In choosing to view the scientific debates over materiality or developmental onset as unresolved, this chapter borrows from Bruno Latour's *We Have Never Been Modern* to acknowledge that speech disability is one of those "hybrids" that cannot be situated purely within social development or observable biological mechanism or even political history, but can only be understood at the convergence of all three. In the previous sections, I have considered the concept of speech disability in its description first by elocution and medicine, then by psychoanalysis and brain science, and finally within behaviorism and cognitivism. Each of these ruptures, which have never been resolved, plays into the ambiguity of speech disability in the political scene. Twin social and natural histories of science produce speech disability as a hybrid object that at first defies disability politics and then is coaxed into submission through its isolation.

6.5. SPEECH DISABILITY SILENCE IN THE ARCHIVE OF DISABILITY HISTORY

In the US context, most major academic treatments of Disability Rights history or disability history in general do not include any mention of the Stuttering Self-Help movement and generally are unclear on whether speech disorders are part of disability or not. What is known is that many disabilities openly included in the canon of disability social movements do have speech-based symptoms, but these symptoms, their need to be treated, and the possible accessibility options related to them seem not to be considered.

Among the arguments made in this chapter, it will be suggested that speech disability has only emerged (as McRuer notes in *Crip Times*) due to the eventual wide acceptance of a post-Chomskyan materialist set of assumptions around speech that suggest it develops regardless of nurture due to its embodiment and universality. Before Chomsky, the influence of Freud and Skinner in psychology had largely allocated speech difference to the fields of the emotional and interpersonal incapacity instead of the realm of biological materialism. This relegation of speech disability to a status of mental illness or mental disorder may have caused it to be overlooked as a physical impairment worthy of inclusion in the physical disability-centered world of disability social movements in the USA, represented most poignantly in Jim Charlton's well-renowned book, *Nothing about Us without Us* (1998). Likewise, many psychiatrists and psychologists as well as psychiatric survivors would have been unlikely to see a stutter alone as a true instance of something worthy of clinical treatment without secondary accompaniment by anxieties that themselves may have come into existence due to the markedness of the seemingly unproblematic difference. Thus, speech disability is displaced from both antipsychiatry social activism and Disability Rights movements because the debate on whether speech disability is in the emotions or in the machinery of the body was as unresolved during the first outpouring of disability activism as it is now.

What presence of speech disability has existed can be found in the Stuttering Self-Help movement. Founded by Bob Goldman and Michael Sugarman in 1977, the then National Stuttering Project (now the National Stuttering Association) organized itself only after nearly one-hundred years of clinical diagnosis and stigmatization had proven that speech language pathologists could not continue to do research about stutterers without stutterer involvement. But the organization and project itself, in terms of the broader arc of disability politics, has taken a fairly apolitical position, outside the initial call to put clinicians in contact with patients.

In the next series of paragraphs, the uneven materiality of speech disability will be considered for how it is brought to bear on the struggle to fight against oppression, as well as its inclusion within the normative categories assumed by the Disability Rights movement such as physical disability and madness.

In the political circumstances in which state remuneration is given to an oppressed population, oppression must be defined as that which is negative and exterior to will or intention. But in the case of stuttering and other speech disabilities, that very problem has been the principle delay to inclusion within politics because of the Freudian/Skinnerian idea that speech disability is simply a poor use of coping skills and because of the tradition that psychology and speech therapy buy into within which William James had once suggested there could be diseases of both instinct and will. Particularly due to politics' explicit limit of the expression and performance of *will* within a capitalist system, it becomes increasingly difficult to suggest that society assists people with speech disabilities until the current political system can be convinced of the Broca/Chomsky conclusion that speech disability is an extra-intentional break in the embodied linguistic–vocal system. But because the schooling of willful misuses of language is such a large part of the knowledge industry, it is unlikely that the justice system will ever consider unsmooth speech as anything more than an aesthetic detail that can and should be enhanced and made more fluid by the bearer of said speech at the demand of the risk of disenfranchisement.

What is new is this chapter's background of the intellectual genealogy of speech therapy. Some of what is highlighted include Freudian and behaviorist tendencies to see speech disability as "developmental" or located in nurture and thus responsive to psychotherapy. Additionally, this locates the origin of speech disorder and speech disability in the postmodern era as a continually uncertain question that defies Cartesian body–mind dualisms. Some of what makes speech disability so anomalous can be attributed to what Charlton (1998: 114) calls "the hierarchy of disability" or the implicit view in the disability rights movement that shows a preference for physical disability over either cognitive or psychiatric (read: invisible) disabilities. This view as well as the ongoing political drama of the later 20th century have resulted in a chaotic discourse around disability and health both within and outside the medical sciences and the political arenas. As will be shown in the following paragraphs, amid such fierce scientific and political debates, speech disability is a paradox that has been only addressed in the most simplistic forms and thus has been left out of deeper consideration in the context of disability activism.

Due to speech disability's unevenness, it is worth considering the ways in which the Stuttering Self-Help movement and National Stuttering Association primarily adopt tactics of resistance used by the health disability movements that critique over-medicalization but nonetheless continue to focus overtly on fixing disability negligence. Such emphases rarely or only provisionally address the topic of speech disability as involving the exposé of violence in the discursive repression and devaluation of speech-disabled individuals. The counter-memory of speech disability as a form of madness might encourage nonprofit, single disability-focused organizations operating under the umbrella of the self-help movement such as the National Stuttering Association to begin to think of how to liberate stutterers, focusing as much on the individual liberty to stutter as it might do on helping people who desire treatment to receive it.

It is notable that Mad Studies as well as the psychiatric survivor movement have pursued a different strategy from that of just correcting negligence, instead pursuing one based on attempting to give psychiatrically diagnosed people more control over their own care and on humanizing such persons to the extent that old institutions of confinement would be eliminated. But speech disability is mired in the model of disability activism that is concentrated on the lack of care for disabled lives instead of the poor quality and low level of autonomy in care for disabled lives that is more often the source of debility, given that quality of care is more determinative of neglect and abuse than is absence of care altogether. One can exist without care and sometimes avoid the violence so endemic to the social support-based care system, but the latter problem is completely off the radar screen of the national debate, as the USA overly prides itself on being the "gold standard" of care for disabled people, as well as global health care in general.

In locating this un-pursued element of stuttering politics that might be omnipresent in its history, I hope to open up space for new reimaginings of both our concept of the disability community as well as the location and meaning of speech disability in the broader world of disability politics. In understanding how speech disability became politicized, we lay bare some elements of the politicization of unequal social conditions. From speech disability, we find out that oppression is presumed to be limited in the area of politics to problems over which the individual is presumed to have no control, and in the democratic, individualist Western polity, speech itself is always presumed to be a mix of intention and embodiedness—thus, the level of intention that coheres even in mis-speech is implicitly removed from the fold of politics around political rights because stuttering and other speech disabilities are presumed to be fixable or, at least, in search of a cure that is always around the corner but rarely materializes. Additionally, unlike body-based disabilities, speech impediment is seen to be sometimes too minor to even consider, while at other times it is considered to be the product of a large enough gap in talent to garner lower overall employment. Once more, the category of speech disability becomes depoliticized precisely because its instability is primed for misunderstanding, especially by simplistic psychoanalytic, behaviorist, and neo-behaviorist analyses that all tend to reduce it to emotion, or by simplistic behaviorism that sees it as an outgrowth of failed nurturing.

6.6. TOWARD AN EPISTEMOLOGICALLY NEUTRAL VOICE

In the preceding pages, I have sought to portray the clash between mentalist and bio-determinist as well as nature-causal and nurture-causal camps in the historical debate about speech disability. In portraying speech and speech disability as a central place of rupture between major theorists of consciousness in psychology, medicine, linguistics, and philosophy, I have hoped to show the extremism on all sides of the debate regarding the materiality of voice and the materiality of speech disability. In sketching the outer extremes of the debate over speech, we are left with a sense of voice itself as not possibly merely madness or symbolic interaction, but also bodily, as well as being composed both of behavioral incentives and disincentives within a normate society. Furthermore, these influences coincide with theories that speaking organisms are predisposed to gain and lose speech differences throughout the maturation process of the brain. Finally, in observing how those scientific debates about speech disability effected its inclusion through pathologization and absence as a worthy subject of phenomenological or policy navigation of difference in both the Disability Rights and psychiatric survivor social movements, I have also aimed to show how speech disability cannot inhabit mere physical or mental disability alone, but must stretch across or transcend the limits of both categories. Not only do I offer this both–and approach, but also I propose that speech disability must ultimately be navigated as a volitional condition of bodily agency itself rather than as a failure of elocution or a symptomatic surface of psychological distress.

In understanding voice as perplexingly occupying multiple fields at once, we are forced to acknowledge that the reductionism around compulsory enhancement via speech therapy can only address speech disability as it is present in the negotiation of body/mental speech with the norms of society. Such negotiations are portrayed complexly in the sociology of disability, such as the work of Erving Goffman, and in histories of madness, such as the work of Michel Foucault, or even in alternative psychiatric institutional settings, such as that supervised by Felix Guattari. The institution can only fix the clinical subjects in connection with the norms of the historical administration of bodies (or bio-power) and can only situate the information of the patient's body in the context of the social reaction to how the body comes across, not to the body and its own experiences (what Goffman might have called "wisdom"). Because clinical science is oriented toward instrumental determinism, speech language pathology cannot address speech disability in its full multidimensional complexity as existing across multiple levels and worlds at any given moment. Instead, within a Merleau-Pontyan framework, all that can be done is to use normative formal judgment to correct errors in communication or sounds not deemed to be legitimate in any natural taxonomy of articulation. However, this move cannot ameliorate the status given in society to speech as a phenomenological measure of adequate cognition that is, in turn, itself an interdependent dialogue between implicit gestural judgment and explicit judgment of meaning, form, and expression in delivery and content.

As Noam Chomsky's viewpoint fused with behaviorism reigns as the current predominant view, we are forced to consider Chomsky's own Cartesian lineage and how the Cartesian limits to the cognitive-dominant model that has arisen as the current panacea to a nearly 200-year debate about speech presume speech itself to be the determining factor that sets the human out from the nonhuman and the machine. This philosophical move simultaneously summons Alan Turing's work on machines and Descartes' *cogito* of human exceptionalism in cognition. In all such works, the ability to form creative or original patterns of language is viewed as the trait that makes the human exceptional and stakes the inherent desirability of anthropocentrism on the novelty of speech. Once a body is in this situation of definition, either via degradation in the case of the disabled human speaker or via total dehumanization in the case of a racialized or ethnicized subject speaking, the speaker is given a provisional humanity within the Descartes–Turing–Chomsky view of voco-anthropocentrism due to the combination of "human" ingenuity and difference in symbols. Chomsky would likely respond to my suggestion that his definition of "human" is overly simplistic by emphasizing that his own turn away from surface structure reflected a need to interrogate the greater capacities of the human, but his work is unable to avoid the core contradiction that may be seen in Merleau-Ponty, but also in literary theories of orality as the need to staple signification to biological cognition. The papering-over of cognition as signification is not just a mass societal process that makes cognition more buried within Western society, but is also a move that is criticized by Merleau-Ponty as Kantian and mentally determinist and by Eric Havelock and Walter Ong as overtly textualist. We turn to the concept of orality offered by Havelock and Ong to provide a sense of voice that is more transcendental.

It is crucial to note that Merleau-Ponty as well as Ong and Havelock are theorists that arrive in the later parts of the twentieth century and thus seemingly prefigure and predict the response to what Stacy Alaimo has called "the linguistic turn" in the possibility of an oral or gestural turn in communication and literary studies. The return of orality here may be historicized as a new development that could be named "post-postmodern," but can certainly be specified as being influenced in part by many areas of academic thought, including environmental studies, "new materialism"/science and technology studies, as well as digital humanities and geo-humanities. The revolt against postmodernism signifies a response to changes in the hegemony of empirical science wherein critical intellectuals abandon more sweeping critiques of scientific positivism and instead follow Haraway and Latour to a balanced respect for cultural studies and scientific thought.

Is it exceptionalizing to read Havelock and Ong as showing that these pieces of speech that are so disruptive may have had a completely different meaning within an oralist epistemology rather than a textualist one, particularly given that Havelock and Ong's conceptualization of orality views orality as extralinguistic and encompassing a range of tonal and gestural forms? In Havelock's work, repetition has a far differing meaning than it does for Chomsky. Rhythm in Havelock sometimes involves failure to generate difference in speech. But repetition means something different in the oralist epistemology than what it means in the textualist ideology that clearly occupies our epoch, as well as Chomsky's Cartesian corpus. Can we stake the claim that much of the pathologization of speech disability comes from textual modernity's painful relationship with the mechanics of oral knowledge during the 500-year technological hegemony of the printing press? Freud and Broca as well as Skinner and Chomsky all seek to intellectualize speech (as even this writing does, to an extent, but more ambiguously) such that it can be reflected as a two-dimensional pattern process either in the material form of the body, in symbols, in measurable behaviors, or in conditioning. But orality has at least three dimensions and operates on multiple levels simultaneously, with one of those levels being on the inside of knowable consciousness. The move to call attention to the oral as a multidimensional category comes from Ong's concept of primary orality, and the idea of levels spanning between objectivity and subjectivity is offered by Maurice Merleau-Ponty's phenomenology, which is the original source for this chapter's multimodal, multimedial notion of speech disability.

Additionally to Ong and Merleau-Ponty's cohering accounts of speech epistemology and gesture epistemology, one can add Lev Vygotsky's account of inner speech in *Thought and Language*. Ehrich (2006) offers that Vygotskyan inner speech reveals an internalization process by which "external operation is reconstructed as an inner one" and "interpersonal processes are transformed into intrapersonal processes." The internalization process is demonstrated by Ehrich's own Vygotskyan reader response theory, which suggests that phonological behaviors while reading demonstrate the connections across the levels of the material, the recognizable, the sensible, and the thinkable. Silent reading or silent repetition of oral language shows this link, as it shows how symbols are translated across dimensions.

With all of these theorists together, we are asked to recognize that speech and speech disability occur on four distinct levels: the materiality of the body; the symbolic recognitions or misrecognitions that impose their effects on the body (Damasio); the focus or unfocus of the sensory world; and finally the inner speech reflection of the dynamic manifestation of all of these processes through Ong's primary orality.

We are brought back, then, to the fundamental problem: speech language pathology as a whole has a limited ability to explain the compounding nature of the sensory, gestural, social structural, and inner aspects of speech. The form in which speech has primarily settled for it to be the subject of diagnosis and self-help activism has been overtly bio-reductionist not because such can be demonstrated as the core element of speech disability, but because of American culture, where bio-determinist psychology has been most successful and has, in turn, demanded all disorders under study to be biologically locatable in genetics, in the body, or in another physical explanation. And in another area, the problem with psychoanalysis is that it ultimately attempts to deconstruct what William James would have called "diseases of will," but will is not merely conditioning, as Freud seems to presume with his developmental model—it might be said to align with the agential nature of bodies as they interact with and re-signify the meanings assigned to them.

The Vygotskyan model is completely synergistic with Merleau-Pontyan thought because both thinkers view habit as something that changes the body through extra-bodily interaction, and both theorists view the body and its perceptions and memories as increasing in complexity and finesse as it is used. Furthermore, Vygotsky's startling suggestion that more advanced systems engage in inner speech and external speech in fact contradicts the Merleau-Pontyan suggestion of a pre-personal realm that is cut off from personal performance. In fact, the pre-personal may be alterable through habit in both of the Vygotskyan and Merleau-Pontyan accounts to some degree. However, Vygotsky is much more mentalist than Merleau-Ponty, even claiming access to inner language and inner cognition. Merleau-Ponty's disinterest in cognition, however, may also need some reconsideration—intention may be the same concept, but his refusal to venture into consciousness beside the sensory–motor schema shows an anti-explanatory strain that refuses to compromise with traditional concepts of the mental as a domain. Where both theorists are consistent is in the concept of multilevel intersubjectivity, which is also supported by psychoanalytic thinker Daniel N. Stern.

6.7. CONCLUSION

I have hoped to convey throughout this chapter the very basic thesis I arrive at from Merleau-Ponty, which is that speech and therefore speech disability exist unevenly across the five dimensions of intersubjectivity. I have shown speech's scientifically undetermined ambiguity through arguing—along with actor network theory accounts—that the debate between the nature and culture of speech is unresolved scientifically and that four major scientific luminaries—Broca, Freud, Skinner, and Chomsky—have never agreed totally on causal relations and have been polarized from each other's theories in this regard. This unresolved quality to the interdisciplinary debate on speech disability means that purely symbolic or purely bio-deterministic framings of speech would be made in error and that instead we must confront speech as a cogno-materiality that is dynamically processed on several levels of experience at once and simultaneously.

CHAPTER SEVEN

Learning Difficulties

A Cultural History of Learning Difficulties in the Modern Age

OWEN BARDEN

7.1. INTRODUCTION

My thesis in this chapter is threefold. Firstly, I contend that "learning difficulties" as we now understand them are phenomena created by certain contingent discursive formations. That is to say, they are not natural, but manufactured, and dependent on particular, peculiar historical conditions. Secondly, I contend that "learning difficulties" is an organizing concept: one that has, over the course of the twentieth and twenty-first centuries, irrespective of the shifting signifying terminology used over this period, radically transformed our sense not only of education and learning, but also of who is or is not deemed entitled to full citizenship and its associated rights, and so who is or is not fully human. Thirdly, I contend that a regime of truth has been constructed around "learning difficulties" that privileges certain knowledges and excludes alternative ways of knowing, most notably those of people labeled with learning difficulties.

In writing a *cultural* history, the emphasis is not on what certain people are or are not learning, nor on what anyone's particular difficulties with learning are perceived to be. Rather, the emphasis is on the role "learning difficulties" play in society. McDermott et al. (2006) put it in the following way in an article elucidating the political work so-called learning difficulties now have to do in Westernized societies:

> A cultural approach to learning difficulties does not address learning difficulties directly but instead addresses arrangements among persons, ideas, opportunities, constraints, and interpretations—what others call the discursive practices of learning difficulties. (McDermott et al. 2006: 13)

In other words, a cultural approach is concerned with the ways in which people who are said to have learning difficulties are conceptualized, spoken about, and interacted with, and with the relational and environmental factors contextualizing and shaping these practices. Through paying attention to these conditions, I aim to demonstrate how intersecting discourses of medicine, education, media, law, economics, colonialism, and eugenics brought into being the phenomenon of "learning difficulties," simultaneously casting professionals as moral agents working for the good of society and people labeled with learning difficulties and its synonyms as immoral or amoral agents. Much as Simpson (2014) has done for intellectual disability in the early modern period, I hope to show how this discursively constructed regime of truth still defines and confines people labeled with learning difficulties.

Atkinson and Walmsley (2010) note that until the late twentieth century, intellectual disability history was subsumed or neglected within accounts from the psycho-medical professions, educational and mental health services, sociologists, and historians. More recently, input from a broad range of disciplines has helped to challenge the assumed truths generated about learning disability—in all its terminological guises—generated by medics, scientists, and medical historians (Philo 2014). Learning difficulties has also emerged as a field of inquiry within its own right within Disability Studies, in tandem with the realization that this aspect of disability has frequently been overlooked in both the turn to the Social Model and the later (re)turn to impairment (Goodley 2001). Meanwhile, Snyder and Mitchell (2005: xi) contend that "[t]here is still much to be learned from historical inquiry into the roots of what has been an unsettling century-and-a-half of rabid segregation and extermination in much of Europe and the US." This chapter offers a contribution to this field. It concentrates on the contemporary period, although in order to develop a fuller appreciation of the evolution of conceptualizations of "learning difficulties," the history will initially consider the nineteenth century.

Much of the evidence I will draw on comes from England, although I will also discuss examples from both the USA and Australia in developing arguments about so-called learning difficulties and how associated norms—with race as a factor—have and continue to vary from one cultural context to another. The material I draw on for my analysis includes primary sources in the Liverpool Hope University Library's Nugent Archive, the Lancashire County Archive in Preston, and the digital archives of the Wellcome Library, as well as a range of secondary sources. The Liverpool Hope University Nugent Archive is named after Monsignor James Nugent, a Roman Catholic priest of the Archdiocese of Liverpool in the late Victorian period. He instituted and influenced a number of local and national health and education organizations, and the Archive's records include those of a number of farm schools, approved and special schools, and other such locations around Liverpool and Merseyside. The Lancashire County Archive holds all manner of official and unofficial records, including those of the Royal Albert Asylum for Idiots and Imbeciles of the Seven Northern Counties and of the Calderstones Institution for Mental Defectives, as well as papers relating to Professor R. J. A. Berry, a prominent early twentieth-century eugenicist. The Wellcome Library houses a globally significant collection of medical history resources. I use these sources and give further examples to show that what was evident in asylums in the mid-nineteenth-century continues to this day in widely dispersed places of confinement, including schools, care homes, and youth detention centers.

7.2. HISTORICAL ONTOLOGY

This chapter draws on Hacking's (2002) interpretation of Foucault's historical ontological method to expose the ways in which, from the mid-nineteenth century onward, professions and institutions of confinement have both stoked and assuaged antipathy toward people with intellectual or cognitive impairments, and consequently profited as a result of the regime of truth they have helped to construct. Under this regime, people with intellectual impairments or perceived deficits are represented as menacing or risky Others; at the same time, the professions and institutions of confinement assume authority over "the problem" by relocating and segregating stigmatized individuals and assuring the public that "the problem" is under control. This move also provides some of those same professionals with captive populations for their own scientific, educational, and capitalist endeavors, which are geared toward either enabling people labeled with learning difficulties to approximate norms or toward keeping them segregated from the population considered normal. These processes of measurement, classification, and segregation bring into being new kinds of people through taxonomies established about perceived intellectual ability. In this way, "Normalization becomes one of the great instruments of power at the end of the classical age" (Foucault, 1979, quoted in Ball 2013: 54), and it continues to be one. The exact pattern of the discourse threads that intertwine to create the enclosing, excluding regime of truth will, as we shall see, evolve over time, but the fabric enveloping the discursive field in which "truths" about learning difficulties are scientifically established is never breached:

> The hegemony of this enclosed space is such that all statements and objects and subjectivities exist only by assuming a position within it .... Different points within the space signify variations in the relative emphasis of different elements. (Simpson 2014: 123)

Hacking (2002), while conceding that the term *historical ontology* is both somewhat pompous and rather vague, nevertheless contends that it represents a useful way of establishing what kinds of things exist, and what makes it possible for them to come into being, by enabling us to illuminate the creation of phenomena and plot their trajectories through discursive formations. I use this method to explain how learning difficulties were brought into being as a phenomenon and how they have subsequently become an organizing concept in Westernized societies: a concept that has radically transformed our sense of what it means to be (or not to be) a person (Goodey 2017). We can draw a parallel with Hacking's (2002) exposition of trauma as an organizing concept in contemporary culture. Noting the shift in the meaning of trauma from principally physical (harm done to the body) to the psychic (harm done to the mind), Hacking (2002: 19) argues that "The story of trauma can be looked at as a sequence of events in the history of psychology and psychiatry. But my concern is the way in which the trauma concept figures in the constitution of selves." He goes on to explicate this history of trauma using the three ontological axes of truth, power, and ethics posited by Foucault, showing how the current conception of trauma shapes our everyday lives in, for example, our responses to natural disasters. Paraphrasing Hacking's argument, substituting the phrase "learning difficulties" for trauma and making a few other minor alterations (swapping mention of soldiers for students, for instance) provides encouraging justification for considering learning difficulties an organizing concept:

> First, there is the person known about, as having a kind of behavior and sense of self that is produced by "learning difficulties." Today there is a vast body of "knowledge" in the burgeoning field of learning difficulties.
>
> Second, in the field of power, we have congeries of possibilities: self-empowerment and advocacy; power of victims over abusers; the power of the courts and legislatures; the power of students to claim reasonable adjustments and other benefits for learning

difficulties. But most importantly, it is the anonymous power of the very concept of learning difficulties that works in our lives.

The third axis is ethical. At the moral level, events, present or remembered, experienced through learning difficulties, exculpate. Learning difficulties are used to explain or excuse an antisocial person, who may also be diagnosed with, for example, "antisocial personality disorder," or, latterly "moral imbecility." Learning difficulties create new moral beings. Learning difficulties offer not only a new sense of who others are, and why some may be that way, but also produce a new sense of self, of who one is and why one is as one is.

This chapter is thus concerned with the sequence of events in the history of psychology and psychiatry—as well as other intersecting discourses—that have helped to establish learning difficulties as an organizing concept: one that generates powerful "truths" about self and Others. These powerful, reflexive, intersecting, inescapable discourses construct a regime of truth in which it is inconceivable not to think of people with apparent learning difficulties as Other: "Truth is linked in a circular relation with systems of power which produce and sustain it, and to effects of power which it induces and which extend it" (Foucault 1980: 133). I begin by considering the rise of the asylums in the mid-nineteenth century and the associated technologies of biopower. Next, I examine the period from 1900 to World War II, paying particular attention to the discourses in the USA, England, and Australia. The following main section concludes at the turn of the millennium, focusing on the progression from institutionalization to "care in the community," while the subsequent main section brings the discussion up to the present day.

7.3. THE NINETEENTH CENTURY: ESTABLISHING THE REGIME

Never has an infant charity made such progress in such a short period. Never has a board of similar character taken up such serious responsibilities; and never, perhaps, has any one been so sustained by public sympathy .... The benefit has already extended beyond the sphere of our exertions. The tone of public feeling in relation to the poor idiot has been raised. He can never again be the forlorn, abandoned, scorned, imprisoned creature he once was. (Telford-Smith and Coupland 1856: 9)

So wrote Dr. Telford Telford-Smith, later to become Medical Superintendent of the Royal Albert Asylum for Idiots and Imbeciles of the Seven Northern Counties (of which more later), and W. H. Coupland in a pamphlet produced for the Edinburgh Home and School for Invalid and Imbecile Children in 1856. By *infant charity* they mean a newly created society formed in 1847 for the establishment of idiot asylums (i.e. not a charity for newborns) in London and Essex that were instituted the following year and shortly afterward incorporated by Royal Charter. Here, sovereign power in the most literal sense combines with religious, psycho-medical, and educational discourses to present a narrative of benevolence, acceptance, and the potential for "improvement," with an initial emphasis on education. Several features are notable in the passage. There is the rather triumphalist tone created by the repetition of *never has*. There is the claim to have elicited and sustained public *sympathy* for the *poor idiot*. And there is the claim to future progress and emancipation: "He can never again be ...." The passage in fact signifies a shifting conception of people who would currently be labeled with learning difficulties, here signified by the term *idiot*. Etymologically, *idiot* comes from the Ancient Greek *idios*, meaning "one's own," and refers to someone deemed self-centered and parasitical, unable to reason or self-regulate, and therefore ineducable and contributing nothing to the common good; someone who represents an obstacle to the perfectible society (Simpson 2014; Anthamatten 2017). Yet the quote suggests a new and public acceptance for the *idiot*, and the asylums instituted during this period initially had the goal of educating their inmates during relatively short-term stays, so that the inmates would ultimately return to—and contribute to—society.

These ideals did not last long, however. Governments and institutions soon sought to confine and control the lives of people labeled (however so) with learning difficulties, largely for their own benefit. During the late nineteenth century, the interests of medical and educational professionals, seeking to define and protect their territories and ensure careers and income, synergized with the interests of capitalist governments newly concerned with productivity, efficiency, imperialism, and "racial hygiene." Trent (1994) comprehensively charts the shift in purpose of US institutions for the "feebleminded" through the 1850s–1890s away from their original educational emphasis and toward a focus on "care" and labor, with this shift being shaped by changing scientific conceptions of cognition in combination with socioeconomic factors (principally the aftermath of the American Civil War, immigration, a move away from trustee to state control of the institutions, and the influence of the UK "colony" and classification systems). Whereas the earlier institutions had attempted to educate people so that they could return to the outside world after relatively short stays—and many did (Rembis 2017)—this shift largely removed the goal of creating "productive" members of the community and society, replacing it with one of containment that is, as we shall see in the final section of this chapter, still in place today.

Colonies, farm schools, reform asylums, and the like sought to become self-sufficient and self-contained: not only through growing and making their own food, clothes, and so on, but by training the "higher-grade" inmates to care for their "lower-grade" peers. This isolation served governments preoccupied with imperialist agendas and maximizing productivity and wealth by keeping "undesirables" away from the rest of the population and—through strict surveillance, gender segregation, and sometimes sterilization—unable to have children, and thereby helping, it was thought, to maximize the health, "fitness," and productivity of the nation. More subtly, perhaps, technologies of learning—literacy, writing, grading, and examination—were developed as forms of accountancy, discipline, and differentiation, means of both measuring and recording learners and distributing them into specialist locations with a "grammocentric world" (Ball 2013: 47). Campbell (2013) describes the ways in which such technologies enabled governments toward the end of the nineteenth century to see inside their citizenries' heads as never before: to know what each individual knew and did not know, could do and could not do, and thus to intervene to control their populations by emplacing individuals according to their academic performance. Snyder and Mitchell (2005) argue that such educational surveillance technologies lay the foundations not only for stigmatization, regulation, and government of the self, but also for the eugenics movement and its ultimate appalling expression in the genocidal Nazi Aktion T4 program. As Foucault (2003: 61) observes, it is at this moment at the end of the nineteenth century that "a technology of human abnormality, a technology of abnormal individuals appears, precisely when a regular network of knowledge and power has been established."

As nodes of this network and agents of this discursive regime, the new institutions and professions of rehabilitation (Stiker 1999) made "mental deficiency" or "feeblemindedness" more visible and helped turn it into a national concern. There was a concomitant shift from a pathetic to a more menacing image of learning difficulties, aided and abetted by isolationist practices (which helped to foster a sense of Otherness), the eugenicist move toward confirming intelligence as hereditary, desirable, and manipulable (Snyder and Mitchell 2005), and the medical professions constituting themselves as "experts" on the problem of mental deficiency in the early twentieth century, writing and discussing articles and books in which feeblemindedness was likened to an organic disease (Digby 1996). Learning difficulties, or idiocy, were conceived of as the root of all human dysfunction, with sensory or physical impairment mere stigmata signifying a deeper malaise. For expansionist nations concerned with maximizing economic and military power, people of "low intelligence" denoted degeneration, threats to the nation's health and security. As such, the rise of Georgian and Victorian institutions and of segregated education systems was driven more by the desire to safeguard the ablenationalist interests of society (Mitchell and Snyder 2015) than to care for or educate the people within them. Clinical judgments were tainted by moral judgments, further clouding some already dubious "scientific" decision-making. By 1911, Charles Paget Lapage and Mary Dendy, who were prominent in the study and education of the "feebleminded" in the UK, were making eugenicist claims in an influential book that:

> valuable as special schools may be, the work done in them must largely be wasted and nullified if the children are discharged at the age of sixteen, the most critical period in their lives, to become in many instances the parents of children similar to themselves. (Lapage and Dendy 1911: 10)

These developments illustrate how, over the latter part of the nineteenth century, a regime of truth was established in which people with apparent learning difficulties represented a threat to the rest of the population, to the extent that many influential scientists, educators, and politicians thought that they should not be allowed to procreate. Learning difficulties was also established as an organizing concept: new "kinds" of people were created, immoral or amoral Others whose existence was not only menacing, but helped to reinforce normalizing ideals. In the next section, I discuss two products of this discursive regime: firstly, the invention of the moron as an exemplar of the way in which new kinds of moral being were constructed; and secondly, the development of arguments around eugenics, sterilization, and extermination in Australia and England.

7.4. THE TWENTIETH CENTURY, 1900–39: INVENTING THE MORON AND THE PROBLEM OF THE UNFIT

Digby (1996: 12) reports that in the UK, entry to special schools was legally dependent after 1914[1] on medical certification, even though, when reporting to the 1908 Royal Commission, "none of the witnesses was able to offer any verbal definition of the degree or want of intelligence which constitutes a defective child." This lack of any scientific basis for decision-making did not deter professionals from developing new taxonomies of people; in fact, they did so enthusiastically. Speaking of his studies of nineteenth-century statistics, Hacking contends:

New slots were created in which to fit and enumerate people …. Social change creates new categories of people, but counting is no mere report of developments. It … creates new ways for people to be. (Hacking 2002: 100)

These new "ways to be" framed possibilities for agency and for control. There was a proliferation of these "ways to be" flowing from the "avalanche of numbers" (ibid.) beginning in the early nineteenth century, an avalanche whose architects were particularly concerned with deviancy. Just as a physicist could make a previously unseen property of light perceptible by manipulating instruments to attain a particular effect, so the medical or educational professional could render visible a new kind of person by manipulating instruments—such as intelligence tests—in order to obtain particular results. The quite literal invention of the "moron" by Henry H. Goddard, discussed below, is a case in point, and it is particularly noteworthy because it was driven by overt ablenationalist, eugenicist concerns about the perceived threat presented to the health of nations by "undesirables" passing as "normal" within the general population.

The 1908 Royal Commission on the Care and Control of the Feeble-Minded adopted the following definitions of what are now commonly called learning difficulties, or perhaps degrees of "mental retardation," as suggested by the Royal College of Physicians of London. The USA had a similar taxonomy based on "mental age":

1. A *feebleminded* person is one who is capable of earning a living under favorable circumstances, but is incapable, from mental defect existing from birth or from an early age, (a) of competing on equal terms with his normal fellows; or (b) of managing himself or his affairs with ordinary prudence.

2. The *imbecile* is one who, by reason of mental defect existing from birth or from an early age, is incapable of earning his own living, but is capable of guarding himself against common physical dangers.

3. An *idiot* is one so deeply defective in mind from birth or from an early age, that he is unable to guard himself against common physical dangers. (Royal Commission on the Care and Control of the Feeble-Minded 1908: 324)

Note that these classifications are given in terms of "risk" of harm to the person (and, as today, with explicit reference to competitiveness or fitness and "productivity"), in spite of the fact that by now the chief aim of the relevant institutions was to protect the "normal" from the "abnormal," and not vice versa. Added to these was the *moral imbecile*, also called in Britain the *moral defective*: a person who, "by reason of an innate defect, displays at an early age vicious or criminal propensities which are of an incorrigible or unusual nature, and are generally associated with some slight limitation of intellect" (ibid.: 325). This fourth classification amplifies the moral connotations of perceived deficiency through emphasizing ablenationalist concerns with degeneracy and the imperative to protect society from crime and corruption, rather than, as with the preceding three, conceits of protecting people portrayed as vulnerable.

Intelligence testing was becoming widespread at this time. Most influential was the Binet–Simon test, which was enthusiastically adopted and adapted by psychologists in the USA. Henry H. Goddard quickly rose to prominence among this group owing to his position as Head of Research at the Training School at Vineland, which enabled him to publish a series of scholarly papers and newspaper articles combining his interests in heredity, intelligence, and social hygiene (Trent 1994). Through manipulating the

Binet–Simon test, Goddard created results that apparently confirmed the existence of a new category of feeblemindedness, and he claimed that 2 percent of all school-aged children belonged in this category. Like a physicist adjusting the properties of his optical instruments to reveal a suspected yet hitherto invisible property of light waves, Goddard's maneuver helped bring into being a new "kind" of person, who was held in many ways to resemble a "normal" child, but was permanently, unimprovably mentally deficient. As such, this new kind of person represented a particular threat to social order because of their potential to pass unnoticed in the general population, combined with their purported propensity for crime and procreation (Trent 1994). In this way, the *moron* (a name Goddard derived from the Ancient Greek *moros*, meaning "dull") was deliberately invented as a new slot into which people could fall and be counted, and a new way for people to be: of low intelligence and a menace to society.

Yet historical ontology teaches us that new kinds of people—and the roles for those people—come into being not through the discoveries of individual scientists, but rather as the contingent products of discourses enacted at particular moments (Reid and Valle 2004). The historical ontologist aims to illuminate the ways in which discursive fields produce particular events from within the space of possible events created by discourse. Here, Foucault is speaking of madness, but the logic extends to other objects brought into being through the interplay of multiple discourses:

> Unity of discourses on madness would not be based upon the existence of the object "madness," or on the constitution of a single horizon of objectivity; it would be the interplay of the rules that make possible the appearance of objects during a given period of time: objects that are shaped by measures of discrimination and oppression, objects that are differentiated in daily practice, in law, in religious casuistry, in medical diagnosis, objects that are manifested in pathological descriptions, objects that are circumscribed by medical codes, practices, treatment and care. (Foucault 1972: 32)

In a historical-ontological interpretation, the moron was not simply a discovery of Goddard's, but rather a new strategic possibility, an object that emerges from a discursive field comprising medicine, education, social Darwinism and social work, scientism in a context of continuing urbanization and population growth, expansionism, capitalism, colonialism, nationalism, and, as a forerunner of today's neoliberalism, a meta-narrative of individualized, meritocratic success (as represented by the American Dream). The ways in which these discourses played out did vary somewhat from place to place, but the overall effect was to establish an irresistible, all-encompassing regime of truth around learning difficulties that made alternative interpretations of this "way of being" virtually inconceivable. I now draw on archive material to illustrate this claim, using examples from Australia and the UK that have connections to Liverpool, where I live and work.

Richard James Arthur Berry was born in 1867 in the village of Upholland, about twelve miles northeast of Liverpool, England. In 1891, he graduated with a degree in medicine from the University of Edinburgh and quickly moved through the ranks of the profession while continuing to work in Edinburgh. In 1905, he left Edinburgh to take up the position of Professor of Anatomy at the University of Melbourne, Australia. During his time there, he had a considerable influence on the teaching of medicine while also pursuing his own research interests. These interests centered on three interrelated topics: cranial anatomy; physical anthropology, especially that of

Australian and Tasmanian aboriginals; and "mental defectiveness" in children. He had his own laboratory and clinic for the study of "mental deficiency," and he published extensively in learned journals, including the *Eugenics Review* (e.g. Berry 1930), gave invited addresses to the British Eugenics Society and the Royal Society of Edinburgh, attended lavish Galton Laboratory dinners, and so on. His influence was considerable, and not limited to fellow academics and medical men. Contemporaneously with the beginning of the Nazi Aktion T4 extermination program, Berry published a book, *Your Brain and Its Story* (Berry 1939), aimed at a general audience, as well as numerous newspaper articles, of which cuttings may be found in the Lancashire County Archives, in which he used his research findings to argue stridently for the segregation, sterilization, and extermination of people with learning difficulties. For example, Berry was convinced that cranial volume was linked causally (as one factor) with intelligence. Put simply, he believed that, by and large, at the population level, bigger skulls equaled bigger brains and therefore higher intelligence. In one study he conducted by measuring skull volumes to deduce the brain weights of different peoples, he arrived at the following results, which were shared both at public lectures and in Melbourne newspapers:

Australian aboriginal: 1189 g
Negro: 1244 g
Malay and Indian: 1266 g
Chinese: 1332 g
Caucasian: 1335 g

The implication of this and other similar work of Berry's was that antipodean Aboriginals and people he termed Negroes (i.e. people of African descent) were of lower average intelligence and more prone to learning difficulties than people of Asian and European stock. An English contemporary of Berry's, Professor Sir E. Ray Lankester, was making similar claims about the heritability of learning difficulties:

congenital feeblemindedness is spontaneous originally and truly hereditary subsequently and is not brought about by starvation and other such conditions: it is more probably due to easy conditions of life and the absence of the selection that obtains amongst more primitive men. (Lapage and Dendy 1911: 17)

The implication here is the same as the basis of Hitlerian eugenics: that because of improvements in living conditions, Nature needs a helping hand in selecting out members of the species who would previously have not survived and bred. But there is a paradox here that neither Berry nor Lankester appear to have acknowledged, constrained as they were by the regime of truth: if selection is indeed more effective among "more primitive men," then surely it would lead to steadily more intelligent humans being born, and fewer incidences of learning difficulties, among those races. So how can those same races also be given as examples of peoples who are less intelligent? Logically, they cannot have both more effective selection and lower intelligence. Nevertheless, not content with neatly classifying intelligence by race, Berry published similar studies that purported to show that criminals and "the lower grades of society" (*Melbourne Argus* 1912: 10) tended to have smaller brains than those "occupying a higher place in the social scale" (ibid.). One such study whose results were also published in the newspapers (ibid.) used an index to tabulate the results, rather than the absolute weights used above:

1—355 Melbourne criminals … 100

2—4 Melbourne students … 102.1

3—British Association males[2] … 103.9

4—215 London Medical students … 104.7

5—5 University college teachers … 105.9

6—35 anatomists … 106.8

Even setting aside the empirical flaws, such as the vastly unequal sample sizes, and the rather remarkable finding by a professor of anatomy that, of all the peoples known to science, anatomists (who are of course invariably Caucasian) turn out to have the heaviest and therefore largest brains and thus greatest intelligence, these results are quite striking. Not only are criminals the lowest of the low, but also British students are superior to Australian students. As such, it is not hard to detect the colonialist, racist, eugenicist ideology underpinning Berry's work. The most succinct and powerful exposition of this ideology I encountered in the archive was a newspaper article written by Berry, afforded a double-page spread in Melbourne's *The Herald* when published on May 3, 1924. The article was called "The Problem of the Unfit" (Figure 7.1).

In person, Berry was reportedly strident and forthright, and his forceful personality is certainly evident in both the tenor and content of the arguments he makes in "The Problem of the Unfit." The article begins by using boxing as a synecdoche for the human condition, managing in the same breath to condescend to his intended audience while also overtly and deliberately dehumanizing people with learning difficulties by equating them to animals. Such animalization was already a well-established tactic of patriarchal disability and racial oppression, aligned to a belief that because animals lack certain traits and abilities, they exist outside our compass of moral responsibility and are therefore fair game for domination and abuse (Taylor 2011):

> That men, like animals, are unequal physically requires no demonstration. It is obvious. The public sees it and accordingly believes it, and does not, therefore, ask the featherweight boxer to contend with a Jack Dempsey. Curiously enough, the same public, not being able to see the human brain, and knowing rather less than nothing about it, seems to expect all men to enter the struggle for existence on terms of equality. (Berry 1924: 10)

Berry goes on to justify the sorting and classifying of individuals according to perceived mental ability in much the same manner as boxers are classified by weight, and then moves to lament the ineducability of the "last" three classes of morons, imbeciles, and idiots, who he seems to believe are subhumans existing outside the law: "Laws are made by normal people for normal people, but it is quite impossible to teach this elementary fact to the more poorly developed grades of mankind." He then contends that people with learning difficulties are essentially more like beasts than humans because of their inability to control their lustful appetites for sex and food, and that this is the source of the great many crimes perpetrated by The Unfit:

> It consequently follows that most crimes of the penal code fall into one or other of these two great groups of animal propensities—crimes against the person and crimes against property …. Mental deficiency, that is, a lack of development of the cells of the controlling and inhibiting brain, is certainly a factor in at least 50 percent of crime, poverty, and prostitution.

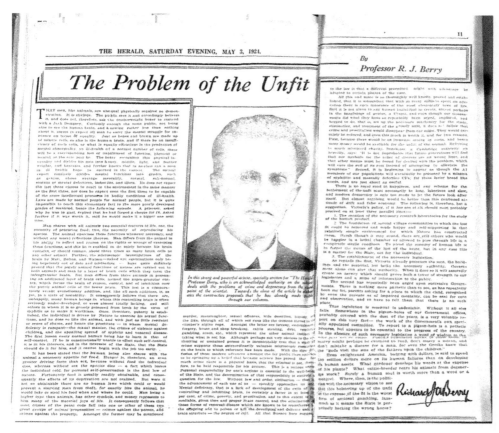

FIGURE 7.1 "The Problem of the Unfit."

Having set out The Problem of the Unfit, Berry then moves, in the final third of the piece, to suggest solutions. This final third is perhaps simultaneously the most revealing and disturbing part of the article. Berry begins it by bemoaning both what he perceives to be a lack of action in respect of the problem and the limitations of such action, even if carried out effectively:

> Still it is not given to any human being to create, except perhaps in the imaginings of a genius, a Utopia, and even though our Governments did what they have so repeatedly been urged, implored, and begged to do, that is, set up the necessary machinery for the study, elimination, and treatment of the grossly unfit, it does not follow that crime and prostitution would disappear from our midst. They would certainly be reduced, and even this much is worth it, and for two reasons. First, because there would be an immense saving in costs, and hence more money would be available for the uplift of the normal …. Second, it is beginning to appear as though the A1 members of our populations will eventually be poisoned by a miasma of syphilitic and mentally defective C3's; for these latter breed like weeds, and are about as useful. (Berry 1924: 11)

Berry here goes beyond even animalization, likening people with learning difficulties to both a cloud of toxic gas and prolific nuisance plants, which ought to be eradicated in order to prevent them from corrupting the "normal" population. He then advocates for enhanced legislation, the establishing of more research laboratories, and the foundation of "special village communities," elsewhere known as colonies, "to which the less fit could be removed." Yet even segregation and isolation are not sufficient, in Berry's estimation, to solve the problem of what he calls elsewhere (*Melbourne Argus* 1912: 10) "the festering human refuse heap":

> Harsh though it may sound, there are still others who would be happier in a lethal chamber or allowed to pass through life in a completely sterile condition. To plead for the sanctity of human life is to forget the victim of the lust of the brute, but in any case, this is a matter for the State, not for the individual.

Berry concludes with a rather desperate call for government intervention:

> Punch's celebrated advice to those about to marry might be extended to read, don't marry a moron, and don't mistake a disease for a man, for even the Greeks knew that the "gods visit the sins of the fathers upon the children."
>
> Even enlightened America, bulging with dollars, is said to spend 500 million dollars more on its human failures than on developing its human assets. What gardener develops his weeds at the expense of his plants? What cattle-breeder rears his animals from degenerate stock? Surely a human soul is worth more than a weed or a mongrel. Where, then, is the politician with the necessary vision to see that this bolstering up of the unfit at the expense of the fit is the worst form of national gambling, inasmuch as it means the State is perpetually backing the wrong horse?

It is difficult to imagine who would be happier inside a gas chamber than outside, yet Berry was not alone in calling for them. Nor did his views only chime with those of the Nazis; the mayors of the English cities of Portsmouth and Nottingham, for instance, had both advocated extermination, with the *Nottingham Evening Post* of June 8, 1909, reporting the Mayor of Portsmouth as saying, "It is possible to submit these idiots to a painless death and release them from the purgatory of non-intelligence" (Stewart 2017: n.p.).

This is not to say that extermination and sterilization were universally accepted as solutions to "the problem of the unfit." The archive of the Calderstones Certified Institution for Mental Defectives near Blackburn in Lancashire, UK, contains a 1933 report of evidence prepared by the institute's medical officers for the Departmental Committee on Sterilization at the Board of Control in London. Its chief author appears to be Dr. Frank A. Gill, Medical Superintendent at Calderstones. Gill's opinion on sterilization, which seems to be based at least in part on the Calderstones admissions data, is as follows:

> As a means of eradicating mental deficiency ... this is a hopelessly futile proposition. The great proportion of defectives are not the progeny of mental defective parents but of apparently normal or subnormal yet more or less self-supporting members of the community ... whom no sterilization laws could touch or seek to touch. (Gill 1933: 1)

Here, Gill is less calling into question the heritability of learning difficulties than admitting that it is not possible to predict which parents will give birth to "the unfit." He also implicitly acknowledges a second paradox in the eugenicist position: that there are so many "undesirables" at large in the population that it not only makes their eradication unfeasible, but also calls into question the statistical basis of determining normalcy. In the USA, Goddard had encountered a similar problem when he applied his IQ tests to military personnel, whose average mental abilities the test found to be equivalent to those of a twelve-year-old.

Like Berry, Gill takes the view that people with learning difficulties are "sex delinquents," but he is less enthusiastic about sterilization, although not out of any higher regard for such people. Rather, he contends that because people with learning difficulties simply cannot understand the consequences of sexual intercourse, removing the consequence of having a child will not alter behavior and hence reduce promiscuity:

> The mental defective is a sex delinquent by nature with strong desires unrestrained by moral control or fear of the consequences, and I question if the release from consequential results of immorality will make much difference in future chastity. (Gill 1933: 1)

Gill may be less enthusiastic than Berry about the efficacy of sterilization as a blanket solution, but his final statement in the report confirms that he thinks it appropriate in certain circumstances:

> Finally, I am strongly in favor of legislation sanctioning sterilization in selected cases and, of course, under proper safeguards. (ibid.)

This evidence shows that although Berry, Gill, and others may have taken varying stances in relation to eugenicist agendas, their beliefs both influenced and helped to reinforce the regime of truth created for learning difficulties. By publishing in medical journals, books, and mainstream newspapers, reporting to committees, and speaking in public, these professionals constructed and manipulated discourses of medicine, education, media, law, economics, colonialism, and eugenics in order both to create "the problem of the unfit" and to position themselves as the experts who can solve "the problem." They are the moral agents who determine what kind of person it is acceptable to be and who must contrast themselves and the wider public against "The Unfit"; here, again, we see learning difficulties as an organizing concept, determining what kinds of persons exist, generating privileged, etic kinds of knowledge about those kinds of person, explaining how they come to be, why they are as they are, and how society should act toward them, while simultaneously reifying normative ideals and enlisting "the unfit" in narratives of degradation.

7.5. FROM 1940 TO THE TWENTY-FIRST CENTURY: BATHS, BLACKCLOCKS AND "BETTER SERVICES"

A gradual transition away from geographical segregation and toward deinstitutionalization and "care in the community" policies and programs characterized the period discussed in this section, at least within the Anglophone countries within the purview of this chapter. However, while wholesale eradication of people with learning difficulties now seemed to be off the agenda, dehumanizing attitudes and practices still prevailed. As the world recoiled from World War II and the Nazi regime and eugenics lost respectability, there appeared to be something of a softening of attitudes toward people with learning difficulties, at least in the public declarations of medical professionals. Whereas Professor Berry and, to a lesser extent, Dr. Gill had advocated for extermination and sterilization, in 1940, Lord Richard Cavendish, Chairman of the Central Committee,[3] published the following in the prestigious British medical journal *The Lancet*:

> The social attitude of most people towards the fate of mentally defective people strikes me nowadays as odd. At one time I shared their opinion and advocated euthanasia was the best: but that was before I had much to do with mentally defective patients. Even after a month or two in the wards I was pretty cocksure—but little by little I found I was wrong. The easy superiority of the eugenicist deserted me, for I found that I was dealing, not with regrettable accidents, but with people, and uncommonly nice people at that.
>
> After five years of their society, and the time has been spent among low-grade defectives, idiots and imbeciles, I know that if someone presented me with a fine new lethal chamber and authority to use it, I should have extreme difficulty in choosing even one victim. On what grounds ought the choice to be made? Mere lack of intelligence seems a dangerous standard. Many high-grade defectives ... would not be noticeably deficient if placed among simple or savage people: they would do pretty well. It seems unreasonable to say that if they had been born scions of a race of savages they would be fit to survive, but that having cropped up in a civilized country they merit death. Most of them are kindly, innocent, easily contented, easily amused and willing to work endlessly at a dull job without losing interest ... on the whole they are good citizens. (Cavendish 1940, quoted in Alston 1992: 78)

In contrast to prior widespread support of euthanasia, here was an outright rejection. Yet despite the apparent sympathy, an infantilizing, dehumanizing attitude can readily be discerned in Cavendish's appreciation of how "uncommonly nice" the "defectives" are, despite being somewhat akin to "savages" or "simple people" who, although they are "good citizens," somehow do not belong in "civilized society." In a similar paternalistic and condescending vein, Dr. F. D. Turner, Medical Superintendent of the Royal Eastern Counties Institution in Colchester, England, at this time, not only referred to adult inmates as "boys and girls," but is on record in an Annual Report as saying, "'Daddy' is the name I like best to hear" (Stevens 1997).

Under a discursive regime of truth that made it difficult for the staff and administrators of such institutions to conceive of people with learning difficulties as adult humans and citizens, rather than as children or even animals, daily disciplinary routines and practices were often aligned more closely with the prison or even the farmyard than the hospital or school. Take the example of bathing: former residents of the Royal Albert Asylum in Lancaster have, in oral history interviews, recalled the routines for bathing in the 1920s through to the 1950s. Some of their statements are corroborated by those of former staff. Baths were communal, with up to six people sharing a bath at any one time. The baths were tepid, with one of the twelve rules for bathing stipulating a temperature of 98°F (i.e. blood temperature). Residents recalled one of their contemporaries having his jaw broken for attempting to resist a bath:

Frank: 'cause he (another resident) wouldn't go in bathroom and have a bath. And then there was three—there was always three staff in the bathroom when you went down ... he wouldn't go in one day so he picks him up and gives him a punch in jaw and throws him in bathroom.

Interviewer: That was the staff?

Frank: Staff. Yes. Anyhow the same day his Dad was coming to see him and of course he had his jaw broken and that. (Unlocking the Past 2010b)

According to former nurse Duncan Mitchell, such practices continued well into the 1980s:

I'll never forget things like bath nights. Everyone had their bath night. You'd probably get two baths a week .... But if it wasn't your night for a bath then you couldn't have one. But it was the way it was done. To be honest it was more like a sheep dip. (Unlocking the Past 2010a)

Of course, bathing routines were not the only evidence of disablist attitudes toward institution residents; clothing was also communal and had to be taken from pre-prepared "bundles"; the food was so poor that Royal Albert residents nicknamed one regular dish as "blackclock soup," blackclock being a dialect term for a beetle. Residents could be sent to a punishment ward for weeks for writing letters to boyfriends or girlfriends. They might be flogged simply for trying to move seats in the dining hall. Even when they were discharged, residents had to exit via a side door; only staff were permitted to use the main entrance. Many such institutions had burial grounds, yet graves were marked with copper tags fastened to nearby trees rather than with headstones: the regime of truth continued to dehumanize people even after they had died.

In 1948 in Great Britain, the National Health Service (NHS) began. On July 5 that year, the Royal Albert was, like other such institutions, absorbed into the newly formed NHS. On the one hand, this meant more money was available, since funding now came from central government rather than solicited subscriptions. As a result, there were improvements in things like clothing, furnishings, and decor. Institutions such as the Royal Albert and nearby Brockhall already resembled hospitals in many ways, having facilities including operating theaters, X-ray rooms, sick bays, pathology laboratories, and mortuaries (Hindmarch 1992). Being subsumed into the NHS meant that the character of such institutions changed, and therefore so did the role of patients. Hitherto, it had been common in institutions in both the UK and the USA for patients to be given work to do. This included domestic work such as cleaning, baking, and laundry duties, crafts such as basket weaving, shoemaking, toolmaking, and so on, as well as agricultural labor, since these isolated organizations strove to be self-sufficient.

It was also commonplace for "high-grade" residents to be given work caring for their "low-grade" fellows (Trent 1994; Wright and Digby 1996). Ostensibly, this work was designed to help prepare residents for the outside world, and this is how it was promoted by institutional agents. It had the added benefit of keeping costs down, which was certainly useful, as many institutions were in frequent financial straits. This exploitation for free or very cheap labor was also defended on the grounds that it gave residents some sense of purpose and dignity. One might remark here that residents only needed a sense of dignity and purpose restored to their lives because the regime of truth around learning difficulties had resulted in its removal. In addition, recalling Lord Cavendish's fond observation above that residents' "willingness to work endlessly at a dull job without losing interest" provides a means to perhaps discern ablenationalism at work: the idea that the only worthwhile life is one that involves productivity and work and that the worthless lives of people with learning difficulties can be made worthwhile through exploitation for labor. Institutions harnessed the labor of one "kind" (Hacking, 2002 100) of resident to govern the conduct of another. With awareness of this, we can appreciate the hegemonic exercise of power: guiding the possibilities of conduct through productive constraints—determining who is able to work, and in what ways, upon whom—while remaining itself concealed (Tremain 2015).

Through the 1950s and 1960s, the purpose of institutions like the Royal Albert became less about education and training and more about custodial care, and they were run in a similar fashion to acute hospitals, despite being long-stay residential sites. Nevertheless, greater recognition of patients' humanity and domestic and social requirements began to develop; in a foreshadowing of the normalization policies of the 1970s, discipline and sexual segregation were relaxed and "parole" was introduced, whereby patients were permitted to make unaccompanied visits into the local town and area. A number of additional factors then contributed to the shift toward "care in the community," again shaped by medical, political, economic, and philosophical discourses. Several institutional scandals, whereby the maltreatment of residents was brought to the public's attention, surfaced in the 1960s, although these were attributed to lack of funding and overcrowding rather than disablist attitudes. Meanwhile, an "explosion" (Alston 1992: 91) of research into "mental handicap" was revealing that the learning abilities of people held in such institutions had been hugely underestimated and their potential was much greater than had previously been thought. At the same time, there was a growing recognition of human rights, with, for example, Goffman's work on stigma and hermetic "total institutions" such as prisons, labor camps and asylums (Goffman 1963, 1968) promoting questioning of whether institutions could provide an environment that would nurture rather than stifle human beings. In the UK, two key pieces of legislation came into force. The 1959/60 Mental Health Acts (England and Wales/Scotland, respectively) repealed the Mental Deficiency Acts, espousing "community care," but providing little funding. The 1971 white paper "Better Services for the Mentally Handicapped" also advocated care in the community.

Historians more qualified than myself have noted that, whatever polices have been in operation at the time, most people marked with intellectual impairments have lived their lives outside institutions rather than in them, simply because such institutions are products of a particular moment in time and existed in only a small number of locations (Digby 1996; Rembis 2017). Nevertheless, "Better Services for the Mentally Handicapped" augured a sea change in government policy on provision for people with what were now starting to be called learning difficulties. This change in policy reflected a change in philosophy, which had its roots in Scandinavian legislation and normalization theory (Wolfensberger 1972; Nirje 1982) and was gaining ground in the USA and Britain. In this philosophy, people with learning difficulties were explicitly recognized as having the same human rights as other citizens. Adherents advocated that disabled people should participate in society and live lives that were as similar as possible to those of nondisabled people, while recognizing that although disabled people and their families would share some needs with other families, they would also be likely to have specific or individual support requirements in order to be able to live and participate in regular communities. Critics of normalization contend that its pursuit of cultural normativity merely represented a strategic reconfiguration of disciplinary biopower (Simpson 2018).

The model of care changed from segregation in institutions that purported to protect patients from the outside world (but whose primary function was arguably to "protect" the outside world from "the unfit") to community care. However, the government did not make any money available with which to implement either the closure of hospitals or the resettlement of residents; hospitals had to use whatever funds were "released" through declining patient numbers and resulting cost reductions. The multiagency support services that replaced the institutions were also poorly resourced. This failure to adequately fund the new policy—that is, to fund the lives of people with learning difficulties—indicates that disablist attitudes still saturated the regime of truth around learning difficulties.

This regime of truth was irresistible even outside the now-withering institutions. People labeled with learning difficulties were no longer necessarily enclosed by their immediate physical environment, within the panoptic architecture of institutions, colonies, and hospitals, but were still enveloped within an all-encompassing regime of truth that characterized people with intellectual impairments or perceived deficits as menacing or risky Others. Although the professions and institutions of confinement had initially attempted to assume authority over this "problem" by relocating and segregating stigmatized individuals and assuring the public that "the problem" was under control, stories from the movement toward care in the community from the early 1970s onward reveal how inescapable the regime was and continues to be. In her autobiography, Mabel Cooper, a former resident of St. Lawrence's Hospital in Caterham, Surrey, describes experiences of, and reflections on, independent living and continuing ableist attitudes:

> There a little Down's Syndrome boy, he comes off the bus to go home .... And the children would not leave him alone, they used to tease him and everything .... They called him names and they squirted water out of the window at me a few times and threw tins .... (Atkinson et al. 1997: 33)

Then, after explaining that writing to the school stopped this abuse:

> It stops the children but then you don't stop the adults because they never learn. One Saturday I was with one of my friends and one of the women was so rude my friend was really shocked .... It really did upset her because she said, "You know, you have told me about it, that people are rude but I had to listen to it to believe it .... It's damn disgusting that people ought to be allowed to do that." (ibid.: 34)

The fear of difference arising from the Othering of people with learning difficulties thus leads to verbal and physical abuse of adults and children. Writing to the school appears to stop the children abusing Mabel and the unnamed boy with Down's Syndrome, though it is impossible to know whether this is due to the abusers developing newfound respect and appreciation for their fellow citizens or simply fear of punishment from the school. It is revealing, however, that Mabel asserts that it is the *adults* who never learn, suggesting that they, too, are discursively positioned within a regime of truth in which their relative power excuses unethical behavior toward people "known about" as having learning difficulties. Exercise of that power helps citizens sustain and extend this "truth" (Foucault 1980).

7.6. THE TWENTY-FIRST CENTURY: THE ARCHIPELAGO OF CONFINEMENT

The move to care in the community and supported or independent living was in part a reaction to the scandalous abuse and neglect evident in many institutions. In theory, it should have led to a more humane, civilized, and inclusive way of life for people labeled with learning difficulties. However, as noted above, even outside such institutions, the all-encompassing regime of truth around learning difficulties still held sway. Moreover, much evidence seems to suggest that rather than these policies and practices leading to the emancipation of people labeled with learning difficulties, all that has happened is a reconfiguration of power relations, "one that is entirely in keeping with the modern drive to greater efficiency" (Drinkwater 2015: 230). Snyder and Mitchell (2005: 3–4) have defined "cultural locations of disability" as sites of violence, restriction, confinement, and the absence of liberty, where disabled people are deposited against their will and that exist largely at odds with the collective and individual well-being of disabled people. In the twenty-first century, we can conceive of such locations forming what might be termed, again following Foucault (1977), the "carceral archipelago" (Adams and Erevelles 2017: 361) or the "archipelago of confinement and control" (Spivakovsky 2017: 366) for people said to have learning difficulties. The islands of this archipelago are scattered across the globe and comprise a continuum of penal, medical, and educational settings, including schools, hospitals, prisons, immigration and detention centers, and care homes. The existence of this archipelago is yet another manifestation of the regime of truth around people deemed to have learning difficulties, who continue to be represented as menacing and risky Others who must be contained and controlled by professionals for their own good, as well as to protect the wider public.

In fact, this disciplinary archipelago now extends beyond the physical realm into the virtual. In 2006, McDermott et al. (2006: 13) wrote about "the concerted activities of millions of people engaging in a surveillance system consisting of professionals—doctors, psychologists, lawyers, educators—and parents," and we can now add in further layers of digitized data, whereby information about people is routinely collected and compared by businesses, organizations, and governments. Disabled people also find themselves exposed, disciplined, and regulated by social media (Lewthwaite 2011; Ellis and Kent 2017). In this section, I draw on evidence from the UK and Australia to illustrate the ways in which the archipelago of confinement operates under a regime of truth now suffused with neoliberal, ablenationalist economic imperatives.

In 2011, the BBC's investigative current affairs program *Panorama* exposed the systematic abuse and neglect of people labeled with learning difficulties at Winterbourne View Hospital, of the kind that was supposedly consigned to history with the demise of the asylums. More recently, the Justice for LB campaign, which highlighted the death of Conor Sparrowhawk (nicknamed Laughing Boy), who drowned in the bath because of inadequate supervision in the hospital that was supposed to be caring for him, has kept the spotlight on these inhumane practices (Ryan 2017). Despite convictions in the Winterbourne View Hospital case and an ensuing government inquiry and publication of a Programme of Action aimed at ensuring that the despicable physical and psychological abuse of people with learning difficulties that took place at Winterbourne View Hospital could never take place again, we are continually presented with evidence of the segregation, maltreatment, and exploitation of people labeled with learning difficulties. A recent review of the deaths of learning-disabled people in England concluded that they not only experienced significant health inequalities and premature mortality, but that delays in care or treatment, gaps in service provision, organizational dysfunction, and neglect or abuse often adversely affected their health (LeDeR 2018). Meanwhile, in June 2017, thirteen directors, managers, and carers were convicted over abuse at two residential homes in Devon, both isolated farmhouses, for adults labeled with learning difficulties (Morris 2017). One such resident had been moved from Winterbourne View Hospital after its closure. One of those convicted was the founder of the company running the homes and is a well-known figure in mental health circles in the UK, having helped formulate national policy on caring for people with learning disabilities in the community. He told the court that he did not know what was going on. However, as at the Royal Albert, residents were punished for trivial transgressions, including staring at a staff member, facial twitches, or asking questions repeatedly. Sometimes residents were punished by being denied food, drink, fun activities, and visits. Other times, they were confined in bare seclusion rooms for hours and sometimes overnight, on occasions wetting or soiling themselves because there were no bathroom facilities. One resident described his experiences thusly:

> It was a room that was disgusting and cold. At night the door was locked. It had a CCTV camera, a smoke detector and a punctured mattress—it was an airbed but it had a puncture in. It was cold, damp. If you wanted to go to the toilet, there was no toilet in there. There was a window but it was locked. No curtains. They made the room as bad as possible and as uncomfortable as possible …. It made me feel terrible in a way … an animal, basically. (Morris 2017: n.p.)

There are strong echoes here of the "farmyard" practices of the Royal Albert. The company running the homes, Atlas Project Team, claimed to provide specialist care for learning-disabled people. The cost of this "care"—or, more accurately, confinement—was reported as being up to £4,000 per week per person. Yet this case is not an isolated incident, a single rogue institution operating outside the law in ways its founder claimed to be ignorant of. Rather, this case is representative of a national and international ablenationalist project of confinement and abuse under the euphemistic guise of managing "risky" individuals with "challenging behavior" and "complex needs." Also in the UK, Brown et al. (2017) have, through interrogating a range of official data as part of the Seven Days of Action campaign to support the rights of people labeled with learning difficulties to live in their own homes, established the following summary facts about the confinement and control of this population: in 2015/16, £477.4 million was spent in keeping approximately 2,500 people labeled with learning difficulties in hospitals, with just over half of those beds provided by the private sector rather than the NHS. Ten years ago, only one in five such beds were in the private sector, meaning that there has been significant growth in private-sector provision—and hence money going to the private sector—over that period, to the point where the private sector now plays the greater role. This "inpatient market" is estimated to be worth £284 million to the private sector: "Most of that provision operates on a for-profit basis and our sons and daughters are its currency" (Brown et al. 2017: 8). On average, a person who has been in hospital for five years will generate £950,000 in income for an independent-sector organization, although significantly higher levels of income are possible. Private providers are tending to locate their institutions where operating costs are lower, as indicated by real-estate prices.

Efficiency and profit thus appear to take precedence over care, support, and education. This leads to people labeled with learning difficulties being sent to hospitals far away from their families. Moreover, under the current funding regime, when such a person is registered with a general practitioner (GP)[4] close to the hospital they are now resident in, as is standard practice, the health authority in that area (known as a clinical commissioning group [CCG]) becomes responsible for the cost of any aftercare, rather than the person's original "home" authority. Inevitably, because these costs are substantial, CCGs are reluctant to meet them, providing further incentive for continued confinement in some cases. In other cases, people are discharged to institutions outside of the area, meaning that they will have to register with a different GP and hence become another CCG's financial responsibility. These factors mean that people labeled with learning difficulties are being traded like commodities in order to generate profits, as providers make exchanges based on the types of provision they do and do not have. These providers unabashedly use the language of commerce in describing what they do. Here is a quote from a report of the Southampton, Hampshire, Isle of Wight, and Portsmouth (SHIP) Transforming Care Partnership (TCP):

> The SHIP TCP is a net importer of people with Learning Difficulties ... plus a net exporter of inpatients as there are no beds on Portsea Island. (quoted in Brown et al. 2017: 8)

And another, from Northamptonshire:

> Northamptonshire is a County with several large providers and this has created an "importer" concern .... St Andrews is a large [independent] provider of services for people with learning disabilities. This hospital is in the process of expanding with a new 100 bed service for people with autism which is a significant concern for the CCGs from an economical and value based perspective. (ibid.)

As if this market in people as though they were livestock was not despicable enough, people labeled with learning difficulties tell us horrible stories of seclusion, assaults, restraint, and self-harm, with those detained in the private sector being 30% more likely to experience an assault and 60% more likely to be detained than those in the NHS:

> One morning he was made to attend a meeting with other patients .... He tolerated this for a while, but then asked to leave. A support worker told him that he couldn't leave, so my son, in a panic, struck the support worker. This same worker retaliated by grabbing him, forcing his arm up behind his back, and manhandling him out of the room.
>
> When I went to visit later, I noticed that my son's arm was badly swollen and I asked about this .... The next morning the manager rang me and said she was organizing for him [the son] to go to A&E [Accident and Emergency] because his arm was still swollen. An x-ray revealed that his humerus was badly broken and that the break was compatible with someone having their arm forced up behind their back. This bone is one of the thickest in the human body and therefore quite difficult to break. (Glover and Olson 2012, quoted in Brown et al. 2017: 16)

Such stories are dispersed through the archipelago of confinement. Returning us to Australia, McCausland and Baldry (2017) report the case of Dylan Voller, a sixteen-year-old held at a youth detention center in the Northern Territory. In August 2016, the Australian Broadcasting Corporation screened footage of guards restraining, secluding, and assaulting children at the facility. Voller, a disabled Aboriginal, was filmed hooded and chained to a chair. The broadcast precipitated a press release from Prime Minister Malcolm Turnbull and Commonwealth Attorney General George Brandis, stating that they were "shocked and appalled" by the images of maltreatment. Yet McCausland and Baldry assert that the incident was neither isolated nor unusual, and that a pattern of treating disabled people as dangerous, Other, and unworthy of full citizenship has been evident throughout Australia's relatively short history, whereby colonialism resulted in the implementation of British models of law, prisons, and other such institutions of control in the eighteenth and nineteenth centuries. As in Britain, "feebleminded" people have been seen as problematic, an issue perhaps more overtly compounded by racism than in the UK. To this day, indigenous Australians in particular, who commonly have multiple impairments and disadvantages, are more likely to encounter the criminal justice system than nonindigenous Australians, and often have their lives "managed" from childhood by the police and judicial systems rather than—in the words of the United Nations Convention of the Rights of Persons with Disabilities—"being afforded care, protection and full and equal enjoyment of all their human rights and fundamental freedoms and respect for their inherent dignity" (UN General Assembly 2007: 292).

People labeled with learning difficulties are routinely being subjected to oppressive, inhumane, and degrading treatment for extended if not indefinite periods, and yet they are not the only ones paying a price for what those of us outside the archipelago and under the auspices of ablenationalism tend to regard as "freedom" (Spivakovsky 2017). The interlocking discourses of policy, legislation, corporate strategy, and the professional "street-level bureaucrats" (Lipsky 1980) or frontline support workers employed in institutions for people labeled with learning difficulties lead those workers inexorably into conceptualizing the people in their care as "risks" to be managed. People labeled with learning difficulties are constituted as risks to wider society, to themselves, to staff, and to profits. This results in restrictive practices that have legislative approval only as measures of last resort becoming normalized and commonplace. Such practices include the administration of drugs approved only for short-term use for years at a time, in addition to seclusion, "aversive technologies" such as inflicting pain, electric shocks, and the forced inhalation of ammonia (Adams and Erevelles 2017), as well as the kinds of physical "restraint" performed on Dylan Voller. A paradox these workers face is that although ablenationalism aims to produce "prudent workers with enhanced responsibility," it also provides "the framework and mechanisms necessary to blame, penalize and ultimately remove from the workforce" anybody who is deemed to be acting irresponsibly, in order that organizational reputation and profit are not put at risk (Spivakovsky 2017: 378). Acting irresponsibly includes workers putting their own health and safety at risk. In an institution where people are frequently violent or where violence is a perceived to be a constant threat, workers respond to this threat to their health and safety—and hence their continued employment—by enacting restrictive practices as a matter of course, all in the name of managing risk. For example, one disability advocate from an Australian disabled people's organization asserted:

> The problem is that a lot of this stuff makes it easier for workers, and sometimes safer for workers—keeping people under control—and I think that means that things like workplace health and safety can be used as a technique for maintaining coercion and control. (ibid.)

My point here is that employees as well as residents find themselves constrained by a discursive regime of truth that constructs people labeled with learning difficulties as risky Others; the power of ablenationalism is exerted through the relationships between, inter alia, these two groups, with the concept of learning difficulties constituting workers as moral agents—protecting everyone from risk, and hence harm—whose apparent professional freedom to act is in fact confined within the very limited space of possibilities afforded by current and historical political, legal, and medical discourses. Of course, disabled people are subjugated to an immeasurably greater degree by this power, and yet ablenationalism denigrates us all.

7.7. CONCLUSION

> From the time people with "the thing," mental retardation, became social problems requiring help and treatment, the contours of this requirement have changed, sometimes dramatically, but the contours of our regard for people with mental retardation have not. This or that must be done to and for them; this and that must be learned about them and said about them to ensure progress in treatment technologies, professional influence, institutional funding, or social control. (Trent 1994: 6)

James Trent introduces his book with this observation, and I would like to conclude with it, capturing as it does the essence of The Problem of Learning Difficulties (as opposed to The Problem of the Unfit). I would also like to suggest that the contours of our regard for people labeled with learning difficulties have not changed because we are enveloped by a powerful regime of truth concerning learning difficulties, created and sustained through multiple intersecting discourses that privilege certain ways of being and of "knowing about" learning difficulties while simultaneously silencing emic ways of knowing. The gaze now directed at people said to have learning difficulties is informed by a long history of condescension, suspicion, and exclusion. Meanwhile, the "work" that learning difficulties has done in Anglophone countries in the twentieth century and continues to do in the twenty-first century is manifold. It includes work to provide Others against which "normals" can be defined and measured; work to legitimate professional medical, legal, educational, and health power knowledge regimes; and work to provide careers for professionals who "care" for fellow humans labeled as defective or risky and profits for companies employing those people. Over the course of this chapter, I have attempted to explain, through the method of historical ontology, how this work is made possible through the constitution of learning difficulties as an organizing concept; one that has radically transformed our sense not only of education and learning, but also of who is or is not deemed entitled to full citizenship and its associated rights, and so who is or is not fully human.

CHAPTER EIGHT

Mental Health Issues

Managing the Mind in the Modern Age

ANNE MCGUIRE

In this chapter, I look to the historical and cultural conditions of possibility that have shaped and reshaped contemporary Western understandings of the "problem mind" in the Modern Age. I examine, in other words, the structures, systems, and assumptions that have and continue to produce particular, non-normative mindbody expressions—behaviors, perceptions, thoughts, responses, affects, etc.—as naturally problematic and thus as being in need of a variety of solutions. I move from the politics and productive effects of changing psychiatric diagnostic regimes and classification schemas to practices of incarceration and policies of deinstitutionalization, to neuroscientific approaches to understanding the mind-as-brain, to the ever-widening field of the contemporary mental health spectrum, and I read these practices of mind management against the social, political, and economic landscapes of the twentieth and twenty-first centuries. This chapter is particularly focused on the cultural politics of the mind in the context of post-World War I America. I have, in other words, chosen to train my gaze on the hegemonic center of psychiatric power in the Modern Age. I do so with the keen awareness that US discourses and diagnostic frameworks exert their influence in ways that spill over and circulate well beyond state borders (Mills 2013; Titchkosky and Aubrecht 2015).

I would like to take a moment to address the language and terminology used throughout this chapter. The Modern Age has seen a proliferation of words seeking to name or describe the terrain of the "problem mind": degenerate, deviant, insane, lunatic, mad, crazy, mental patient, disordered, mentally ill, psychiatric survivor, client, consumer, ex-patient, ex-inmate, neurodivergent, on the spectrum. What is more, as the number of psychiatric diagnostic categories have expanded over the years, so too have the number of possible ways of naming—and so understanding—the problem mind. And so we might add to this list: person with schizoaffective disorder; with oppositional defiant disorder; with hoarding disorder; with autism spectrum disorder, level 1. In the pages to follow, I utilize different words in relation to different and corresponding moments in history to describe the broad range of labels, identities, behaviors, and ways of relating, sensing, interacting, experiencing and being in the world that have been or continue to be interpreted as "problem minds." In so doing, I hope to historicize, de-medicalize and indeed de-naturalize the category of "mental problem" and underscore the historical, political, and material contingency of our ways of naming and knowing the mind and its many variances.

8.1. CONTAGION AND CONTAINMENT: WORLD WAR I AND THE INTERWAR YEARS

The pull to classify and order the mind and its so-called problems reaches back for centuries, with, for example, the taxonomical work of Hippocrates in Antiquity, Burton's *The Anatomy of Melancholy* (1661), or Thomas Sydenham's *Epistolary Dissertation on the Hysterical Affections* (1682). However, the psychiatric classifications that emerged at the beginning in the nineteenth century represent uniquely modern phenomena that can be traced to the civilizing spaces of the asylum (Rose and Abi-Rached 2013). In fact, the first attempts to formally gather data on madness in the USA were only made possible by the prior existence of a diverse assemblage of people—"displaced, desolate, despairing, deranged"—both confined and defined within the walls of the asylum (Rose and Abi-Rached 2013: 115). The heterogeneous collection of asylum inmates grouped together within the presumed homogenous space of the asylum produced the necessary conditions for classification to emerge as a key management strategy. As Rose and Abi-Rached remind us, in the USA, the "clinical desire to classify was supplemented by … a statistical project driven by the national census, and its demand that every person within the national territory should be enumerated" (2013: 115). The project of gathering meaningful census data was, in the asylum, near impossible, as the available means of classifying mental disorder were, at the time, "chaotic": writes Sanders, "diagnostic systems were about as varied as the institutions and individuals that created them" (2011: 395–6). A lack of agreement between psychiatrists translated into what the American Psychiatric Association (APA) would refer to as "a polyglot of diagnostic labels and systems" that "effectively block[ed] communication and the collection of medical statistics" (American Psychiatric Association 1952: v). Against this backdrop, there emerged a new and distinctly modern push for a classificatory systems approach to managing the apparent problems of the twentieth-century mind.

The close of World War I marked a watershed moment for psychiatric classification. In 1917, the Committee on Statistics of the American Medico-Psychological Association (which would later become the APA) issued a series of recommendations for the development of a uniform classification system of mental disorder (Sanders 2011). By 1918, the Committee on Statistics, together with the Bureau of the Census and the National Committee for Mental Hygiene, published the *Statistical Manual for the Use of Institutions for the Insane*, the first "formal, standardized nomenclature of psychopathological conditions," and the precursor to the diagnostic categories laid out in the APA's contemporary "bible" of psychiatric diagnosis, the *Diagnostic and Statistical Manual of Mental Disorders* (DSM) (Kawa and Giordano 2012: 2; Rose and Abi-Rached 2013). Composed of twenty-two diagnostic categories, the *Statistical Manual* of 1918 was initially developed for application strictly within the bounds of the asylum: "to provide the U.S. census with a better basis for its classification of those confined" (Rose and Abi-Rached 2013: 116). Reflecting the dominant biologically oriented frame for understanding madness of the day, most of the categories described in the *Statistical Manual* were psychotic conditions with presumed somatic etiologies (Kawa and Giordano 2012).

A genealogy of the *Statistical Manual* reveals changing historico-cultural perspectives on the mind and its problems. The first editions of the manual were primarily concerned with counting and classifying a seemingly ever-expanding population of "mental defectives" being quarantined in state-run institutions, a concern that bears the markings of a eugenic philosophy endemic to North America and Western Europe at the time. Indeed, eugenic thinking had reached great popularity in the early half of the twentieth century, a time period that also saw the culmination of a variety of state-sponsored practices on both sides of the Atlantic (Mitchell and Snyder 2003). These eugenic practices encouraged the reproduction of "fit" individuals and families, while discouraging or even prohibiting the reproduction of those deemed "unfit." The "problem mind" was of particular interest to the operational logics of eugenics. Those classed as "mentally unfit" were targeted by various eugenic controls and measures, which included segregation (e.g. the incarceration of people in state-run asylums, schools, and hospitals), forced sterilization (e.g. the 1927 US Supreme Court decision in *Buck v. Bell* permitted the involuntarily sterilization of the "feebleminded"), and genocidal elimination (e.g. psychiatric patients were among the first to be "euthanized" under the Nazi Aktion T4 program). As the principal means of discerning and treating the "problem mind," psychiatry played a key role in the machinery of eugenic surveillance and selection (Lifton 1986). Indeed, it was in large part due to pre-World War II psychiatry's close ties to the project of eugenics that the field underwent a series of radical transformations in the years immediately following World War II.

8.2. CRISIS, CLASSIFICATION, AND THE COUCH: WORLD WAR II AND THE POSTWAR YEARS

The late 1930s and 1940s marked a distinct and deeply political shift in psychiatry as the field moved away from somatic understandings of the so-called disorders of the mind. As the West grappled with World War II, biological modes of defining and ordering people became unpalatable, invariably tainted by the violent biological racism of the Nazi death camps. As received notions of a strictly somatic mind began to lose traction, room was made for an increased interest in the role played by socioenvironmental factors in the production of the problem mind. The persecution against the Jews in Europe saw waves of European refugees migrating to the USA. Among them were a significant number of psychoanalysts seeking to keep alive Freudian thinking vis-à-vis fascist attempts at its eradication. Thus, the political climate of postwar America worked to nurture the flourishing of psychodynamic theories of the mind, which understand human psychological functioning to be premised on a complex interaction of internal energies, drives, and forces that, in turn, shapes the individual's personality, responses, feelings, and behaviors.

Also driving the postwar rise of psychoanalysis were the large numbers of soldiers returning home from World War II: veterans bearing the considerable psycho-emotional weight of their experiences of and reactions to the violence and trauma of combat (Kawa and Giordano 2012). The phenomenon of soldiers returning home from the trenches with a variety of traumas was nothing new. Indeed, the idea of "shell shock" began to proliferate during World War I, when it was first understood as an organic problem (a "wound" or "neurological lesion" resulting from exposure to explosive forces), and later as a form of "traumatic neurosis" displayed by weak or malingering soldiers (Shephard 2000; Jones et al. 2007). What made the World War II moment somewhat distinct, however, was that, at this historical juncture, trauma-induced psychosis or neurosis started to be viewed as neither organic nor as a matter of personal or individual moral character. At the close of World War II, the overarching characterization of the nature of veteran trauma had shifted from the realm of the biological/moral to the socioenvironmental, a change that is exemplified, for example, in the writing of Dr. William C. Menninger—the head of what was then a brand new Neuropsychiatric Division of the US Army. Writing in 1947 on treating war-induced neuroses, Menninger emphasized the need for psychiatry to consider the patient's "whole environment ... everything outside ourselves, the thing to which we have to adjust—our mates and our in-laws, the boss and the work, friends and enemies, bacteria and bullets, ease and hardship" (W. Menninger [1947] 1994: 352, quoted in Rose and Abi-Rached, 2013: 118).

During this shift toward psychoanalysis, psychiatry underwent a period of rapid expansion. This growth seemed to take root in the US Army—with its preponderance of distressed or anguished military personnel—and then expanded outward to settings in the community. Writes Grob:

> In 1941, the status of psychiatrists in military as well as civilian life was marginal. Only 35 members of the Army Medical Corps were assigned to neuropsychiatric sections in hospitals. During the war, psychiatrists slowly increased their presence and importance. At the beginning of 1944 the specialty was raised to the level of a division within the Office of the Surgeon General and placed on an equal organizational level with medicine and surgery .... By the end of the war about 2,400 physicians had been assigned to psychiatry, although perhaps less than a third had previous training in the specialty. (1991: 427)

Outside of the military, the number of American psychologists in 1939 was ten times greater than in 1919, growing from 300 to 3000, and this number only increased following World War II (Halliwell 2014).

In addition to the high numbers of traumatized soldiers, there were a number of other sociocultural factors that made the time ripe for psychiatry's expansion. Argues Houts, the "unbounded optimism" that flowed from the favorable social and economic conditions of the postwar period in the USA coupled with an attendant push for social welfare provided the necessary conditions for psychiatry to flourish during this time period (2000: 939). The postwar period also saw the proliferation of a variety of dedicated public mental health policies and state practices: the era saw the establishment of mental health legislation (e.g. the Mental Health Study Act of 1955), prevention initiatives (e.g. the first suicide prevention center opened in Los Angeles, California, in 1958), the emergence of community mental health centers, and the growth of patient- and parent-run advocacy groups focused of the disordered mind. There was, writes Houts, "a clear sense that mental-health professionals could and should do more" (2000: 938). He continues by noting that this "was certainly in keeping with the postwar optimism of American culture and the utopian belief that America could do anything and achieve anything now that the machinery of war could be harnessed for the production of a better world" (Houts 2000: 938).

The historically particular optimism surrounding mental health and illness is perhaps most dramatically captured by the 1950s-era creation of the "Mental Health Bell" by the oldest and largest mental health nonprofit organization in the USA, Mental Health America (MHA). In the early years of the 1950s, MHA issued a call to hundreds of past and present asylums and state hospitals from across the country, requesting their "discarded shackles and chains" (MHA of South Central Kansas n.d.). In 1952, MHA volunteers collected the restraints and heaped them in the lobby of the organization's national headquarters in New York (MHA of South Central Kansas n.d.). On April 13, 1953, at the McShane Bell Foundry in Baltimore, politicians, philanthropists, and organization staff gathered to melt down the shackles, recasting them into a 300-pound "Mental Health Bell" inscribed with the words "Cast from shackles which bound them, this bell shall ring out hope for the mentally ill and victory over mental illness" (MHA of South Central Kansas n.d.; MHA 2016). Infused with a new mission of compassionate caring for the mentally ill while also promising to help a broader society navigate for a better future, psychiatry came to occupy an esteemed place within a new postwar world order. Of course, the expansion of psychiatry was not limited to North America and Western Europe; with the founding of the World Psychiatric Association in 1951, psychiatry took its first steps toward becoming the globalized, transnational phenomenon it is today (Mills 2013; Titchkosky and Aubrecht 2015).

This period saw significant changes as to the spaces in which psychiatry could be found. While prior to World War II, with few exceptions, most psychiatrists worked in custodial hospitals and asylums, the postwar period ushered in an important new era of clinical psychiatry. By 1947, more than half of American psychiatrists had a private practice, working their trade in outpatient clinics (Scull 2015). By 1958, a fraction—only 16%—of all US psychiatrists practiced in state hospitals (Scull 2015). The flourishing of psychiatry outside of the institution was at once a condition and an effect of another significant period in this history: deinstitutionalization. Just as psychoanalysis presented a disruption to the biologically based, eugenically inflected contagion narrative of the mad mind in need of containment, the paradigm also challenged the long-held belief that the proper place for those determined to have psychiatric disorders or conditions was within the bounds of the state-run asylum. Though it would go on for many more decades, the 1950s marked the first beginnings of the deinstitutionalization movement in the USA, which I discuss at length in the following section.

The beginnings of the ideological and policy-driven move away from the asylum coincide rather neatly with developments in pharmaceutical treatments for the disorderly mind. For example, the mid-century discovery of chlorpromazine—the first antipsychotic drug to be put on the market—and its associations with "cure" promised an efficient means of managing the problem mind outside of the confines of the psychiatric hospital. The rise of drugs also served to bring psychiatry more in line (albeit, as we shall see, tentatively) with the biological and medical sciences, an alliance that served to further substantiate psychiatry's growing cultural authority (Scull 2015). Perhaps surprisingly, the pharmaceutical revolution that followed the discovery of psychopharmaceutical drug protocols did not present a significant challenge to the dominance of psychoanalysis, or at least not yet. Indeed, the acceptance of psychopharmaceuticals in the 1950s and 1960s was not held in opposition with nonbiologically oriented psychoanalytic therapies and treatments, but rather as complementary. As Rose and Abi-Rached note, at the time "one of the main advantages of the drugs was that it made the patients who had been treated more amenable to psychotherapy" (2013: 35–6).

Alongside this slow shift away from large, state-run institutions and against the backdrop of soldiers returning home from war with a variety of environmentally induced conditions of the mind and body, psychiatrists began to train their gaze toward the everyday minutiae of psychopathology, with many advocating for more, better, and earlier means of recognizing, assessing, and diagnosing psychiatric illness. This historical moment gave rise to an uptick of state-sponsored public mental health campaigns targeting caregivers, teachers, employers, and other members of the lay public, schooling them in the signs and symptoms of mental disorder as well as in the proper environmental conditions for good development and mental flourishing (Grant 1998). And so, as the bounds of psychiatry expanded, so too did the scope of madness, which became inclusive of everything from the most severe or profound cases so routinely cast as naturally in need of containment in prison-like facilities to varied, everyday neuroses and ailments of the mind endemic to the population at large (Rose and Abi-Rached 2013). The psychoanalyst was less interested in one-size-fits-all diagnostic labels and categories, instead focusing on the underlying psychopathology of the specific individual in treatment. "Psychoanalysis approached mental illness dimensionally," notes Scull, which meant that "rather than sharp discontinuities between the mad and the rest of us, all of us were to some degree pathological, flawed creatures, and the sources of mental disturbances were rooted in all our psyches" (2015: 360). Here, we have a first glimpse of what is now a much more commonplace understanding of mental illness on a continuum ranging from mild to severe, a spectrum device that I will further explore in its current twenty-first-century usage later in this chapter.

As we have seen, the postwar period led to a rapid expansion of the range of possible problems or disorders attributable to the mind and to a related expansion of the available means of solving such problems: from psychoanalytic couch culture to various forms of interventionist surveillance to drug protocols. Once again, psychiatry was faced with an overabundance of "problem minds" and, once again, this apparent chaos was met with calls for more precise taxonomies. The US Army and the Veterans Administration developed a new system of classification that was at once broad enough "to better incorporate the outpatient presentations of World War II servicemen and veterans" and precise enough to differentiate between "psychophysiological, personality, and acute disorders" (American Psychiatric Association n.d.a). Thus, the 1950s marks the birth of what remains to this day the most influential means of classifying psychiatric disorder. With translations into over twenty languages, the APA's DSM is often colloquially referred to as the "bible" of psychiatric diagnosis. Writes Kawa and Giordano, it "enjoys a nearly hegemonic status as *the* reference for the assessment and categorization of mental disorders of all types—not only in the United States, but increasingly in Europe and more recently Asia" (Kawa and Giordano 2012: 1). Indeed, since its first publication in 1952, it has become integral to the practice of clinicians, legislators, prosecutors, policy-makers, and insurers, and it is increasingly mediating the work of educators, social workers, and others in public service. In addition to being an effect of culture, the birth (and subsequent rebirths) of the DSM made possible a range of effects that reverberated through the sociocultural landscape and indeed shaped it in turn. First and foremost, the DSM was then—as it is now—a cultural artifact with much to teach us about the social, historical, and political conditions rendering it intelligible as a means of interpreting and understanding the mind and its problems. I turn now to a further exploration of some such conditions.

8.3. ANTI-PSYCHIATRY, DEINSTITUTIONALIZATION, AND THE FALL OF PSYCHOANALYSIS: THE 1960S AND 1970S

The release of a standardized, universal diagnostic tool served to further legitimize the discipline of psychiatry, and it began to play an increasingly powerful role in public policy and popular discourse (Rose and Abi-Rached 2013). Of course, out of accumulations of power always grow cultures of resistance. While, "contention surrounding psychiatry is as old as psychiatry itself," the North American postwar conformity of the 1940s and 1950s gave way to a decidedly nonconformist, antiauthoritarian cultural turn in 1960s (Crossley 2006: 73). Alongside and, at times (as we shall see), intermingling with the feminist movements and the movements for African-American and LGBT civil rights of the 1960s and 1970s, emerged a formidable antipsychiatry movement. This movement was by no means homogenous, being composed of a diverse group of people with a wide variety of psychiatric labels and institutional experiences, variously self-identifying as mad, crazy, consumers, survivors, and/or ex-patients (Morrison 2005; Crossley 2006; Lewis 2016). Despite this heterogeneity, writes Lewis: "early founders of the movement shared common experiences of disrespect, disregard and discrimination at the hands of psychiatry" (2016: 105). Many also had experienced violent, nonconsensual confinements and treatments, and various other kinds of institutional abuse, ranging from neglect to assault (Lewis 2016). In response to their lived experiences, antipsychiatry activists advocated for more humane treatment of the so-called "mentally ill" and, indeed, questioned the very concept of madness itself, as well as the power and control afforded to those authorities operating within the "psy" disciplines and systems (Morrison 2005; Crossley 2006; Lewis 2016). Participants in the antipsychiatry movement were connected through their shared desire to challenge medicalized understandings of madness: the naturalized assumption that madness is something that is internally experienced, biologically rooted, and, as such, a fixed state unrelated to powerful cultural norms and social institutions of control. At this historical juncture, madness came to be understood as an "essentially contested category" (Rose and Abi-Rached 2013: 113).

Antipsychiatry activist critiques resonated with popular concepts emanating from academic studies in the sociology of deviance, which contended that "mental illness was a residual category, applied to those whose violation of cultural norms could not be explained in any other way" (Rose and Abi-Rached 2013: 113). Indeed, the 1960s and 1970s saw the proliferation of influential academic and fiction texts that did not just challenge psy-systems and knowledges, but pushed for a complete reassessment of medical normativity (e.g. Laing's *The Divided Self* [1960], Michel Foucault's *Madness and Civilization* [1960], Tomas Szasz's *The Myth of Mental Illness* [1961], and Erving Goffman's *Asylums: Essays on the Condition of the Social Situation of Mental Patients and Other Inmates* [1961]). Critiques of psychiatry and the social production of the problem mind also began to infiltrate general public awareness and popular culture; this time period saw the publication of a number of high-profile journalistic exposé's replete with shocking images of inhumane conditions of confinement (e.g. Geraldo Rivera's widely watched 1972 documentary *Willowbrook: The Last Great Disgrace*). It also saw the notable release of novels such as Silvia Plath's *The Bell Jar* (1963), Joanne Greenburg's *I Never Promised You a Rose Garden* (1964), and Ken Kesey's *One Flew over the Cuckoo's Nest* (1962). *One Flew over the Cuckoo's Nest*, which was adapted in 1972 into an Academy Award-winning film by Miloš Forman, received much critical success and mainstream popularity. The book, and later the film, seemed to capture the American cultural ethos of postwar antiauthoritarianism, with Nurse Ratched figured as the embodiment of a bureaucratic totalitarianism and patients McMurphy and Chief as captives of the unchecked power of psychiatry from within the oppressive space of the "total institution" (Goffman 1961). Taken together, such pieces of 1960s and 1970s popular culture served to amplify and popularize some of the specific critiques being advanced by antipsychiatry activists of the 1960s and 1970s (e.g. the violence of forced incarceration and drugging of mad people, the harm of aversive therapies such as electroconvulsive therapy, etc.). With regard to the discipline of psychiatry, the tide of popular sentiment was now tinged with suspicion, and the "solution" of large, state-run facilities was increasingly met with public disapproval. Through lobbying, direct action, and class action lawsuits, civil rights lawyers and patient advocates joined activists, academics, and members of the general public in putting pressure on governments to grant civil rights to psychiatric patients and, indeed, to abandon the state-run psychiatric hospital as a primary model for care. In response to mounting pressure, the state bureaucracy responded as bureaucracies typically do: by instituting further bureaucratic measures and developing a new set of policies and programs aimed at ending the era of large, state-run schools and hospitals that served to warehouse people labeled with psychiatric or intellectual disabilities. I turn now to a more nuanced discussion of the critical cultural period of deinstitutionalization in the USA, yet another key moment in the history of the production of the "problem mind" in the Modern Age.

Although there were variances across states, it is generally thought that deinstitutionalization occurred in two distinct waves, with people labeled as "mentally ill" starting to be moved out of psychiatric facilities beginning in the 1950s, followed by the deinstitutionalization of people with the label of "mentally retarded" in the 1970s (Ben-Moshe 2013; Rembis 2014). We have already touched upon a number of cultural conditions that have influenced a gradual movement away from the state institution as a primary site of care: e.g. the overcrowding of asylums in the early twentieth century, the mid-century emergence of psychopharmaceutical therapies promising to render individuals fit for life in the community, and the 1960s and 1970s culture of egalitarian politics and its role in nurturing the popular belief in the dehumanizing effects of forced incarceration, etc. Scull (2015) contends that alongside and beneath this confluence of factors lie important questions of political economy: the state-run mental hospital was becoming just too costly to operate, thus rendering it a nonviable solution to the problems of the mind at this time. In the words of 1960s-era Massachusetts Commissioner of Mental Health, Milton Greenblatt, "In a sense, our backs are to the wall; it's phase out before we go bankrupt" (quoted in Scull 2015: 320). Scull (2015) emphasizes the link between deinstitutionalization, the growth of capitalism, and the social and economic context of the US welfare state. With "the tighter post-war labour market and the unionization of state workers … work-weeks fell from the 65 or 70 hours that had been typical of the 1930s to 45 hours a week or less" (Scull 2015: 319–20). The postwar years also saw the expansion of federally administered social security and social assistance programs, culminating with the passing of Medicaid and Medicare in the late 1960s. As the federal government began administering (albeit meager) funds to individuals with qualifying diagnoses to cover health care costs (i.e. direct-to-consumer payments), the states soon caught on that they no longer needed to bear the financial burden of institutional care. The shuttering of institutions thus left a host of ex-psychiatric patients-turned-consumers with the responsibility of purchasing their own custodial care from a growing number of private enterprises (e.g. private practice clinics/clinicians, nursing homes, group homes, etc.).

In keeping with the cultural ethos of change endemic to the 1960s and 1970s, the movement out of the state institution was understood as at once liberal and humane. Deinstitutionalization was buffered by the political promise that life "in the community" was unambiguously superior to life in the institution. Yet, while ex-patients benefited from the move out of the confines of the institution—particularly those who were able to secure employment and housing, find communities of care, etc.—deinstitutionalization also presented a new set of problems. The shuttering of institutions left many ex-patients unemployed, in poverty, on the streets, and/or under new (less regulated, for-profit) forms of institutional care. Writes Scull, "[T]he ramshackle network of [private] establishments, intended as a cheap alternative to the state hospital, and the swelling presence of the seriously mentally disabled among the ranks of the homeless, stand as an indictment of contemporary American mental health policy" (2015: 324). As I go on to discuss in further detail momentarily, the decrease in state-run institutions and subsequent increase in the underemployment and/or under-housing of ex-patients ought not to be interpreted as straightforwardly causally connected. Structural inequities such as inadequate health and social supports underpin the abuses endemic to the state institution, as well as a range of post-deinstitutionalization problems such as the underemployment and under-housing of mad people. What is more, as mentioned earlier, the closing of the large state-run institutions did not put an end to institutional styles of care. At this historical juncture, the "problem mind" became the object of a new, often un- or de-regulated privatized industry of residential care where an emphasis on profit often translated into the reduction of services for the people most dependent upon them.

The post-deinstitutionalization period saw the increased criminalization of mental illness in the USA. As the (physical) walls of the institution began to come down, both literally and figuratively, the resultant mixing of those people labeled as mad with those presumed sane enflamed centuries-old anxieties and respectability politics that transformed the ex-patient into a new kind of threat. Many cultural historians have noted, for example, a relationship between deinstitutionalization, the rise of poverty and homelessness among ex-patients, the criminalization of mental illness, and the subsequent growth of mass incarceration in the USA (Ben-Moshe 2013; Rembis 2014). Rembis reports that, "in 1973, there were approximately 93,000 New York residents in state hospitals and approximately 12,500 New Yorkers in the Department of Corrections. By 2000, those numbers had flipped, with only 5,000 New Yorkers in state hospitals and approximately 72,000 individuals in the New York State Department of Corrections" (2014: 150). Indeed, according to a 2006 report by Human Rights Watch, the estimated number of prisoners with psychiatric labels is approximately 1.25 million, which is, Rembis (2014) points out, double the number of people in state psychiatric facilities in their heyday in the mid-1950s. Drawing on the words of Angela Davis, Rembis argues that, like psychiatric institutionalization, "[prison] incarceration has become a powerful means of 'disappearing … dispensable populations from society … in the false hope of disappearing the underlying social problems they represent'" (2014: 140). While there is an undeniable relationship between deinstitutionalization and mass incarceration—a relationship that is punctuated by the fact that many of the state hospital buildings that closed down, were later reopened as prisons—Ben-Moshe critically cautions against oversimplified theories of "transincarceration," which rely on a logic wherein deinstitutionalization leads to unemployment, which leads in turn to poverty, homelessness, and, ultimately, to the reincarceration of many ex-patients in jails (Ben-Moshe 2013). With respect to those incarcerated in prisons versus state institutions or hospitals, Ben-Moshe importantly reminds us that "we are not speaking about the same population" (2013: 396). She continues, "[G]enerally speaking the inmate population in mental hospitals tended to be white, older and more equally distributed by gender then those [predominantly younger, racialized male inmates currently] incarcerated in prisons" (2013: 396). Ben-Moshe shows us how the "new asylum thesis"—this idea that prisons are simply the new asylums of the late twentieth/twenty-first centuries—inaccurately cites the "easy target" of deinstitutionalization as the cause of housing insecurity and the growth of the prison industrial complex (2017: 277). Marking deinstitutionalization as the primary source of the problematic proliferation of other contemporary state practices of incarceration dangerously undermines the importance of anticolonial, antiracist, and antipsychiatry critiques of structural injustice and institutional forms of care. It represents a conceptual sleight of hand that trains our collective, critical gaze away from a constellation of neoliberal social and economic policies that work together to nurture the growth of prison systems and private nursing homes, to reduce the availability of accessible and affordable housing, and to increase the criminalization and policing of mad and/or racialized people/communities (Ben-Moshe 2017; Ritchie 2017).

By the late 1970s, the American public was routinely confronted with stories of a suspect psychiatry: stories, for example, of political dissenters labeled as insane and incarcerated in the Soviet Union or, in the USA, of the high numbers of black civil rights protesters diagnosed with schizophrenia (or "protest psychosis," as it was sometimes referred to); stories of psychiatry's unreliability (e.g. David Rosenhan's infamous 1973 experiment in which researchers pretending to be patients presented themselves to psychiatric hospitals claiming to hear voices but who otherwise "acted normally" and were admitted and diagnosed as schizophrenic); and stories of abuse (e.g. the mind-control experiments on mad subjects conducted by Donald Cameron as part of the MKUltra project at McGill University in Canada) (Duffin 2010; Metzl 2010). In addition, it was not just the public that was crying foul. Above and beyond such public relations problems, psychiatry faced myriad other problems emanating from within the field itself. At this juncture, there was mounting concern coming from APA insiders over the unreliability of hazy diagnostic categories and criteria too open to clinician interpretation and judgment (Cooper et al. 1972; Rosenhan 1973). What is more, with deinstitutionalization, psychiatry had lost a dedicated space (i.e. the hospital and the asylum), and while community care had, in one sense, broadened the reach of psychiatry, it also meant that psychoanalysts were now working alongside (and facing competition from) other health professions interested in the troubled mind (e.g. clinical psychologists, social workers, etc.) (Mayes and Horwitz 2005; Scull 2015, Das 2016). Psychiatry had become "troubled ... to its core" (Rose and Abi-Rached 2013: 112).

A lynchpin in the 1960s- and 1970s-era challenges to psychiatry was the debate over the inclusion of homosexuality as a diagnostic category of psychological disorder (Bayer 1987; Rose and Abi-Rached 2013). Classed as a form of "paraphilia," homosexuality was listed as a discrete disease category in DSM-I, as well as in the first six printings of DSM-II (American Psychiatric Association 1968). This inclusion was directly challenged by a Stonewall-era groundswell of LGBT civil rights activists who, together with their allies in the antiwar and feminist movements, organized a variety of instrumental direct action protests targeting conferences and other gatherings of the APA. While these actions were specifically protesting the APA's inclusion of homosexuality in the diagnostic criteria, the critiques and rhetoric that were drawn upon by LGBT activists reflected ideological frameworks endemic to the antipsychiatry narratives of the time. "Psychiatry is the enemy incarnate," famously shouted Gay Liberation Front activist Frank Kameny as he and others occupied a 1971 APA convention in Washington, D.C. (Bayer 1987: 105). By this time, it was becoming more and more clear that the APA was not a monolithic entity: indeed, queer protesters received important supports from allies and closeted psychiatrists from within the ranks of the APA, including a group of high-ranking members who called themselves the "GAYPA" (Das 2016). The depathologization protests of the early 1970s paved the way for the removal of homosexuality from DSM-II's seventh printing in 1974. The final resolution to depathologize homosexuality was largely credited to Dr. Robert Spitzer, who, as we shall see in the following section, went on to play a key role in the making of DSM-III and related efforts to increase psychiatry's credibility as a legitimate and objective science.

Uncomfortably positioned between mounting popular cynicism, internal debates over diagnostic reliability, and, as we shall explore more in the upcoming section, the new demands of a private economy, psychiatry began to loosen its ties with the psychoanalytic order of things. The thirty-year-long period when psychoanalysis dominated American minds, institutions, and culture came to a close, fueled by what is near-universally described by historians of psychiatry as a "paradigm shift" toward the biological mind that culminated with the publication of DSM-III in 1980 (Mayes and Horwitz 2005; Decker 2013).

8.4. DSM-III, "NEUROMANIA," AND THE NEOLIBERAL BUREAUCRACIES OF THE 1980S AND 1990S

Psychiatry underwent yet another period of monumental change culminating in the early 1980s, a time marked by deep philosophical and practical questions about the ontological nature of madness and its relationship to sanity. In the 1980s, as today, no quantitative scientific measure—be it a blood test or brain scan—could be relied upon to definitively point to the existence of mental illness. In light of this, a crisis-ridden psychiatry turned toward the next best thing: the order and precision of a universal system of classification. As we have seen throughout this chapter, the project of diagnosing and managing the "problem mind" in the Modern Age cannot be disentangled from the project of psychiatry itself and its own attendant claims to power and respectability. This shift toward standardization not only promised better, more reliable diagnosis, it also promised that, in a changing world, psychiatry itself would retain and ultimately expand much of the power and authority it had accumulated in earlier decades of the twentieth century.

On the heels of his high-profile successes with the removal of the homosexuality entry from DSM-II—and, surely, to a significant degree as a direct result of these successes— Robert Spitzer was selected to head up the task force for a new edition of the DSM. The tie that binds the end of the homosexuality diagnostic category with the birth of DSM-III raises important questions about the progress narrative that is commonly ascribed to depathologization in the history of psychiatry. In one sense, the depathologization of homosexuality seemed to represent a reluctant admission on the part of the APA that its understanding of mental illness could, in fact, be biased, influenced by (nonobjective, contingent, and politically mediated) social norms. Yet, the removal of homosexuality from the DSM did not deliver us a more critical psychiatry, a psychiatry more committed to examining the complex interplay between norms and diagnosis. After all, as Das points out, depathologization was "not entirely anti-heteronormative or egalitarian" (2016: 393). It did not, for example, completely sever the pathological ties framing the queer bodymind as an object of psychiatric concern: after all, the manual's entry on homosexuality was merely replaced with "Sexual Orientation Disturbance," a new category that even retained the same diagnostic code as its predecessor (Das 2016). Second, the performance of depathologization ultimately served to uphold and confirm the biological "truth" and "realness" of the other forms of "mental pathology" that remained enshrined in the pages of the DSM. As Das compellingly argues, the formal demedicalization of homosexuality was "both progressive and conservative: progressive in its rejection of past wrongs against gays and lesbians in particular, and conservative when it came to retaining and consolidating [psychiatric] power" (2016: 394). Indeed, this worked to produce "new normativities," which we will explore later in this chapter (Das 2016: 394). But first, let us return to a more precise discussion of the emergence of the deeply culturally influential systems of classification in DSM-III.

First published in 1980, the third edition of the DSM (DSM-III) marked a major paradigm shift in the history of modern psychiatry, one that flowed from the field's 1970s-era "crisis of legitimacy" (Mayes and Horwitz 2005). The previous two editions of the DSM were relatively short and psychoanalytically inflected. They were criticized for being too interested in theories of causation and too open to clinician judgment. In contrast to such interpretive modes of knowing and managing the mind, DSM-III was framed as an empirically derived, multiaxial, "atheoretical" (i.e. not interested in theories of causation) classification system. Building on previously published systems of classification such as the Feighner Criteria and the Research Diagnostic Criteria, DSM-III introduced "specified diagnostic criteria": neo-Kraeplinian checklists of observable symptoms, a certain number of which the patient was required to display in order to receive a diagnosis (Rose and Abi-Rached 2013; Cooper 2014). The adoption of this standardized systems approach promised to decrease clinician interpretation and so increase the uniformity and reliability of psychiatric diagnosis. Of course, it behooves us to question the presumed good of this move away from clinical interpretation and toward biologically oriented notions of objectivity. Psychiatry's claim to objective, calibrated, reliable diagnostics problematically smoothed over differing and even contesting epistemologies and/or theoretical frameworks with respect to the human mind, as well as divergent approaches to responding to the mind and its troubles. In other words, DSM-III ensured that clinicians who may have been previously "speaking different languages" were pulled in "under one professional and institutional umbrella" (Das 2016: 394). Notes Das, "the DSM-III model presupposed that they were talking about the same thing and extended its jurisdiction over them all" (2016: 394). This conflation engendered an "impression of commensurability" that, in fact, extended across a non-homogenous constellation of theories, methodologies, and clinical practices and foregrounded the APA's "agenda of the bureaucratization of knowledge production for diagnosis" (Das 2016: 394).

We can better understand 1980s psychiatry's "agenda of the bureaucratization of knowledge production" as we place it against the backdrop of the diffuse set of social and economic policies and ideologies that make up neoliberalism. Following from previous decades that, as we have seen, were defined by the liberal optimism of the welfare state, a more conservative, laissez-faire economic mandate began to take hold in the 1980s during the Reagan administration, and it has been mediating economic policy and ideology in the USA ever since. Neoliberalism is generally characterized by the privatization of public services, the liberalization of trade, the deregulation of labor and markets, and the reconfiguration of "all spheres of existence" in "economic terms and metrics" (Harvey 2005; Birch and Mykhnenko 2010; Brown 2015: 10). The neoliberalization of psychiatry in the 1980s is made particularly clear, as I touch on below, in DSM-III's moves to: (1) medicalize and thus individualize madness and mental distress; and (2) bureaucratically arrange these new disease entities into clear-cut and coded categories of disorder.

Distinct from earlier psychoanalytic interest in reactions, neuroses, and shades of gray, the new psychiatry born in the 1980s stressed the objective biological existence of psychiatric illness. Under DSM-III, psychiatric disorder was not understood to be relational or situational (e.g. a patient who had recently lost their child could not be classified as depressed), but was instead defined as a manifestation of inner psychobiological dysfunction. As per the APA: "[N]either deviant behavior (i.e. political, religious, or sexual) nor conflicts that are primarily between the individual and society are mental disorders unless the deviance or conflict is a symptom of a dysfunction in the individual" (American Psychiatric Association 1980). And so, the birth of DSM-III was an important hallmark of a new era wherein the mind was reconfigured as something that was not only objectively knowable, but, indeed, biological in nature. This idea of inner mental disorder fit well within a dominant neoliberal model of human health and flourishing that takes the responsibility of care away from the state, instead thrusting it onto a self-managing individual who must take responsibility for their own personal health and wellness through behavioral and financial investments in the body and mind. DSM-III's recasting of mental distress as an individual health condition produced a new "mindful" subject of psychiatry that was, in keeping with the demands of neoliberalism, cast as deeply personally responsible for their states of health and illness: the sole site of illness, but also the primary source of resiliency.

The systematic organization of coded and categorically distinct kinds of mental illness also opened up new possibilities for the neoliberal administration and governance of mental health. The organization of observable communicative and/or behavioral signs into clear-cut categories of pathology translated into an all-or-nothing approach to understanding mental health and illness. With diagnostic borders rigidly delineated, the category of "mental disorder" entered into sharpened focus. Mental illness was now something one could have or not have, or, ontologically speaking, be or not be. And, under DSM-III, there were more ways to "be" mentally ill. DSM-III underwent a dramatic thickening at this time (McGuire 2017). Published in 1952, the first edition of the manual described 106 unique diagnostic categories and was only 130-pages long. Three decades later, DSM-III was, at almost 500 pages, four times as long and described three times as many diagnostic categories. This thickening is, of course, not altogether surprising, particularly as we look, here again, to the social, historical, and economic conditions of the time. In the decades leading up to the publication of DSM-III, drug companies were becoming increasingly aware that treating chronic mental illness could be immensely profitable, and yet the psychoanalytic paradigm presented a problem for the free flow of capital. Interpretive and unreliable, psychodynamic theories did not lend themselves to the administrative needs of pharmaceutical research and development, for example, or to the bureaucratic requirements of the Food and Drug Administration. Notes Scull:

> For drug development to proceed ... and for the regulatory authorities to grant licenses to release new drugs to the market, it was vital to have access to homogeneous groups of patients. To demonstrate that one treatment was statistically superior to another required increasingly large numbers of patients who could be assigned to the experimental and control groups that double-blind testing relied upon. (2015: 386)

Psychoanalysis' non-categorical approach also represented a problem for insurance companies. Rose and Abi-Rached explain:

> As funding for psychiatry was restricted in the United States in the 1970s, government and private health insurers became concerned about the lack of specificity of classification, the confusions of terminology, and the difficulty of establishing clear boundaries between those who were eligible for treatment—and hence for insurance reimbursement—because they were suffering from an illness and those who were not. (2013: 119–20)

Reflecting the neoliberal economic ethos of the time and producing it in turn, DSM-III instigated new modes of managing the mind and its problems, which brought patients/ clients, clinicians, researchers, state regulators, drug manufacturers, and insurance companies into a complicated web of market relations, relations that continued to extend and reproduce within the context of the "neuromania" of the 1990s. Indeed, it was at this historical juncture that "the brain ... entered popular culture, and mind seems visible in the brain itself" (Rose and Abi-Rached 2013: 5).

Julie Passanante Elman observes that "while NASA may have dominated the public and popular scientific imaginations of the 1970's and 1980's, the 'gelatinous three-pound world called the brain' had replaced the moon as the great undiscovered country of the 1990s" (2014: 136). While neuroscientific initiatives have been around since as far back the 1960s, the 1980s and 1990s marked a sharp uptick in social, cultural, and scientific interest in the mysteries of the human brain (Rose and Abi-Rached 2013). This flourishing of neuroscience was far from apolitical. In the midst of the economic conservatism of the 1980s and 1990s, the competition for federal and state funding was fierce: the boom of neuroscientific research was the result of decades of lobbying on the part of individual neuroscientists, patient advocacy groups, and professional societies. These voices of advocacy routinely conjured up paternalistic images of victims of mental illness or neurological impairment who desperately needed neuroscientific innovation, discoveries that promised to unlock the tragic mysteries of the mentally ill or neurologically impaired mind and enable "tens of millions" of presumed-suffering citizens "to live more productive and less disabled lives in the future" (Passanante Elman 2014: 137). The lobbying efforts paid off on July 17, 1990, when then-President George H. W. Bush declared the 1990s as the "Decade of the Brain." This declaration further cultivated an explosion of cultural interest, economic investment, and scientific research in the neurological origins of the so-called "problems of the mind" and, indeed, in their elimination by available neuroscientific means. While previous decades had sought to manage the problem mind by, for example, containment in asylums, social welfare, or hours on the couch, the 1990s saw the culmination of yet another strategy of management: the treatment of the problem mind through its biomedical elimination in the form of prevention or cure.

Born out of neoliberal economic conservativism, the "Decade of the Brain" was not simply driven by a benevolent desire to save or improve the lives of those living with mental illness and/or neurological conditions. As Passanante Elman reminds us, "[T]he Decade of the Brain proclamation was also a federal response to simultaneous reports, issued by the National Institute of Neurological Disorders and Stroke and the National Advisory Mental Health Council, which declared neurological disorders to be among the most pervasive and costly problems facing America in the coming decade" (2014: 137). The cost of mental illness was then, as it is now, routinely measured by number of days absent from work and by the expense of (publically funded or subsidized) medical tests, treatments, procedures, and supports. With this notion of economic burden in mind, Passanante Elman importantly connects the Decade of the Brain with the contemporaneous emergence of the Americans with Disabilities Act (ADA), which was signed into law by Bush just nine days after he signed the resolution declaring the Decade of the Brain. Taken together, these two historic signings represent what Passanante Elman calls a "complex and interrelated neoliberal proposition" (2014: 138). While in one way "cures for neurological disabilities promised to stem the economic drain posed by the disabled," she writes, "access to employment would 'mainstream' disabled workers into full participation in American capitalism by alleviating their dependence on costly government services" (Passanante Elman 2014: 138).

While on the one hand promising to eliminate the (presumed) fiscal drain of disability, on the other hand, the "Decade of the Brain" nurtured the growth of the US economy via the development of a number of important advances in medical research, as well as diagnostic and therapeutic technologies. For example, 1991 saw the introduction of functional magnetic resonance imaging (fMRI), a device that measures brain activity by detecting changes in blood flow. fMRI does not measure brain structure, but rather functioning—"[W]e seemed to be able to see the neural correlates of the activities of mind itself in real time," write Rose and Abi-Rached, "and once we did, it seemed impossible to doubt that mind is what brain does" (2013: 13). Indeed, they write, "[T]he very interior processes of the living and dynamic brain, its anatomical normalities and pathologies, its activity in delusions and normal perception, its secretion or blockade of neurotransmitters, could be rendered visible and correlated with a phenomenology of mental life" (Rose and Abi-Rached 2013: 73). The discovery of fMRI and its promised insights into the mind-as-brain were especially significant in bringing the brain sciences together with psychiatry and bolstering the growing hybrid field of neuropsychiatry. Insights into the inner workings of the mind-as-brain were now not only visualized in research or clinical settings. In the 1990s, images of brightly colored brain scans began to pepper Western popular culture. In so doing, they confirmed and delivered a new kind of "cerebral subject" (Ortega and Vidal 2007). As they seemed to render transparent and visible previously secret inner processes of the mind, functional neuroimages also promised the potential for objective, visually based diagnoses. Observes Joseph Dumit, "The brain scans that we encounter in magazines and newspapers, on television, in a doctor's office, or in a scientific journal make claims on us. These colorful images with captions describe brains that are certifiably smart or depressed or obsessed" (2004: 5). Thus, in addition to shaping a variety of novel bio-identities and biosocial communities— the neurodiversity community being one noteworthy example here, with its common symbolic usage of the rainbow-colored brain—the functional scans seemed to confirm the post-DSM-III's categories approach. As notes Dumit, "[W]e are placed among the categories that the set of images offers. To which category do I belong? What brain type do I have? Or more nervously: Am I normal?" (2004: 5).

Color-coded fMRI scans and clear-cut diagnostic categories gestured toward the possibility of a definitive snapshot of the human mind/brain. And yet, such approaches are nonetheless born of and responsive to a historically and culturally particular bureaucratic style of management and its attendant need for clarity of kind. It is a need that, as I will discuss momentarily, seems to be shifting underfoot. Despite its (purportedly) increased transparency in the late twentieth and early twenty-first centuries, the mind/brain continues to evade the certainty of neuropsychiatric capture. "Each of the pathways that neuropsychiatry has attempted to trace through the brain seems to run, not into the bright uplands of clarity," write Rose and Abi-Rached, but rather "into the murky, damp, misty, and mysterious forests of uncertainty" (2013: 138). This uncertainty has anticipated the emergence of a new style of mind management in the Modern Age, one that is premised on flexible and graded spectrums of mental health and illness and one that anticipates customized as opposed to strictly bureaucratized solutions.

8.5. THE MAINSTREAMING OF MENTAL HEALTH, SPECTRAL DIAGNOSTICS, AND THE CUSTOMIZED SOLUTIONS OF THE TWENTY-FIRST CENTURY

During the waning days of the twentieth century, the US Department of Health and Human Services released the first ever Surgeon General's Report dedicated to mental health. In the preface to the report, Surgeon General David Satcher reminds us that while "the past century has witnessed extraordinary progress in our improvement of the public health through medical science and ambitious, often innovative, approaches to health care services … concerns regarding mental illness and mental health too often were relegated to the rear of our national consciousness" (US Department of Health and Human Services 1999: vi). Collapsing the diagnostic with the prognostic, Satcher continues by reminding the American public that, despite the many biomedical advances of the twentieth century, "tragic and devastating disorders such as schizophrenia, depression and bipolar disorder, Alzheimer's disease, the mental and behavioral disorders suffered by children, and a range of other mental disorders" continue to affect "nearly one in five Americans in any year," yet often remain "spoken of in whispers and shame" (US Department of Health and Human Services 1999: vi). Vis-à-vis the "tragic" and "devastating" specter of these disorders is a critical mass of "fiercely dedicated advocates, scientists, government officials, and consumers" insisting "that mental health flow in the mainstream of health" (US Department of Health and Human Services 1999: vi). Central to the "mainstreaming of mental health" is yet another kind of problem mind. Satcher states: "[C]ommon sense and respect for our fellow humans tells us that a focus on the positive aspects of mental health demands our immediate attention" (US Department of Health and Human Services, 1999: vi). Formally taken to be, merely, an absence of mental illness, Satcher here describes mental health in positive terms, a distinct and bounded object worthy of attention in its own right. While the mentally abnormal, deviant, or ill mind continues to be held up in the twenty-first century as a problem mind, the "normal" or mentally "well" or "healthy" mind has emerged alongside it as a contemporary problem of a different order.

Satcher's 1999 report makes it clear that underpinning the desire to "mainstream mental health" are familiar concerns over economic cost and state burden. Yet, at the same time as it reminds us that "the burden of mental illness on health and productivity in the United States and throughout the world has long been profoundly underestimated," the report also alerts us to the fact that not all "mental illness burdens" are created equal. The report uses the disability-adjusted life-years (DALYs) measure to calculate, order, and compare mental illness categories in terms of the degree of economic burden these place on the state, with "major depression" listed as "equivalent in burden to blindness or paraplegia," and the "active psychosis seen in schizophrenia is equal in disability burden to quadriplegia" (US Department of Health and Human Services 1999: 4). In relation to this sliding scale of economic burden emerge equally slippery notions of mental health and illness. At the turn of the century, we see that "'mental health' and 'mental illness' are not polar opposites," says the report; instead, these categories "may be thought of as points on a continuum" (US Department of Health and Human Services 1999: 4). The "Report on Mental Health" (1999) names an idea that would grow into another shift in science and culture, away from the DSM-III categories approach and toward this idea of a graded field of unbounded affective intensities anchored by a notion of "full" mental health or normalcy on the one side and "severe" abnormal pathology on the other. We have heard talk of this kind of graded range before. The notion of a mental health continuum has been around since Freud (and likely even before this). Still, there is something rather different about its usage today. In its contemporary twenty-first-century application, the mental health continuum—or, as it is commonly referred to, the mental health spectrum—is at once a conceptual, rhetorical, and diagnostic tool that is organizing a wide variety of bodies and minds in ways that seem to breach and defy traditional designations such as normal/abnormal, health/illness, and mad/sane, and yet it does not completely vanquish these. Psychiatry's move toward spectrums was thrust into the spotlight in first decade of the twenty-first century with the controversy-plagued development of the most recent edition of the DSM, DSM-5.

As we look to the contemporary moment, it is apparent that Western psychiatry is in the midst of (yet another!) crisis of legitimacy, this time fueled by new discoveries in twenty-first-century neurobiology and epigenetics, discoveries that seem to disrupt the categories approach to diagnosis. Whereas for the better part of the twentieth century the mind-as-brain was understood to be biologically inflexible and categorically determined (i.e. "fixed for life"), twenty-first-century research on neuroplasticity tells the story of a brain structure that is fluid and responsive: ever-changing in relation to the environment, experiences, and conditions under which it is living (Pitts-Taylor 2016: 17). A resonant narrative of biological non-fixity has taken hold in recent studies of human genetics. Research in the field of epigenetics is showing us that gene expression can be altered through interactions with the environment without changing the underlying genetic code. This means that even if two people have the exact same genetic sequence, depending on their personal histories, environmental exposures, and life experiences, one may express a given trait while the other might express it differently or not at all. Such novel discoveries in the biomedical sciences have led psychiatric researchers, clinicians, and consumers alike to a radical questioning of the field's categorical grounds (Rounsaville et al. 2002; Adam 2013). Studies emanating from within the field of psychiatry also point to the insufficiency of the categorical approach, citing high rates of comorbidities among disorders, an overreliance on catchall categories, low diagnostic stability over time, and the insufficiency of the one-size-fits-all treatment protocols (Kupfer et al. 2002; American Psychiatric Association 2013). Taken together, this evidence led the authors of *A Research Agenda for DSM-V* to issue a dramatic call in 2002 for yet another "paradigm shift" with respect to how mental disorders are recognized and diagnosed: a move from the categorical to the dimensional (Kupfer et al. 2002: xix; Adam 2013; American Psychiatric Association 2013).

Distinct from the categorical model wherein the clinician is charged with the task of discerning the presence or absence of disorder, the dimensional diagnostic framework encourages the clinician to "recognize, measure, and monitor disorder by degree" (McGuire 2017: 407). In keeping with the fluidity of neuroplasticity and epigenetics, the dimensional approach does not imply a clear or fixed threshold between "normality" and "disorder" (American Psychiatric Association n.d.b; Pitts-Taylor 2016; McGuire 2017). Dimensional spectra of mental health and illness thus replace categories of being with thresholds of intensity. As I have written about elsewhere, "When thinking about dimensional spectrums of mental health and illness ... the pertinent question is not 'is disorder present or absent?' but rather 'how much disorder is present?'—that is to say, 'how intense are the symptoms?'; 'how often do they occur?'; 'how long do they last?'; 'how severe are the incapacitations?', and so on" (McGuire 2017: 407–8). And so while, on the one hand, dimensional psychiatry moves us away from the long-held belief that normalcy and pathology are mutually exclusive binary categories, it does not do away with oppositional notions of "normal" and "abnormal." Under a dimensional diagnostic framework, classifications of normal and abnormal, healthy and ill minds rather become diametrically opposed poles anchoring a graded spectrum of diagnostic possibilities.

With the publication of DSM-5's draft criteria in 2010 and with the release of the published manual in 2013, it was apparent that a full "paradigm shift" would not (yet) take place. Still, according to the APA, DSM-5 introduces an "integration of a dimensional approach to diagnosis and classification," one that is to be complementary to the still-current categorical approach (American Psychiatric Association n.d.b: para. 1). What this means is that while diagnostic categories remain intact in the new manual, the APA has made a few dimensionally inspired adjustments as to how "mental disorders" are interpreted and measured by clinicians. The new diagnostic criteria for autism and schizophrenia, for example, replace previous disorder subclassifications (e.g. "PDD-NOS" or "Asperger's Syndrome" for autism and "paranoid," "disorganized," or "catatonic" for schizophrenia) with the all-inclusive "schizophrenia spectrum" and "autism spectrum" designations (American Psychiatric Association 2013). Yet, despite their increased flexibility and stretchiness, DSM-5's spectrum categories do not invite a diagnostic free-for-all: accompanying these wide-reaching spectrums are new "measures indicating degree of [symptom] acuteness" (American Psychiatric Association n.d.b: para. 2). Autism, schizophrenia, and other DSM-5 spectrum diagnoses include new diagnostic modifiers: point-based scales measuring gradations of symptom severity. And so, while these new dimensionally inflected diagnostic categories do emphasize a sense of continuity between mental pathology and health, they also introduce more sensitive, discerning means of differentiating the infinite gradations of pathology that lie between these two still-opposing extremes. DSM-5's turn toward dimensionality can be also glimpsed in the adjustment to the new manual's format and organizational structure. For example, diagnostic categories are now grouped together by shared risk factors and symptom characteristics (American Psychiatric Association n.d.b, n.d.c). The new chapter sequence, according to the APA, "reflects what has been learned during the past two decades about how the brain functions and how genes and environment influence a person's health and behaviour" (American Psychiatric Association n.d.c: para. 2). In so doing, the chapter reorganization orients to a future in which mental health and illness are made measurable in scientifically more precise ways (i.e. where a susceptibility/risk biomarker tracked through an individual's DNA profile or from a personal wearable device can inform a tailored/customized therapeutic protocol, be it pharmacological or behavioral), paving the way for a future of customizable, personalized mental health care.

While the cultural landscape of the contemporary West seems to be defined by this "mainstreaming of mental health," it is also plagued by much talk of "mental health crises." Jasbir Puar argues that, in twenty-first-century neoliberal biomedical societies, "there is no such thing as an 'adequately abled' body anymore," and the same can be said of the "abled" or normative mind (2012: 155). More and more people are falling under the purview of psychiatry, and this growing mass of people understanding them/ ourselves to be "less than well" is placing unique demands on systems of education, work, law enforcement, and so on. That the nature of the contemporary "mental health crisis" is most often framed as a crisis of *health* and not, say, as a crisis of *illness*, is telling. Let us think back to the turn-of-the-new-century US Surgeon General's report and its problematization of the mind that might be readily understood to be "healthy" alongside the more traditionally problematized "mentally unhealthy" mind. As the report moves seamlessly from its sliding DALY scales measuring the economic burden of mental illness on the state to its turn toward graded continua of individualized notions of mental health, it makes explicit the fraught relationship between spectrum thinking and the "economization of life" (Murphy 2017). Both rationalities, it would seem, turn on a question of degree. On the surface, shifts away from binarized, categorical designations of mental normalcy and abnormalcy, health and illness, toward the colorful multidimensionality of a "mental health spectrum" promise to open up possibilities for living differently from the norm. Indeed, the spectrum approach is often taken to be straightforwardly empowering, a disavowal of individualized biological destinies or static ontologies. "There's no such thing as normal," we might be tempted to cry, and "biology is not destiny." Yet, even as twenty-first-century theories of brains, genes, and minds seem to disavow normal and "offer a reprieve from biological determinism," we must also confront, following Pitts-Taylor, the "'dual association' with freedom and control" (2016: 18). In other words, we need to address the ease with which the story of the mind's flexibility, adaptability, and responsiveness to its environment aligns with highly normative neoliberal demands for ongoing acts of self-care and personal health management in the name of optimization and enhancement (Pitts-Taylor 2016: 18; McGuire 2017; Fritsch and McGuire 2019).

I have argued elsewhere that psychiatry's movement toward dimensionality can be read as a kind of neoliberal deregulation strategy (McGuire 2017). As the boundaries between mental health and illness, normalcy and abnormalcy seem to be disappearing, we are also confronted with new and less visible modes of surveillance and regulation that are being extended over more and more bodies and minds. As we have seen, while graded continua of mental health are widening the field of pathology and risk, they are at the same time providing the grounds for an inclusive, optimistic, and—from the vantage point of market capitalism—highly lucrative narrative of personal responsibility, improvement, recovery, and resiliency (McGuire 2017, Fritsch and McGuire 2019). The failure of the half-century-old, one-size-fits-all bureaucratic approach to managing mental illness anticipates what Ajana calls "preventative, participatory and personalized models of healthcare" (2017: 13). Often privatized and for profit, these customizable approaches to mental health management interpolate the patient as a kind of para-practitioner in their own biomedical regimens, consciously and endlessly measuring and monitoring unstable states of health so as to "catch" the earliest of "non-vital" signs and work toward revitalization. This cultural climate of hyper-individualized "mental problems" functions to depoliticize and thus naturalize the social conditions working to differentially produce mental distress among those in the crosshairs of sometimes multiple systems of oppression. At the same time, the personalization and customization of (often for-profit) therapeutic solutions work to dramatically limit health access for those most in need. Thus, even as the spectrum undermines the category of the normal mind, its detailed risk profiles and severity measures still uphold a normative subject; a spectrum subject who possesses the functional capacity, flexibility, and capital to move along the pathological gradations of a continuum that is tilted toward a neoliberal "compulsory normativity" (McRuer 2006; McGuire 2017, Fritsch and McGuire 2019).

Vis-à-vis spectrum severity measures and claims to neoliberal normativity, the mind/brain is nonetheless rebellious, defiant, and disruptive. Indeed, over the course of the past century, the mind/brain can perhaps best be characterized by a certain remarkable—and, as we have seen, often remarked upon—refusal to be managed. And so, while I was initially tasked with tracing the cultural history of "mental problems" in the Modern Age, what I found instead was a plethora of ways in which the human mind has been, on the one hand, *problematized* (e.g. by a vast network of actors including doctors, investors, lawmakers, and prison guards, as well as whole structures of legislative, judicial, governmental, and medical/psychiatric control) and, on the other hand, how it has been troublesome or *problematic* to those very structures always looking for better, more efficient modes of government and control over people. It is toward this latter sense of the unruly, rebellious, severe, or otherwise "problematic" mind that I think we need to turn, for in its constant refusal of the models and systems seeking to contain it—and, indeed, in its continued destabilization of these models and systems of management—we might encounter, grapple with, and let flourish a means of living differently from the norm.

NOTES

CHAPTER 2

1. In this chapter, I use *ablement* or *abledment* (enacting abledness) to express a productive relation, in contrast with the terminology of *ability/abled* or *able-bodied*, which is not axiomatic and requires problematization.

2. When I wrote this piece, Scotland had been under a Red Alert for snowfall, and as a wheelchair user, my mobility had been dramatically impacted by that snow. Yet this hindrance is *differentiated* in the access I may have to a vehicle (a small car or a four-wheel drive) and the kinds of work conditions available to me (an academic can avail themselves of working from home, whereas a zero-contract worker will not have that flexibility and may be docked pay as a consequence). There are stories of poor people walking five miles through heavy snow to access foodbanks in order to avoid starvation.

3. The existence or absence of papers produces parallel and fictional identities that matter. Take the example of people living in Nazi Germany referred to as *U-boat Jews* who used their German papers to create new identities that erased their Jewishness (Hahn-Beer 2001), or a more recent example of the changing marital status for people whose same-sex marriage is not recognized in certain nation-state jurisdictions: they fly into one country where they are regarded as "married" and then another where they are considered "single."

4. Unless otherwise cited, all etymological renderings are from Brown (1993).

5. In some countries, equality laws can become barriers when organizations successfully argue the fact that they have *met the minimum legal requirements* for building accessibility, even though "access" that stimulates mobility is still not available. For example, a building where university graduations occur is held to be accessible, yet it is not possible for wheelchair users in the academic procession to access the podium as there is no ramp provided, resulting in exclusion from full access to the graduation-day journey in pursuance of their academic roles. In this instance, fulfillment of equality laws is weaponized to deny full accessibility.

6. Disability activist Sheila King took Jetstar Airways, a subsidiary of Qantas, to the Australia Federal Court (*King v. Jetstar Airways Pty Ltd* (No 2) 11 [2012] FCA 8, 2012; 286 ALR 149). Available online: http://www7.austlii.edu.au/cgi-bin/viewdoc/au/cases/cth/FCA/2012/8.html.

7. The language of "perfection" saturates much of Buddhist literature. Perfection is not used in the Greek sense of corporeal idealization; rather, "perfection" used in the translations and descriptions of Indic Buddhist terms tends to carry a different connotation. For example, the *mahāpurusha lakshanas* (signs of a great person) are characteristics of an ideal without necessarily the connotations of complete (beyond *saṃsaric*) perfection. They are therefore not denoted as "perfect" in our sense (Bee Scherer, personal communication).

8. This idea of the ableist-right has close associations with the alt-right, which I explore more fully in Campbell (2019).

9. In 2014, the Research Institute for Consumer Affairs (Barton et al. 2014) conducted a market study of scooters. The methodology is extremely problematic. The purview of stakeholders is limited (e.g. no aged-person organizations). Despite there being 330,000 scooter users in

the UK, five user personas were developed based on a narrowly distributed survey to which 480 people responded. The research presumes mobility scooters to be only a disability issue. Nowhere is usage by people deemed not to be mobility impaired (anatomically) factored into the research survey questions. Absent are any questions exploring socioeconomic or environmental issues that might have influenced scooter usage.

10. The media's role in these mobility debates and the ensuing comments from members of the public could be construed as a hate crime in the form of disability vilification, or "stirring up" hatred under UK legislation (see the Criminal Justice Act 2003, for England and Wales, and Walters, Brown, and Wiedlitzka 2016 for a discussion of motivations and causes).

11. This argument was also used to deny women in the third trimester of a pregnancy access to disabled parking permits (see Campbell 2009).

12. Mark Mason seems to have some "issue" with diversity. Although disability is not explicitly mentioned, his piece "Compulsory Subtitles? I Read 'em and Weep" (Mason 2018) is another assault on the increased use of subtitles in video media.

13. *Nationalist investments* in disability pop up in rather strange places. One example is rhetoric opposing the usage of cochlear implants for Deaf people, which is viewed as antipatriotic, given that these devices contribute significantly to the economies of certain countries (see Campbell 2009).

14. See Endnote 10, above.

CHAPTER 3

1. In disability and chronic pain and illness communities, having a certain amount of "spoons" per day is a frequently used shorthand used to describe limited energy and ability (Cowley 2015).

2. Christine Labuski's recent book, *It Hurts Down There: The Bodily Imaginaries of Female Genital Pain*, goes into depth on the impact of not being able to talk about the body part that is in pain, for example (Labuski 2015).

3. Here, a proliferation of recent scholarship in Disability Studies can be easily turned to (Patsavas 2014; Mitchell and Snyder 2015; Puar 2017; McRuer 2018; Schalk 2018; and many more). "Capacities of incapacity" is a phrase that David T. Mitchell and Sharon L. Snyder use in their 2015 *The Biopolitics of Disability: Neoliberalism, Ablenationalism, and Peripheral Embodiment* (Mitchell and Snyder 2015).

4. In their 1991 book, *Deadly Dust: Silicosis and the On-Going Struggle to Protect Workers' Health*, David Rosner and Gerald Markovitz brought silicosis, a deadly occupational disease with a devastating and continuing toll, back into public discourse (2006). The book was republished in 2006 as a testament to its great importance to the cultural geography and epidemiology of chronic pain and illness.

5. Perhaps the most contentious association with chronic pain in the contemporary moment is the "epidemic" of opioid addiction in the USA. This chapter's discussion of chronic pain and illness in the Modern Age does not dwell on opioid addiction. Instead, I lay out in the chapter some important transformations brought about by attending to the experience of chronic pain and illness, which has and is effecting greater intersectionality in the politics and field of Disability Studies. That said, the racial dynamics of the opioid problem are complex enough to merit a chapter of their own. I will lay out here some threads that are in urgent need of more research. First, because of racist bias regarding vulnerability to pain, the black population has been less impacted by opioid addiction that traces its origins to painkiller abuse *because* of some of the problems of delegitimation and lack of access to

adequate care. As Dr. Andrew Kolodny put it in an interview from November 4, 2017, on the "All Things Considered" program on National Public Radio (NPR):

> doctors prescribe narcotics more cautiously to their non-white patients. It would seem that if the patient is black, the doctor is more concerned about the patient becoming addicted, or maybe they're more concerned about the patient selling their pills, or maybe they are less concerned about pain in that population. But the black patient is less likely to be prescribed narcotics, and therefore less likely to wind up becoming addicted to the medication. So what I believe is happening is that racial stereotyping is having a protective effect on non-white populations. (King and Kolodny 2017)

This lack of access has paradoxically allowed the narrative of the opioid epidemic to have a "white" face for many years now. However, a lack of access that might on the surface appear to be a saving grace has perpetuated heroin use instead, and many older African-Americans in urban areas have been functional addicts for years, and some for decades. As this chapter goes to publication, media attention has finally begun to attend to this demographic of opioid users because overdose-related deaths among urban African-American heroin users have skyrocketed since the synthetic opioid fentanyl has begun to be mixed in with the supply as of 2014 or 2015 (Jamison 2018a; Nnamdi 2019). As reporter Peter Jamison put it in a tweet on December 18, 2018, "Opioid abuse is often associated w/ white, rural/ suburban parts of the U.S. But a new wave of the epidemic is decimating black heroin users in cities" (Jamison 2018b).

6. The work of disability scholars and activists Eli Clare, Liz Crow, Nirmala Erevelles, Anna Mollow, Tobin Siebers, Susan Wendell, and all of those mentioned in this chapter has played an important role in conceptualizing this shift (Crow 1996; Wendell 2001; Siebers 2008; Erevelles 2011; Mollow 2014; Clare 2015).

7. David T. Mitchell and Sharon L. Snyder's recent book, *The Biopolitics of Disability: Neoliberalism, Ablenationalism, and Peripheral Embodiment*, develops an understanding of peripheral embodiments and capacities of incapacity that sheds even more light on the particularities of what modes of knowledge and being are available to us from human variation (Mitchell and Snyder 2015: 180).

8. Of course, one of the biggest reasons for access to medications being blocked in the context of chronic pain is the panic around opioid addiction. Opioid addiction, as Patrick Radden Keefe has written in his October 30, 2017 *New Yorker* piece on the Sackler family, has itself been created and fed by corruption and bribery within pharmaceutical companies and sustained by direct-to-consumer marketing (Keefe 2017). Given this, we can also lay the blame for the consequent regulation and anxiety that cause a greater incidence of people in chronic pain being blocked from receiving medication at the feet of profit-driven pharmaceutical marketing. This tight regulation and constant surveillance of opioid prescriptions adds the specter of moralization, a ubiquitous presence in the lives of those who require such medications, subjecting them to greater bureaucracy and expense, more frequent doctor visits required for refills, the need for hard-copy original scripts, and higher costs of prescriptions. Notably, due to the greater credibility that comes with white male privilege and financial means, opioid addiction—and access to the treatment of such addictions—is also a chronic illness directly deriving from "states of privilege," hence the moralizing atmosphere of states of privilege and bodies of abuse that permeates and radiates out from the white, oblong Vicodin pill.

9. Crip-of-color critique, drawing on a lineage of queer-of-color critique, attends to "systemic de-valuation ... of non-normative bodies and minds," which is also frequently correlated

with impairment and disablement (Kim 2017). Crip-of-color materialism is yet another articulation of what Critical Disability Studies as a methodology *does*. A crip-of-color *materialism* particularizes crip-of-color critique to engage what the Black Marxist tradition refers to as Racial Capitalism. Feminist Disability and Mad Studies scholar Tanja Aho makes a more explicit connection to "crip-of-color-materialism" in *Lateral*, drawing on and extending feminist Disability Studies scholar Nirmala Erevelles' "materialist disability studies" (Erevelles 2011; Aho 2017). In *Disability and Difference in Global Contexts*, Nirmala Erevelles turns to a consideration of the history of transatlantic slavery in her analysis of the coupling of disability and fungibility that the slave trade effected, imbricating attributes of disability and debility with commodification and the material and discursive dispossession that capacitated the institution of slavery in the USA (Erevelles 2011). In Erevelles' analysis, it becomes clear that disability and commodification were co-constitutive in the transformative dehumanization that was the transformation of violent enslavement upon which the capitalist economy of "modernity" has been predicated. Erevelles' approach has some affinity with Jasbir Puar's 2017 book, *The Right to Maim: Debility, Capacity, Disability*. Puar uses the term "debility" to describe what crip-of-color materialism or materialist Disability Studies describes as a culturally and politically produced demographic vulnerability to illness, impairment, and injury ("maiming," to use Puar's word) (Puar 2017). That is, "debility" in Puar's book descriptively names what I have been outlining in my discussion thus far of the intersectional evolution of the field of Disability Studies that attentiveness to the quandary of impairment and compounded identities has been generating, especially over the last decade.

10. Schalk argues that the methodological attunement that Minich, Kim, and herself—among others—are advocating allows "critical disability studies [to] better engage in conversations about the ways both ability and disability operate in representations, language, medicine, the law, history, and other cultural arenas," and to attend to historically variable definitions of disability (Schalk 2017). With regard to *social norms*, Schalk formulates "*(dis)ability*" as a designation of "social norms which categorize, rank, and value bodyminds" (Schalk 2017, 2018). For Schalk, here, *disability* is "a historically and culturally variable category within this larger system" (Schalk 2017).

11. Jasbir Puar's book, *The Right to Maim: Debility, Capacity, Disability*, discusses at length the bio-politics of certain populations being available for injury with regard to Israel and Palestine (Puar 2017).

12. In line with the "crip-of-color materialism" that Aho and Erevelles gesture toward, Geary's project works to reclaim a "black materialist" tradition of health analysis, reaching back to W. E. B. Du Bois, which "defines the social causes and origins of health and disease, relating them to the power relations" (Erevelles 2011; Geary 2014: 7; Aho 2017). A "materialist epidemiology," such as the one Geary's book presents, takes "welcoming biosocial conditions" into account, rather than limiting itself to biomedicalizing discourse.

13. Naming "state intimacy" or "the violent intimacy of the racist state" as the primary risk factor paints a more accurate picture (Geary 2014: 2). He writes:

> I argue that the racial blackness of the US AIDS epidemic has been produced not by the behaviors of African Americans but by the conditions of structured, racist domination. Racism, not race, ethnicity, or culture. In dominant social and scientific discourses, HIV infection has been understood to index perverse intimacies of sex and drug use, what are politely named "risk behaviors." AIDS has been considered a consequence of these intimacies. For black Americans, however, I argue that the primary structuring factor that has determined risk of HIV infection has been what I call *state intimacy*, or the violent intimacy of the racist state. (Geary 2014: 2)

Geary cites "structured impoverishment" and segregation as contributing to "increased malnutrition, concurrent infection, and overall immiseration that lend toward increased susceptibility to HIV infection," noting that "racially unequal health and healthcare must ... be recognized as significantly structuring risk and vulnerability to infection" (Geary 2014: 5).

14. Mollow notes that Freddie Gray was a victim of environmental racism before dying from police brutality—having been raised in an environment with unremediated lead, he was diagnosed with learning disabilities and had high levels of lead in his blood (Mollow 2017: 114). Further, she writes:

> Historically and contemporarily, black neighborhoods have been used as dumping grounds for toxins that white people have the political and economic clout to keep out of their communities. People of color are far more likely than whites to have little choice but to live near landfills, hazardous waste facilities, coal-fired plants, and chemical factories; they also face disproportionate levels of water contamination and air pollution. (Mollow 2017: 115)

Mollow also notes that lead gets into household dust and is ingested via breathing, and "it is virtually impossible for people who live in lead-painted homes to avoid breathing or ingesting this contaminant," contrary to the popular behavioral assumption that one must eat lead paint to be affected (Mollow 2017: 115).

15. Notably, as a "developing" nation in whose politics the USA has had a heavy—and disavowed—hand, Brazil presents an exceptional example of the violences of rapid industrialization followed by rapid neoliberalization, and the economic inequalities and the immiseration of the poor are stark and vast (Parker 1998; Amar 2013; Biehl 2013).

16. Notably, Biehl's published account is accompanied by photographs, as though to attest to the incredible conditions here.

17. This is an excerpt from Book XI of *The Dictionary*, which is an expansive collection of the poems that Catarina wrote in her tenure at Vita. In this excerpt, Catarina makes a quite lucid assessment of her situation and of the origin of Vita in the bankruptcy of the nation (Biehl 2013: 336).

18. With a great deal of time and energy, Biehl arrives at a diagnosis for Catarina's actual illness, which is quite different from psychosis, enacting a reverse hysteria on her case—or rather, revealing her social and familial contexts to be themselves performing a social psychosis—though too late for her life to be recuperated.

19. Although *Figures* is the official project title, Crow's piece has the phrase "We Are Figures" associated with it, which is a pointed expression of her work as embodying what these abstract figures in statistics and finance might represent, and resisting such abstraction.

CHAPTER 4

1. Maya Chacaby, personal communication 2017; for a full discussion of this sense of story, see King (2003) and Chacaby (2011).

2. In launching its "20/20 Right to Sight" campaign, the WHO (2017) has claimed that "Today, there is an estimated 180 million people worldwide who are visually disabled. Of these, between 40 and 45 million persons are blind and, by definition, cannot walk about unaided. They are usually in need of vocational and/or social support. The loss of sight causes enormous human suffering for the affected individuals and their families. It

also represents a public health, social and economic problem for countries, especially the developing ones, where 9 out of 10 of the world's blind live. In fact, around 60% of them reside in sub-Saharan Africa, China and India."

3. In contrast to this understanding, some artistic, autobiographical, and theoretical accounts of blind authors grapple with sight conceived of as a powerful cultural character. Consider, for example, Georgina Kleege, John Hull, Ved Mehta, Hema Karah, Lynn Manning, Ryan Knighton, Robert Scott, Rod Michalko, Hellen Keller, Cathy Kudlick, Stephen Kuusito, David Bolt, and Hannah Thompson. Particular to this incomplete list of authors is an orientation toward questioning the place of sight in organizing the meaning of life and thereby not suggesting that adjustment to a sighted world is the only thing interesting about blindness.

4. Some disability memoirs, life writing, and the popularity with the contemporary digital story-telling industry act as a kind of ventriloquism, encouraging disabled people to speak their debasement (see editors' introduction in this volume).

5. There is, of course, no right to sight in any of the international Declarations of Human Rights; this "right to sight" is a metaphor that may be tied more to unquestioned versions of human nature than to human rights. Humans, or so the medical story goes, ought to see (Titchkosky 2014, 2015).

6. This epistemological interest in blindness may also be enhanced by the numbers of blind people whose blindness is caused by the use of chemical weapons in both World Wars, as well as the use of Agent Orange in Vietnam and other chemicals in the Middle East. The interest in rehabilitation since World War I and World War II also enhanced the interest in blindness and epistemology.

7. Georgina Kleege (2005: 179) suggests, "The Hypothetical Blind Man ... has long played a useful, though thankless role, as a prop for theories of consciousness. He is the patient subject of endless thought experiments." It should be noted that an implicit invocation of a hypothetical sighted person comes along with the explicit invocation of a hypothetical blind person.

CHAPTER 5

1. After leaving home, I serendipitously gravitated toward Deaf communities. My college, although a hearing–speaking institution, was a short walk from the Kentucky School for the Deaf; I read for my MPhil at Trinity College Dublin, where the Deaf community in Ireland holds critical mass; and I now live in Washington, D.C. a short distance from Gallaudet University. Thus, while my childhood experiences of the Deaf community were either singular or voyeuristic, as an adult I have had the good fortune to live in communities with a rich local Deaf culture. I identify as "deaf," having been raised in a hearing family and cultural space. This chapter is grounded in my experiences of having to "pass" as hearing in some instances, or being hailed as "too deaf" in others, and a resulting search for work in the crosshairs of hearing and d/Deaf experience.

2. It is not lost on me that both films are film adaptations of popular theatrical productions, each with its own complicated relationship to oralism. *The Miracle Worker* tells the story of the deaf-blind Helen Keller's language acquisition with the assistance of Anne Sullivan; *Children of a Lesser God* is concerned with Sarah's desire to communicate in ASL instead of oral speech, despite her husband James' requests. As the 2017 Oscar-winning live action short *The Silent Child* demonstrates, oralism is still prevalent in families with deaf children who have little to no contact with the broader Deaf community and its culture.

3. In 1902, the first known use of film to record ASL captured a young woman signing the US national anthem. The ninety-second film, "Deaf Mute Girl Reciting Star Spangled Banner," captures the signer's passionate recitation in a full-body shot set against an American flag (Clark 2017). Eleven years later, in 1913, two-time president of the National Association of the Deaf George W. Veditz filmed *Preservation of the Sign Language* to argue for manual sign language education against the prevailing oralist mode of Deaf education. Veditz's film was later preserved in the National Film Registry by the Library of Congress. For more information, see Carol Padden (2004).

4. *Signing the Body Poetic* (2006), edited by Bauman et al., features a concise timeline of the "Video Period of ASL Literature" from 1960 to 2006 in their appendix A (pp. 244–50). This timeline traces how film technology and ASL have coeval developments throughout the twentieth century.

5. Woodward's capitalization of "Hearing" grammatically demonstrates a cultural orientation toward sound and spoken language instead of sign languages. I have maintained his capitalization in this specific citation, but throughout my work I do not capitalize hearing because most hearing people do not consciously identify "hearing" as a cultural identity marker.

6. The 21st Century Communications and Video Accessibility Act (CVAA) updates laws enacted before the early 1980s to reflect changes in technology, most significantly video and the internet. A full version is published online (see Federal Communications Commission 2017).

7. "Visucentric" refers to a cultural product or space created with visual access in mind. Optimal visual accessibility is preferable for d/Deaf persons, who may rely on visual cues and or prefer communicating vis-à-vis sign languages. This term, sometimes written as "visu-centric," has its lineage in the 2005 "DeafSpace Project" (DSP), a collaboration between architect Hansel Bauman and Gallaudet University's ASL Deaf Studies Department. Visucentric design was developed as a solution to intuitive architectural access for deaf experiences in the built environment, but as I argue, it has utility in cultural products, particularly cinema. For more information on visucentrism and Deaf Space, developed with architect Hansel Bauman (of hbhm Architects), see H-Dirksen L. Bauman (2004), Ansel Bauman (2008), Millam-Porteos (2008). See also Charlene A. Johnson's thesis on enhancing Deaf Space Design Guidelines (DSDG) by developing spatial practices using a Deaf cultural lens (2010).

8. I purposefully use "deaf" to describe characters who are functionally deaf but raised or presented as being outside of Deaf culture.

9. Scholarship in the *Deaf Studies Digital Journal* is available in both video-recorded ASL and as written English translations. To better understand the homological relationship between ASL and film, view the retelling of Clayton Valli's "Lone Sturdy Tree." The story uses various cinematic techniques, including medium- and low-angle shots, pan movements, and cross-cuts. Bauman and Murray ask viewers to "imagine the possibilities if we gave cameras to Deaf children so that they could tell their stories through the medium of film" (2009: 9).

10. For robust and thorough consideration of d/Deafness in television, see the results from Katherine A. Foss' 2014 study analyzing representations of deafness across forty programs with 254 episodes. The findings call for a diversity of d/Deaf characters and storylines to combat mainstream stigmatization and stereotypes.

11. SimCom, or "simultaneous communication," is the simultaneous use of spoken word and ASL, often by a hearing individual whose first or primary language is not ASL. SimComming often privileges the grammar of the spoken language, which fragments the meaning in ASL

due to inverted syntax or unclear topicalization, as well as other signing inconsistencies or errors. ASL usually follows Subject-Verb-Object or Time-Subject-Verb-Object word orders. Given my experience with lip-reading as a hearing aids-user raised in hearing culture, the temptation to SimCom in mixed company is frequently offset by the miscommunications that inevitably occur—communication errors are exacerbated when linguistic specificity is lost.

12. Chirsty Smith, the first Deaf contestant on the popular *Survivor* reality competition, is a notable example of a reality star who used her newfound visibility to advocate for the Deaf community and its culture. Following her 2003 appearance on *Survivor: The Amazon*, Smith created a children's show for Colorado's Rocky Mountain PBS called *Christy's Kids: Challenge Yourself* (2005) and co-founded the nonprofit Discovering Deaf Worlds, which endeavors to increase education access to deaf persons in developing countries.

13. Ridloff, like Frelich, was nominated as Best Actress in the three major American theatrical competitions: the Tony Awards, the Drama Desk Awards, and the Outer Critics Circle Awards.

14. Sanchez's reading of ASL language and poetry, as well as written-English poems and prose, attends to how signed language creates a palimpsestic layering of meanings when someone signs a story or poetry—the formal grammar and performative aspects of signed language ensures the body remains visible where it might otherwise be obscured in the printed language of words on a page.

15. Wailes has advised on most of the major Deaf culture productions from 2015 to 2018, including *Wonderstruck* (2017, dir. Todd Haynes), the third season of the ABC series *Quantico* (which features Marlee Matlin as an ex-FBI agent who lost her hearing following a bomb explosion), and Sundance Now's Deaf-created series *This Close*.

16. Harvard provides a direct link between the two short films. In *Signage*, he played one of Jonathan's Deaf who actively discouraged Jonathan from starting a relationship with Lex because he is hearing.

17. Fernandez was set to succeed I. King Jordan, Gallaudet's first Deaf president. Jordan was appointed in 1988 following Deaf President Now (DPN), an eight-day protest during which students advocated for a Deaf president following the Board of Trustees' selection of Elizabeth A. Zinser, the sole hearing candidate under consideration. Jordan later endorsed Fernandez, who was deaf but only learned ASL later in life. Organized under the banner "Unity for Gallaudet," Deaf students, faculty, and administrators felt that they were ignored during the selection process. Although reports that the oust was rooted in "Deaf politics" circulated in the media, many Gallaudet faculty, staff, students, and alumni maintained that their displeasure was rooted in Zinser's current performance and popularity as provost at the school.

18. For an account of the wide implications of the American eugenicist response to deafness, particularly concerning "racial hygiene" during the era of National Socialism in Germany, see Biesold (1999). Biesold's study details how d/Deaf persons were subjected to euthanasia, forced abortions, and sterilizations in attempts to eradicate hereditary deafness from the public body.

19. The hyperlink to *Sign*'s Indiegogo campaign created by co-writer and director Keenan-Bolger, "sign-a-silent-short-film-gay," indicates an early classification of *Sign* as a "gay film" instead of as a "Deaf film." As I am arguing, these categories are not an either/or, although the tag label does indicate which classification would be deemed more marketable on a crowdfunding platform.

CHAPTER 7

1. Subsequent to the 1908 Royal Commission on the Care and Control of the Feeble-Minded.
2. No sample size given.
3. The top administrative layer for asylums in the UK until they were incorporated into the NHS.
4. Family physician.

REFERENCES

Abeysekara, Ananda (2011), *The Politics of Postsecular Religion: Mourning Secular Futures*, Colombo: Social Scientists Association.

Adam, David (2013), "Mental Health: On the Spectrum," *Nature*, 496: 416–18.

Adams, D. L., and Nirmala Erevelles (2017), "Unexpected Spaces of Confinement: Aversive Technologies, Intellectual Disability, and 'Bare Life'," *Punishment & Society*, 19 (3): 348–65.

Adar, Einat (2017), "From Irish Philosophy to Irish Theatre: The Blind (Wo)man Made to See." *Estudios Irlandeses – Journal of Irish Studies*, 12 (1). Available online: https://www. estudiosirlandeses.org/2017/02/from-irish-philosophy-to-irish-theatre-the-blind-woman-made-to-see.

Aho, Tanja (2017), "Neoliberalism, Racial Capitalism, and Liberal Democracy: Challenging and Emerging Critical Analytic," 6 (1). Available online: https://csalateral.org/issue/6-1/forum-alt-humanities-institutionality-neoliberalism-racial-capitalism-aho.

Ajana, Btihaj (2017), "Digital Health and the Biopolitics of the Quantified Self," *Digital Health*, 3: 1–18.

Alston, Joe (1992), *The Royal Albert. Chronicles of an Era*, Lancaster: Centre for North-West Regional Studies, University of Lancaster.

Amar, Paul (2013), *The Security Archipelago: Human-Security States, Sexuality Politics, and the End of Neoliberalism*, Durham: Duke University Press.

American Psychiatric Association (n.d.a), "DSM history." Available online: https://www. psychiatry.org/psychiatrists/practice/dsm/history-of-the-dsm.

American Psychiatric Association (n.d.b), "DSM-5's Integrated Approach to Diagnosis and Classifications." Available online: http://www.psychiatry.org/File%20Library/Psychiatrists/ Practice/DSM/APA_DSM-5-Integrated-Approach.pdf.

American Psychiatric Association (n.d.c), "The Organization of DSM-5." Available online: https://www.psychiatry.org/File%20Library/Psychiatrists/Practice/DSM/APA_DSM_ Organization-of-DSM-5.pdf.

American Psychiatric Association (1952), *Diagnostic and Statistical Manual of Mental Disorders*, Washington, D.C.: American Psychiatric Association.

American Psychiatric Association (1968), *Diagnostic and Statistical Manual of Mental Disorders: DSM-II*, Washington, D.C.: American Psychiatric Association.

American Psychiatric Association (1980), *Diagnostic and Statistical Manual of Mental Disorders: DSM III*, Washington, D.C.: American Psychiatric Association.

American Psychiatric Association (2013), *Diagnostic and Statistical Manual of Mental Disorders: DSM-5*, Washington, D.C.: American Psychiatric Association.

Amesbury, Richard (2016), "Is the Body Secular? Circumcision, Religious Freedom, and Bodily Integrity," *Journal of the British Association for the Study of Religion*, 18: 1–10.

Anderson, Eric (2009), *Inclusive Masculinity*, London and New York: Routledge.

Anthamatten, Eric (2017), "Trump and the True Meaning of 'Idiot'." *The New York Times*. Available online: https://www.nytimes.com/2017/06/12/opinion/trump-and-the-true-meaning-of-idiot.html.

A Quiet Place (2018), [Film] Dir. John Krasinski, Hollywood, CA: Paramount Pictures, DVD.

Assmann, Jan (2009), *The Mosaic Distinction or The Price of Monotheism*, Redwood City: Stanford University Press.

Atkinson, Dorothy, and Jan Walmsley (2010), "History from the Inside: Towards an Inclusive History of Intellectual Disability," *Scandinavian Journal of Disability Research*, 12 (4): 273–86.

Atkinson, Dorothy, Mark Jackson, and Jan Walmsley (eds.) (1997), *Forgotten Lives: Exploring the History of Learning Disability*, Kidderminster: BILD.

Babel (2007), [Film] Dir. Alejandro G. Iñárritu, Hollywood, CA: Paramount Home Entertainment, DVD.

Baby Driver (2017), [Film] Dir. Edgar Wright, Culver City: Sony Home Pictures, DVD.

Baker, Bernadette, and Fiona Campbell (2006), "Transgressing Non-crossable Borders: Disability, Law, Schooling, And Nations," in Scott Danforth and Susan Gabel (eds.), *Vital Questions in Disability Studies and Education*, 319–46, New York: Peter Lang Publishers.

Ball, Stephen J. (2013), *Foucault, Power and Education*, New York and London: Routledge.

Barasch, Moshe (2001), *Blindness: The History of a Mental Image in Western Thought*, New York: Routledge.

Barney, Chuck (2011), "Chuck Barney: 'Switched at Birth' Another Winner for ABC Family," *The Mercury News*, June 28. Available online: www.mercurynews.com/2011/06/28/chuck-barney-switched-at-birth-another-winner-for-abc-family.

Barnhart, Robert (2015), *Chambers Dictionary of Etymology*, London: Chambers Harop Publishers.

Barton, Cassie, Jasper Homes, and Caroline Jacobs (2014), *Mobility Scooters: A Market Study*, London: Research Institute for Consumer Affairs.

Bateman Cannon, M. (2006), "Silent Stereotypes: The Representation of Deafness in Film," *Deaf Studies Today*, 2: 247–62.

Bauman, Hansel (2008), "Deaf Diverse Design Guide." Identifying the Principles of Deaf Space, November 9. Available online: http://www.dangermondarchitects.com/blog.

Bauman, H-Dirksen L. (2003), "Redesigning Literature: The Cinematic Poets of American Sign Language poetry," *Sign Language Studies*, 4 (1): 34–47.

Bauman, H-Dirksen L. (2004), "Audism: Exploring the Metaphysics of Oppression," *Journal of Deaf Studies and Deaf Education*, 9 (2): 239–46.

Bauman, H-Dirksen L., Jennifer L. Nelson, Heidi M. Rose (eds.) (2006), *Signing the Body Poetic*, Berkeley and Los Angeles: University of California Press.

Bauman, H-Dirksen L., and Joseph J. Murray (2009), "Reframing: From Hearing Loss to Deaf Gain," translated by Fallon Brizendine and Emily Schenker, *Deaf Studies Digital Journal*, 1: 1–10. Available online: http://dsdj.gallaudet.edu/assets/section/section2/entry19/DSDJ_entry19.pdf.

Bauman, H-Dirksen L., and Joseph J. Murray (eds.) (2014), *Deaf Gain: Raising the Stakes for Human Diversity*, Minneapolis: University of Minnesota Press.

Bayer, Ronald (1987), *Homosexuality and American Psychiatry: The Politics of Diagnosis*, Princeton: Princeton University Press.

Ben-Moshe, Liat (2013), "Disabling Incarceration: Connecting Disability to Divergent Confinements in the USA," *Sage Journals*, 39 (3): 385–402.

Ben-Moshe, Liat (2017), "Why Prisons are Not 'The New Asylums'," *Sage Journals*, 19 (3): 272–89.

Bentley, Peter (2012), Britain is Mobility Scooter Capital of Europe: 300,000 on Our Roads and Streets as Obesity and Number of Pensioners Soar, *The Daily Mail Online*, May 12. Available online: http://www.dailymail.co.uk/news/article-2143307/Britain-mobility-scooter-capital-Europe-300-000-roads.html.

Berker, Ennis Ata, Ata Husnu Berker, and Aaron Smith (1986), "Translation of Broca's 1865 Report: Localization of Speech in the Third Left Frontal Convolution," *Archives of Neurology*, 43 (10): 1065–72.

Berlant, Lauren (2011), *Cruel Optimism*, Durham: Duke University Press.

Bernstein, Elizabeth (2010), "Militarized Humanitarianism Meets Carceral Feminism: The Politics of Sex, Rights, and Freedom in Contemporary Antitrafficking Campaigns," *Signs*, 36 (1): 45–72.

Berry, Richard J. A. (1924), "The Problem of the Unfit," *The Herald*, May 3: 10–11.

Berry, Richard J. A. (1930), "The Physical Basis of Mind and the Diagnosis of Mental Deficiency," *Eugenics Review*, 22 (3): 171–82.

Berry, Richard J. A. (1939), *Your Brain and Its Story*, London: Oxford University Press.

Bérubé, Michael (2016), *The Secret Life of Stories: From Don Quixote to Harry Potter, How Understanding Intellectual Disability Changes Transforms the Way We Read*, New York: New York University Press.

Betcher, Sharon V. (2014), *Spirit and the Obligation of Social Flesh: A Secular Theology for the Global City*, New York: Fordham University Press.

Bhabha, Homi ([1994] 2012), *The Location of Culture*, London and New York: Routledge.

Biehl, João ([2005] 2013), *Vita: Live in a Zone of Social Abandonment*, Berkeley: University of California Press.

Biernoff, Suzanna (2017), *Portraits of Violence: War and the Aesthetics of Disfigurement*, Ann Arbor: University of Michigan Press.

Biesold, Horst (1999), *Crying Hands: Eugenics and Deaf People in Nazi Germany*, Washington, D.C.: Gallaudet University Press.

Birch, Kean, and Vlad Mykhnenko (eds.) (2010), *The Rise and Fall of Neoliberalism: The Collapse of an Economic Order?* London: Zed Books.

Birnbaum, Morton (1960), "The Right to Treatment," *American Bar Association Journal*, 46 (5): 499–505.

Bishop, Rollin (2012), "Are Women Really Being Electronically Tracked in Saudi Arabia?" *The Mary Sue*, November 23. Available online: https://www.themarysue.com/saudi-electronic-tracking.

Boisvert, Donald L., and Jay E. Johnson (eds.) (2012), *Queer Religion. Vol. 1: Homosexuality in Modern Religious History. Vol. 2: LGBT Movements and Queering Religion*, Santa Barbara: ABC-CLIO.

Bolt, David (2014), *The Metanarratives of Blindness: A Re-Reading of Twentieth-Century Anglophone Writing*, Ann Arbor: University of Michigan Press.

Bolt, David (2016). The Metanarrative of Blindness; A Re-reading of Twentieth-Century Anglophone Writing, Ann Arbor: University of Michigan Press.

Bolt, David (2018), *Cultural Disability Studies in Education: Interdisciplinary Navigations of the Normative Divide*, London: Routledge.

Boon, Marcus, Eric Cazdyn, and Timothy Morton (2015), *Nothing: Three Inquiries in Buddhism*, Chicago: University of Chicago Press.

Bourne, Rupert (2013). "WHO Global Burden," in *Global Burden of Blindness and VisualImpairment*. https://iapb.org/wp-content/uploads/Global-Burden-of-Disease-and-Vision-Impairment_Rupert-Bourne_16Sept2013.pdf.

Breaking Through (aired December 30, 1996), [TV Movie] Dir. Fred Gerber, *Lifetime*.

Brim, Matt (2014), *James Baldwin and the Queer Imagination*, Ann Arbor: University of Michigan Press.

Brown, Lesley (1993), *The New Shorter Oxford English Dictionary on Historical Principles*, Oxford: Clarendon Press.

Brown, Mark, Elaine James, and Chris Hatton (2017), *A Trade in People: The Inpatient Healthcare Economy for People with Learning Disabilities and/or Autism Spectrum Disorder*, University of Lancaster: CeDR Briefing Paper 2017:1. Available online: http://wp.lancs. ac.uk/cedr/files/2017/06/A-Trade-in-People-CeDR-2017-1.pdf.

Brown, Wendy (2015), *Undoing the Demos: Neoliberalism's Stealth Revolution*, Brooklyn: Zone Books.

Brueggemann, Brenda Jo (2009), *Deaf Subjects: Between Identities and Places*, New York: New York University Press.

Burstow, Bonnie, Brenda A. LeFrançois, and Shaindl Diamond (eds.) (2014), *Psychiatry Disrupted: Theorizing Resistance and Crafting the (R)Evolution*, Montreal: McGill-Queen's University Press.

Burton, Stacy (1995), "Benjy, Narrativity, and the Coherence of Compson History," *Cardozo Law and Literature* 7 (2): 207–28.

Butler, Judith (1990), *Gender Trouble: Feminism and the Subversion of Identity*, London and New York: Routledge.

Caldwell, Felicity (2018), New Queensland Trains Denied Human Rights Exemptions, *Brisbane Times*, March 3. Available online: https://www.brisbanetimes.com.au/politics/queensland/ new-queensland-trains-denied-human-rights-exemption-20180302-p4z2iz.html.

Campbell, Fiona Kumari (2009), *Contours of Ableism: The Production of Disability and Abledness*, Basingstoke: Palgrave Macmillan.

Campbell, Fiona Kumari (2014), "Geodisability Knowledge Production and International Norms: A Sri Lankan Case study," in Karen Soldatic and Helen Meekosha (eds.), *The Global Politics of Impairment and Disability: Processes and Embodiments*, 87–106, London: Routledge.

Campbell, Fiona Kumari (2017), "Queer Anti-Sociality and Disability Unbecoming: An Ableist Relations Project?" in O. Sircar and D. Jain (eds.), *New Intimacies/Old Desires: Law, Culture and Queer Politics in Neoliberal Times*, 280–316, New Delhi: Zubaan Books.

Campbell, Fiona Kumari (2019), "Precision Ableism: A Studies in Ableism Approach to Developing Histories of Disability and Abledment," *Rethinking History*, 22 (3): 138–56.

Campbell, Tom (2013), *Dyslexia. The Government of Reading*, Basingstoke: Palgrave Macmillan.

Carter, Angela, Theodora Danylevich, and Alyson Patsavas (2018), co-written call for papers on "Cripistemologies of Continuous Crisis" for the 2018 American Studies Association Meeting.

Carver, Raymond (2015), *What We Talk about When We Talk about Love: Love Stories*, New York: Vintage Books.

Chacaby, Maya (2011), "Kipimoojikewin: Articulating Anishinaabe Pedagogy Through Anishinaabemowin (Ojibwe Language) Revitalization," MA thesis, OISE of the University of Toronto. Available online: https://tspace.library.utoronto.ca/handle/1807/30080.

Charlton, James I. (1998), *Nothing about Us without Us: Disability Oppression and Empowerment*, Thousand Oaks: University of California Press.

Charlton, James I. (2010), "Peripheral Everywhere," *Journal of Literary & Cultural Disability Studies*, 4 (2): 195–200.

Children of a Lesser God (1986), [Film] Dir. By Randa Haines, Hollywood: Paramount Pictures, DVD.

Cholden, Louis S. A. (1958), *A Psychiatrist Works with Blindness*, New York: American Foundation for the Blind.

Chomsky, Noam (1959), "A Review of BF Skinner's Verbal Behavior," *Language*, 35 (1): 26–58.

Clare, Eli ([1999] 2015), *Exile and Pride: Disability, Queerness, and Liberation*, Durham: Duke University Press.

Clark, John Lee (2017), "ASL and 'The Star Spangled-Banner'." *Wordgathering* 11 (2). Available online: http://www.wordgathering.com/past_issues/issue42/essays/clark.html (accessed May 2, 2019).

Claustrophobia (2011), [Film] Dir. Harlan Schneider, Intelligent Pictures, streaming.

Clayton, Phillip (2007), "Boundaries Crossed and Uncrossable: Physical Science, Social Science, Theology," in Kevin Vanhoozer and Martin Warner (eds.), *Transcending Boundaries in Philosophy and Theology*, 91–104, Aldershot: Asgate Publishing.

Clegg, Joshua W. (2012), "Teaching about Mental Health and Illness through the History of the DSM," *History of Psychology*, 15 (4): 364–70.

Cole, Steven, Sarah Keenan, and Bob Diamond (eds.) (2013), *Madness Contested: Power and Practice*, London: PCCS Books.

Comstock, Gary D., and Susan E. Henking (eds.) (1997), *Que(e)rying Religion: A Critical Anthology*, New York: Continuum.

Corker, Marian, and Tom Shakespeare (2002), "Mapping the Terrain," in Marian Corker and Tom Shakespeare (eds.), *Disability/Postmodernity: Embodying Disability Theory*, 1–17, London: Continuum.

Cook, Hera (2004), *The Long Sexual Revolution: English Women, Sex, and Contraception 1800–1975*, Oxford: Oxford University Press.

Cooper, John Edward et al. (1972), *Psychiatric Diagnosis in New York and London: A Comparative Study of Mental Hospital Admissions*, Oxford: Oxford University Press.

Cooper, Rachel Valerie (2014), *Diagnosing the Diagnostic and Statistical Manual of Mental Disorders*, London: Karnac.

Cowley, Sophie (2015), "'Coming Out' as a Spoonie." *HuffPost Blog*, April 8. Available online: https://www.huffingtonpost.com/sophie-cowley/coming-out-as-a-spoonie_b_7013638.html.

Crossley, Nick (2006), *Contesting Psychiatry: Social Movements in Mental Health*, London: Routledge.

Crow, Liz (1996), "Including All of Our Lives: Renewing the Social Model of Disability," first published in *Encounters with Strangers: Feminism and Disability*, Jenny Morris (ed.), Toronto: Women's Press. Available online: http://www.roaring-girl.com/wp-content/uploads/2013/07/Including-All-of-Our-Lives.pdf.

Crow, Liz (2015), *Figures*, mass-sculptural durational performance. Available online: www.wearefigures.co.uk.

Crutchfield, Susan, and Marcy Epstein (2000), "Introduction," in Susan Crutchfield and Mary Epstein (eds.), *Points of Contact: Disability, Art, and Culture*, 1–20, Ann Arbor: University of Michigan Press.

Crow, Liz (2018), Keynote talk given at "Composing Disability: Crip Politics and the Crisis of Culture" at the George Washington University in Washington, D.C., March 22.

Das, Geeti (2016), "Mostly Normal: American Psychiatric Taxonomy, Sexuality, and Neoliberal Mechanisms of Exclusion," *Sexuality Research and Social Policy*, 13 (4): 390–401.

Davidson, Michael (2008), *Concerto for the Left Hand: Disability and the Defamiliar Body*, Ann Arbor: University of Michigan Press.

Davis, Lennard J. (1995a), *Bending over Backwards: Essays on Disability and the Body*, New York: New York University Press.

Davis, Lennard J. (1995b), *Enforcing Normalcy: Disability, Deafness, and the Body*, New York: Verso.

Davis, Lennard J. (2008), *Obsession: A History*, Chicago: University of Chicago Press.

Davis, Lennard J. (2018), "Quiet Places," *The Los Angeles Review of Books*, April 30. Available online: https://lareviewofbooks.org/article/quiet-places.

De Beer, E. S. (ed.) (1979), *The Correspondence of John Locke*, vol. 4, Oxford: Clarendon Press.

de Beauvoir, Simone ([1949] 2011), *The Second Sex*, trans. Constance Borde and Sheila Malovany-Chevallier, with an introduction by Judith Thurman, New York: Vintage.

Deafula (1975), [Film] Dir. Peter Wolf (as Peter Wechsberg), Signoscope, theatrical release.

Decker, Hannah S. (2013), *The Making of DSM-III: A Diagnostic Manual's Conquest of American Psychiatry*, New York: Oxford University Press.

Department for Transport (DfT) (2010), Consultation on proposed changes to the laws governing powered mobility scooters & powered wheelchairs (DfT-2010-10). Available online: https://www.gov.uk/government/uploads/system/uploads/attachment_data/file/2392/consultation-document.pdf.

Derrida, Jacques (1981), *Dissemination*, Chicago: University of Chicago Press.

Devlieger, Patrick J. (2005), "Generating a Cultural Model of Disability," *19th Congress of the European Federation of Associations of Teachers of the Deaf (FEAPDA)*, October 14–16. Available online: https://is.muni.cz/el/1441/jaro2015/SP_0002/um/50945627/51056873/culturalmodelofdisability.pdf.

Diderot, Denis ([1796] 2004), *Supplement to Bougainville's "Voyage"*, Salt Lake City: Project Guttenburg.

Diderot, Denis, and John le Rond d'Alembert (1750), *Encyclopédie de Diderot et d'Alembert Tome l – A à E*, Paris: A Geneve.

Didion, Joan ([1979] 2009), *The White Album*, New York: Farrar, Straus, Giroux.

Digby, Anne (1996), "Contexts and Perspectives," in David Wright and Anne Digby (eds.), *From Idiocy to Mental Deficiency. Historical perspectives on people with Learning Difficulties*, 1–21, London: Routledge.

Difficult People (2016), [TV show] Dir. Jeffrey Walker, Season 2, Episode 2, "Kessler Epstein Foundation," Hulu.

Donahue, Wendy (2013), "5 Myths about Being Deaf," *Chicago Tribune*, October 30. Available online: http://www.chicagotribune.com/lifestyles/health/sc-health-1030-justin-leblanc-20131030-story.html.

Donnelly, Grace (2017), "What You Don't Know, but Should, about the Slave Trade Happening in Libya Right Now", *Fortune Magazine*, November 29. Available online: http://fortune.com/2017/11/29/libya-slave-trade.

Drinkwater, Chris (2015), "Supported Living and the Production of Individuals," in Shelley Tremain (ed.), *Foucault and the Government of Disability*, 229–44, Ann Arbor: University of Michigan Press.

Duffin, Jackie (2010), *History of Medicine: A Scandalously Short Introduction*, 2nd edn., Toronto: University of Toronto Press.

Dumit, Joseph (2004), *Picturing Personhood: Brain Scans and Biomedical Identity*, New Jersey: Princeton University Press.

Durr, Patti (2016), "Deaf Cinema," in Genie Gertz and Patrick Boudreault (eds.), *The SAGE Deaf Studies Encyclopedia*, SAGE Publications, Inc: EBSCOhost. Available online: http://search.ebscohost.com/login.aspx?direct=true&db=nlebk&AN=1163208&site=ehost-live.

Ehrich, J. F. (2006), "Vygotskian Inner Speech and the Reading Process," *Australian Journal of Educational & Developmental Psychology*, 6: 12–25.

Eiesland, Nancy L. (1994), *The Disabled God: Towards a Liberatory Theology of Disability*, Nashville: Abingdon Press.

Elkins, Stanley (2000), *The Magic Kingdom*, New York: Dalkey Archive Press.

Ellis, Katie, and Mike Kent (eds.) (2017), *Disability and Social Media*, Abingdon: Routledge.

Engel, Antke (2013), "Lust auf Komplexität: Gleichstellung, Antidiskriminierung und die Strategie des Queerversity," *Feministische Studien*, 13 (2): pp. 39–45.

Erevelles, Nirmala (2011), *Disability and Difference in Global Contexts: Enabling a Transformative Body Politic*, New York: Palgrave Macmillan.

Farley, Wendy (1999), "'The Pain-Dispelling Draft': Compassion as a Practical Theology," *Perspectives in Religious Studies*, 26 (3): 291–302.

Faulkner, William ([1929] 1990), *As I Lay Dying: The Corrected Text*, New York: Vintage International.

Federal Communications Commission (2017), "Twenty-First Century Communications and Video Accessibility Act of 2010—Pub. L. 111-260," *FCC*, September 8. Available online: https://www. fcc.gov/consumers/guides/21st-century-communications-and-video-accessibility-act-cvaa.

Felman, Shoshana (1993), *What Does a Woman Want? Reading and Sexual Difference*, Baltimore and London: Johns Hopkins University Press.

Fitzgibbon, Kathleen (2003), "Modern-Day Slavery? The Scope of Trafficking in Persons in Africa," *African Security Review*, 12 (1): 81–9.

Foss, Katherine A. (2014), "Constructing Hearing Loss or 'Deaf Gain'? Voice, Agency, and Identity in Television's Representations of d/Deafness," *Critical Studies in Media Communication*, 31 (5): 426–47.

Foucault, Michel ([1966, 1970] 2005), *The Order of Things: An Archaeology of the Human Sciences*, London and New York: Routledge.

Foucault, Michel (1972), *The Archaeology of Knowledge*, London: Tavistock Publications.

Foucault, Michel (1977), *Discipline and Punish: The Birth of the Prison*, New York: Vintage.

Foucault, Michel (1980), *Power/Knowledge: Selected Interviews and Other Writings 1972–1977*, New York: Pantheon.

Foucault, Michel (1990), *The History of Sexuality, Volume 1: An Introduction*, New York: Vintage.

Foucault, Michel (2003), *Abnormal: Lectures at the College de France*, New York: Picador.

Foucault, Michel (2005), *History of Madness*, New York: Routledge.

Fraiberg, Selma (1977), *Insights from the Blind: Comparative Studies of Blind and Sighted Infants*, New York: Basic Books.

Fraser, Ben (ed.) (2016), *Cultures of Representation: Disability in World Cinema Contexts*, New York: Wallflower Press.

Freeman, Elizabeth (2016), "Hopeless Cases: Queer Chronicities and Gertrude Stein's 'Melanctha'," *Journal of Homosexuality*, 63 (3): 329–48.

Freud, Sigmund (1953), *On Aphasia: A Critical Study*, Oxford: International Universities Press.

Friedman, Thomas L. (2005), *The World Is Flat: A Brief History of the Twentieth-Century*, New York: Farrar, Straus, and Giroux.

Fritsch, Kelly, and Anne McGuire (2019), "Epigenetic Risk and the Spectral Politics of Disability," *Body and Society*, doi: 10.1177/1357034X19857138.

Frost, Robert (1995), *Mending Wall, Collected Poems, Prose and Plays*, New York: Library of America.

Frye, Lezlie (2018). "From U.S. Disability Rights Historiography to Crip Pasts: On Truth's Excess," Conference presentation at "Composing Disability: Crip Politics and the Crisis of Culture" at George Washington University, Washington, D.C., March 23.

Gaete-Reyes, Mariela (2015), "Citizenship and the Embodied Practice of Wheelchair Use," *Geoforum*, 64: 351–61.

García, Ofelia, and Debra Cole (2014), "Deaf Gains in the Study of Bilingualism and Bilingual Education," in H-Dirksen L. Bauman and Joseph J. Murray (eds.), *Deaf Gain: Raising the Stakes for Human Diversity*, 95–111, Minneapolis: University of Minnesota Press.

Garland-Thomson, Rosemarie (1997), *Extraordinary Bodies: Figuring Physical Disability in American Culture and Literature*, New York: Columbia University Press.

Garland-Thomson, Rosemarie (2004), "Integrating Disability, Transforming Feminist Theory," in Bonnie G. Smith and Beth Hutchison (eds.), *Gendering Disability*, 73–103, New Brunswick: Rutgers University Press.

Geary, Adam (2014), *State Intimacies: Antiblack Racism and the AIDS Epidemic*, New York: Palgrave Macmillan.

Gentleman, Amelia (2012), "The Trouble with Mobility Scooter," *The Guardian*, May 2. Available online: https://www.theguardian.com/society/2012/may/02/trouble-with-mobility-scooters.

Gevisser, Mark (2018), "House of Rainbow: LGBT Rights Balanced on the Pink Line," *Griffith Review*, 59. Available online: https://griffithreview.com/articles/house-of-rainbow-lgbt-rights-balanced-pink-line.

Gibson, William (1995), *The Difference Engine*, New York: Bantam.

Giddens, Anthony (1990), *The Consequences of Modernity*, Oxford: Oxford University Press.

Giddens, Anthony (1991), *Modernity and Self-Identity: Self and Society in the Late Modern Age*, Cambridge: Polity Press.

Gill, Frank A. (1933), *Evidence Prepared by the Medical Officers of Calderstones Institution for the Departmental Committee on Sterilization*, Calderstones Certified Institute for Mental Defectives, Lancashire County Archives Item HRBC/10/2.

Ginsberg, F., and Rayna Rapp (2015), "Making Disability Count: Demography, Futurity, and the Making of Disability Publics," *Somatosphere*. Available online: http://somatosphere.net/2015/05/making-disability-count-demography-futurity-and-the-making-of-disability-publics.html.

Goffman, Irving (1959), *The Presentation of Self in Everyday Life*, New York, NY: Anchor Books, Doubleday.

Goffman, Erving (1963), *Stigma. Notes on the Management of Spoiled Identity*, London: Penguin.

Goffman, Erving (1961, 1968), *Asylums. Essays on the Social Situation of Mental Patients and Other Inmates*, London: Penguin.

Goldenberg, Naomi R. (2015), "The Category of Religion in the Technology of Governance: An Argument for Understanding Religions as Vestigial States," in Trevor Stack, Naomi Goldenberg, and Timothy Fitzgerald (eds.), *Religion as a Category of Governance and Sovereignty*, 280–92, Leiden: Brill.

Goode, Erich, and Nachman Ben-Yehuda (2009), *Moral Panics: The Social Construction of Deviance*, 2nd edn., Chichester: Wiley-Blackwell.

Goodey, C. F. (2016), *Learning Disability and Inclusion Phobia: Past, Present and Future*, Abingdon: Routledge.

Goodley, Dan (2001), "'Learning Difficulties', the Social Model of Disability and Impairment: Challenging Epistemologies," *Disability & Society*, 16 (2): 207–31.

Goodley, Dan (2013), "Dis/entangling Critical Disability Studies," *Disability & Society*, 28 (5): 631–44.

Goodley, Dan (2017), *Disability Studies: An Interdisciplinary Introduction*, 2nd edn., London: SAGE.

Gopal, Guru (2011), *Humiliation: Claims and Context*, Delhi: Oxford University Press.

Gould, Stephen Jay (1996), *The Mismeasure of Man*, New York: W.W. Norton & Company.

Gould, Stephen Jay (2002), *The Structure of Evolutionary Theory*, Cambridge, MA: Belknap Press.

Grant, Julia (1998), *Raising Baby by the Book: The Education of American Mothers*, New Haven: Yale University Press.

Gretton, Richard H. (1913), *A Modern History of The English People, Vol. I, 1880–1898*, London: Grant Richards.

Griffin, John Howard (2004), *Scattered Shadows*, Maryknoll: Orbis Books.

Grob, Gerald N. (1991), "Origins of DSM-I: A Study in Appearance and Reality," *American Journal of Psychiatry*, 148 (4): 421–31.

Grunbaum, Adolf (1984), *The Foundations of Psychoanalysis: A Philosophical Critique.* Thousand Oaks: University of California Press.

Hacking, Ian (1983), "Biopower and the Avalanche of Printed Numbers," *Humanities in Society*, 5: 279–95.

Hacking, Ian (2002), *Historical Ontology*, Cambridge, MA, and London: Harvard University Press.

Hahn-Beer, Edith (2001), *The Nazi Officer's Wife: How One Jewish Woman Survived the Holocaust*, New York: Abacus Publishers.

Halfacree, Keith (1996), "Out of Place in the Country: Travellers and the 'Rural Idyll'," *Antipode*, 28 (1): 42–72.

Hall, Lesley A. (2012), *Sex, Gender, and Social Change in Britain since 1880*, 2nd edn., London: Macmillan Press.

Halliwell, Martin (2014), *Therapeutic Revolutions: Medicine, Psychiatry, and American Culture, 1945–1970*, New Brunswick: Rutgers University Press.

Haraway, Donna J. (1991), *Simians, Cyborgs, and Women: The Reinvention of Nature*, New York: Routledge.

Hardt, Michael, and Antonio Negri (2005), *Multitude: War and Democracy in the Age of Empire*, New York: Penguin.

Harmon, Kristen (2010), "Deaf Matters: Compulsory Hearing and Ability Trouble," in Susan Burch and Alison Kafer (eds.), *Deaf and Disability Studies: Interdisciplinary Perspectives*, 21–47, Washington, D.C.: Gallaudet University Press.

Harvey, David (2005), *A Brief History of Neoliberalism*, Oxford: Oxford University Press.

Hatfield, Mark (1995), "'The War against Disease and Disability', Albert Lasker Public Service Award," *Journal of the American Medical Association*, 274: 1077.

Havelock, Eric Alfred (1986), *The Muse Learns to Write: Reflections on Orality and Literacy*, New Haven: Yale University Press.

HBBM Architecture (n.d.), *Deaf Space Design Guidelines*. http://www.hbhmarchitecture.com/index.php?/ongoing/Deaf-space-design-guide.

Healey, Devon (2019), *Blindness in V Acts: Disability Studies as Critical Creative Inquiry*, Toronto: University of Toronto, unpublished PhD diss.

Hear Me (2009), [Film] Dir. Fen-fen Cheng, KAM, DVD.

Heidegger, Martin ([1953] 1977), "The Question Concerning Technology," in David Krell (ed.), *Martin Heidegger Basic Writings*, 284–317, New York: Harper & Row.

Hindmarch, Heather (1992), "Lisieux Hall and the Provision of Services to People with Learning Difficulties in Lancashire," Ch. 3, MA diss. submitted to Lancashire Polytechnic. Available online: http://www.lancslearningdisabilityinstitutions.org.uk/content/catalogue_item/heather-hindmarch/calderstones-brockhall-examples-institutional-care.

Hobsbawm, Eric J. (2012), *Nations and Nationalism since 1780: Programme, Myth Reality*, Cambridge, UK: Cambridge University Press.

Houts, Arthur C. (2000), "Fifty Years of Psychiatric Nomenclature: Reflections on the 1943 War Department Technical Bulletin, Medical 203," *Journal of Clinical Psychology*, 56: 935–67.

Hubley, J., and C. Gilbert (2006), "Eye Health Promotion and the Prevention of Blindness in Developing Countries: Critical Issues," *British Journal of Ophthalmology*, 90 (3): 279–84.

Hughes, Bill (2009), "Wounded/Monstrous/Abject: A Critique of the Disabled Body in the Sociological Imaginary," *Disability and Society*, 24 (4): 399–410.

Hull, John M. (1997), *On Sight and Sightedness: A Journey into the World of Blindness*, Oxford: Oneworld Publications.

Human Flow: A Film (2017), [Documentary film] Dir. Ai Weiwei, Participant Media & Amazon Studios, in association with AC Films.

I Love You, But (1998) [Film] Dir. Peter Wolf, Peter Wolf Production, theatrical release.

Inaba, Carrie Ann (2016), "'Dancing With The Stars' Season 22 Blog: Week 2," *Access Hollywood*, March 29. www.accessonline.com/articles/carrie-ann-inabas-dancing-stars-season-22-blog-week2/#uwmYQqpEgT3m3oA0.99.

Isherwood, Lisa, and David Harris (2014), *Radical Otherness: Sociological and Theological Approaches*, London and New York: Routledge.

Jamison, Peter (2018a), "D.C.'s Opioid Epidemic: As African American heroin overdoses skyrocketed the city ignored life-saving strategies," *The Washington Post*, December 19. Available online: https://www.washingtonpost.com/graphics/2018/local/dc-opioid-epidemic-response-african-americans.

Jamison, Peter (2018b), Twitter post, December 18, 9:55 a.m. Available online: https://twitter.com/PeteJamison/status/1075041855824412673.

Jericho (2006–8), [TV series] Created by Stephen Chbosky, Josh Schaer, and Jonathan E. Steinberg, aired September 20, 2006–March 25, 2008, on CBS.

Jenseits der Stille (Beyond Silence) (1996), [Film] Dir. Caroline Link, Vancouver, British Columbia: Lionsgate, DVD.

Johnson, Charlene A (2010), "Articulation of Deaf and Hearing Spaces Using Deaf Space Design Guidelines: A Community Based Participatory Research with the Albuquerque Sign Language Academy." Available online: https://digitalrepository.unm.edu/arch_etds/18 (accessed December 2, 2018).

Johnson, Merri Lisa (2010), *Girl in Need of a Tourniquet: Memoir of a Borderline Personality*, Berkeley: Seal Press.

Johnson, Merri Lisa, and Robert McRuer (2014), "Cripistemologies: Introduction," *Journal of Literary & Cultural Disability Studies* 8 (2): 149–69.

Jones, Edgar, Nicola T. Fear, and Simon Wessely (2007), "Shell Shock and Mild Traumatic Brain Injury: A Historical Review," *American Journal of Psychiatry*, 164 (11): 1641–5.

Kabachnik, Peter (2010), "Place Invaders: Constructing the Nomadic Threat in England," *Geographical Review*, 100 (1): 90–108.

Kafer, Alison (2013), *Feminist Queer Crip*, Bloomington: Indiana University Press.

Karah, Hemchandran (2019), "Blind Culture and Cosmologies: Notes from Ved Mehta's Continent of India," in Anita Ghai (ed.), *Disability in South Asia: Knowledge and Experience*, Thousand Oaks: Sage Publications.

Kassell, Lauren (2013), "Medical Understandings of the Body, c.1500–1750," in Sarah Toulalan and Kate Fisher (eds.), *The Routledge History of Sex and the Body: 1500 to the Present*, 57–74, London and New York: Routledge.

Kawa, Shadia, and James Giordano (2012), "A Brief Historicity of the *Diagnostic and Statistical Manual of Mental Disorders*: Issues and Implications for the Future of Psychiatric Canon and Practice," *Philosophy, Ethics and Humanities in Medicine*, 7: 2.

Keefe, Patrick Radden (2017), "The Family That Built an Empire of Pain," *The New Yorker*, October 30.

Keenan-Bolger, Andrew (2016), "SIGN—A Silent Short Film," *Indiegogo*. Available online: https://www.indiegogo.com/projects/sign-a-silent-short-film-gay#.

Keller, Helen (1904a; 2004b), *The World I Live in*, New York: The New York Review.

Kemp, Jonathan (2009), "Queer Past, Queer Present, Queer Future," *Graduate Journal of Social Science*, 6 (1): 3–21.

Kim, Jim Yon, Joyce V. Millen, Alec Irwin, and John Gershman (eds.) (2000), *Dying for Growth: Global Inequality and the Health of the Poor*, Monroe: Common Courage Press.

Kim, Jina B. (2017), "Toward a Crip-Of-Color Critique: Thinking With Minich's 'Enabling Whom'?" *Lateral*, 6 (1). Available online: http://csalateral.org/issue/6-1/forum-alt-humanities-critical-disability-studies-crip-of-color-critique-kim.

Kimmel, Michael S. (1994), "Masculinity as Homophobia: Fear, Shame, and Silence in the Construction of Gender Identity," in Harry Brod and Michael Kaufman (eds.), *Theorizing Masculinities*, 119–42, Thousand Oaks: SAGE Publications.

Kincheloe, Pamela (2018), "'A Quiet Place' Falls into a Tired Trope about Deafness," *Huffington Post*, April 14. Available online: https://www.huffingtonpost.com/entry/opinion-kincheloe-quiet-place-deaf-people_us_5ad10645e4b0edca2cb9acc6.

King, Noel, and Andrew Kolodny, Interview (2017), "Why is the Opioid Epidemic Overwhelmingly White?," *All Things Considered*, National Public Radio, November 4. Available online: https://www.npr.org/2017/11/04/562137082/why-is-the-opioid-epidemic-overwhelmingly-white.

King, Thomas (2003), *The Truth About Stories: A Native Narrative*, Toronto: House of Anansi Press.

King v Jetstar Airways Pty Ltd (No 2) 11, [2012] FCA 8, 2012; 286 ALR 149. Australia.

Kleege, Georgina (1999), *Sight Unseen*, New Haven: Yale University Press.

Kleege, Georgina (2005), "Blindness and Visual Culture: An Eye-Witness Account," *Journal of Visual Culture*, 4 (2): 179–90.

Klobas, L. E. (1998), *Disability Drama in Television and Film*, Jefferson: McFarland.

Knighton, Ryan (2007), *Cockeyed: A Memoir of Blindness*. New York: PublicAffairs.

Knittel, Susanne (2014), *The Historical Uncanny: Disability, Ethnicity, and the Politics of Holocaust Memory*, New York: Modern Languages Initiative.

Kohl, Herbert (1993), "The Myth of 'Rosa Parks the Tired'. Teaching about Rosa Parks and the Montgomery Bus Boycott," *Multicultural Education*, 1 (2): 6–10.

Konik, Adrian (2009), *Buddhism and Transgression: The Appropriation of Buddhism in the Contemporary West*, Leiden and Boston: Brill.

Krentz, Christopher B. (2016), "The Camera as Printing Press: How Film Has Influenced ASL Literature," in Dirksen L. Bauman, Jennifer L. Nelson, and Heidi M. Rose (eds.), *Signing the Body Poetic*, 51–70, Berkeley and Los Angeles: University of California Press.

Kress, Gunther (2009), *Multimodality: A Social Semiotic Approach to Contemporary Communication*, London: Routledge.

Kudlick, Catherine (2005), "The Blindman's Harley: White Canes and Gender Identity in America," *Signs*, 30 (2): 1589–606.

Kumar, Naveen (2018), "Pushing Deaf Storytelling Past The Tipping Point," *Entertainment Tonight*, May 4. Available online: https://www.etonline.com/how-nyle-dimarco-shoshannah-stern-and-others-are-pushing-deaf-storytelling-past-the-tipping-point?linkId=51329392.

Kupfer, David J., Michael B. First, and Darrel A. Regier (eds.) (2002), *A Research Agenda for DSM-V*, Washington, D.C.: American Psychiatric Association.

Kuppers, Petra (2014), *Studying Disability Arts and Culture: An Introduction*. London and New York: Palgrave Macmillan.

La vida secreta de las palabras (*The Secret Life of Words*) (2005), [Film] Dir. Isabel Coixet, Universal City: Universal Pictures Home Entertainment, DVD.

Labuski, Christine (2015), *It Hurts Down There: The Bodily Imaginaries of Female Genital Pain*, Albany: SUNY Press.

Lakoff, George (1987), *Women, Fire, and Dangerous Things: What Categories Reveal about the Mind*, Chicago and London: University of Chicago Press.

Lane, Harlan (2002), "Do Deaf People Have a Disability?" *Sign Language Studies*, 2 (4): 356–79.

Lane, Harlan (2005), "Ethnicity, Ethics, and the Deaf-World," *Journal of Deaf Studies and Deaf Education*, 10 (3): 291–310.

Langan, Celeste (2001), "Mobility Disability," *Public Culture*, 13 (3): 459–84.

Lapage, Charles P., and Mary Dendy (1911), *Feeblemindedness in Children of School Age*, Manchester: University of Manchester Press.

Laplanche, Jean, and Jean-Bertrand Pontalis (1973), *The Language of Psycho-Analysis*, London: Hogarth Press.

Latour, Bruno (2012), *We Have Never Been Modern*, Cambridge, MA: Harvard University Press.

LeDeR (2018), *Learning Disabilities Mortality Review (LeDeR) Programme Annual Report*. University of Bristol Norah Fry Centre for Disability Studies. Available online: http://www.bristol.ac.uk/sps/news/2018/leder-report.html.

Leibetseder, Doris (2016), "Reproductive Ethics: An Example of an Allied Dis/Ability-Queer-Feminist Justice," in Bee Scherer (ed.), *Queering Paradigms VI: Interventions, Ethics, and Glocalities*, 131–46, Oxford: Peter Lang.

Leigh, Irine W. (2009), *A Lens on Deaf Identities*, New York: Oxford University Press.

Lerner, Miriam Nathan, and Edna Edith Sayers (2016), "Film: Deaf Characters," in Genie Gertz and Patrick Boudreault (eds.), *The SAGE Deaf Studies Encyclopedia*, SAGE Publications: EBSCOhost. Available online: search.ebscohost.com/login.aspx?direct=true&db=nlebk&AN=1163208&site=ehost-live.

Levin, David Michael (1997), *Sites of Vision: The Discursive Construction of Sight in the History of Philosophy*, Cambridge, MA: MIT Press.

Lewis, Bradley (2016), "A Mad Fight: Psychiatry and Disability Activism," in Lennard Davis (ed.), *The Disability Studies Reader*, New York: Routledge.

Lewis, Charlton (1991), *Elementary Latin Dictionary*, Oxford: Oxford University Press.

Lewthwaite, Sarah (2011), "Disability 2.0: Student Dis/Connections. A Study of Student Experiences of Disability and Social Networks on Campus in Higher Education," Unpublished thesis submitted to the University of Nottingham. Available online: http://etheses.nottingham.ac.uk/2406/1/Final_Thesis_Accessible.pdf.

Lifton, Robert Jay (1986), *The Nazi Doctors: Medical Killing and the Psychology of Genocide*, New York: Basic Books.

Lipsky, Michael (1980), *Street-Level Bureaucracy: Dilemmas of the Individual in Public Services*, New York: Russell Sage Foundation.

Listen To Your Heart (2010) [Film] Dir. Matt Thompson, Osiris Entertainment, DVD.

Longmore, Paul K. (2003), "Screening Stereotypes: Images of Disabled People in Television and Motion Pictures," in *Why I Burned My Book: And Other Essays on Disability*, 131–47, Philadelphia: Temple University Press.

MacPherson, Crawford Brough (1964), *The Political Theory of Possessive Individualism: Hobbes to Locke*, London: Clarendon Press.

Magee, Bryan, and Martin Milligan (1995), *On Blindness: Letters between Bryan Magee and Martin Milligan*, Oxford: Oxford University Press.

Manderson, Lenore, and Carolyn Smith-Morris (2010), *Chronic Conditions, Fluid States: Chronicity and the Anthropology of Illness*, New Brunswick: Rutgers University Press.

Manning, Lynn (2000 [revised unpublished script 2007]), *Weights*, written and performed by Lynn Manning; Off Broadway Premiere by Theatre By The Blind, 2004.

Marcus, Mary Brophy (2016), "Celebrex Arthritis Drug Study Surprises Heart Experts," *CBS News*, November 13. Available online: https://www.cbsnews.com/news/celebrex-arthritis-nsaid-drug-study-surprises-cardiovascular-heart-experts.

Martel, Yann (2012), *The Life of Pi*, Edinburgh: Canongate Books.

Mason, Mark (2015), "The Mobility Scooter Plague," *The Spectator*, April 11. Available online: http://www.spectator.co.uk/2015/04/the-mobility-scooter-plague.

Mason, Mark (2018), "Compulsory Subtitles? I Read 'Em and Weep," *The Spectator*, January 6. Available online: https://www.spectator.co.uk/2018/01/compulsory-subtitles-i-read-em-and-weep.

Master of None (2017), [TV series] Dir. Alan Yang, Season 2, Episode 6, "New York, I Love You," Netflix, May 12, streaming.

Masters, Robert A. (2010), *Spiritual Bypassing: When Spirituality Disconnects Us from What Really Matters*, Berkeley: North Atlantic Books.

Mayes, Rick, and Allan V. Horwitz (2005), "DSM-III and the Revolution in the Classification of Mental Illness," *Journal of the History of the Behavioral Sciences*, 41 (3): 249–67.

Mbembé, J.-A., and Libby Meintjes (2003), "Necropolitics," *Public Culture*, 15 (1): 11–40.

McCausland, Ruth, and Eileen Baldry (2017), "'I Feel Like I Failed Him by Ringing the Police': Criminalising Disability in Australia," *Punishment & Society*, 19 (3): 290–309.

McDermott, Ray, Shelley Goldman, and Hervé Varenne (2006), "The Cultural Work of Learning Disabilities," *Educational Researcher*, 35 (6): 12–17.

McGinn, Robert (1990), "What is Technology?" in Larry Hickman (ed.), *Technology as a Human Affair*, 10–25, New York: McGraw Hill.

McGuire, Anne (2017), "De-regulating Disorder: On the Rise of the Spectrum as a Neoliberal Metric of Human Value," *Journal of Literary and Cultural Disability Studies*, 11 (4): 402–21.

McRuer, Robert (2006), *Crip Theory: Cultural Signs of Queerness and Disability*, New York: New York University Press.

McRuer, Robert (2018), *Crip Times: Disability, Globalization, and* Resistance, New York: New York University Press.

Medoff, Mark (1987), *Children of a Lesser God*, Salt Lake City: Gibs M. Smith, Inc.

Mehta, Ved (1987), *Vedi*, New York: Norton.

Melbourne Argus (1912), "Criminals and Brains. A Professor's Deductions," November 6.

Merleau-Ponty, Maurice ([1945] 1958), *Phenomenology of Perception*, New York: Routledge Classic.

Meseguer, Alicia Z. (2012), "Reviews: Moshe Barasch, *Blindness: The History of a Mental Image in Western Thought* (London and New York: Routledge, 2001)," *Oxford Literary Review*, 26 (1), 197–202.

Metrocosm (2017), *Visualizing the Flow of Asylum Seekers into the Industrialized World*, February 9. Available online: http://metrocosm.com/asylum-seekers.

Metzl, Jonathan Michel (2010), *The Protest Psychosis: How Schizophrenia Became a Black Disease*, Boston: Beacon Press.

MHA (2016), *The Mental Health Bell*. Available online: http://www.mentalhealthamerica.net/bell.

MHA of South Central Kansas (n.d.), *The Bell*. Available online: http://www.mhasck.org/who_ we_are/thebell.html.

Michalko, Rod (1998), *The Mystery of the Eye and the Shadow of Blindness*, Toronto: University of Toronto Press.

Michalko, Rod (1999), *The Two in One: Walking with Smokie, Walking with Blindness*, Philadelphia: Temple University Press.

Michalko, Rod (2002a), *The Difference That Disability Makes*, Philadelphia: Temple University Press.

Michalko, Rod (2002b), "Estranged-Familiarity," in Marian Corker and Tom Shakespeare (eds.), *Disability and Postmodernity: Embodying Disability Theory*, 175–84, London: Continuum.

Minich, Julie Avril (2016), "Enabling Whom? Critical Disability Studies Now," *Lateral*, 5 (1). Available online: http://csalateral.org/issue/5-1/forum-alt-humanities-critical-disability-studies-now-minich.

Milam, Lorenzo W. (1993), *CripZen: A Manual for Survival*, San Diego: Mho & Mho Works.

Milam-Porteous, Amanda (2008), "Designing for the Deaf," *Accommodations for the Deaf: Designing*, LifePrint, November 28. Available online: http://www.lifeprint.com/asl101/ topics/accommodationsforthedeaf02.htm.

Miller, Brian R. (2015), "History of the Blind," in *Encylopaedia Britannica Online*. Available online: https://www.britannica.com/topic/history-of-the-blind-1996241.

Mills, China (2013), *Decolonizing Global Mental Health: The Psychiatrization of the Majority World*, London: Routledge.

Milroy, Lesley, and James Milroy (2002), *Authority in Language: Investigating Standard English*, London: Routledge.

Mitchell, David (2002), "Narrative Prosthesis and the Materiality of Metaphor," in Sharon Snyder, Brenda Jo Brueggemann, and Rosemarie Garland-Thomson (eds.), *Disability Studies: Enabling the Humanities*, 15–30, New York: The Modern Language Association of America.

Mitchell, David T., and Sharon L. Snyder (2005), *Cultural Locations of Disability*, Chicago: University of Chicago Press.

Mitchell, David T., and Sharon L. Snyder (2000), *Narrative Prosthesis: Disability and the Dependencies of Discourse*, Ann Arbor: University of Michigan Press.

Mitchell, David T., and Sharon L. Snyder (2003), "The Eugenic Atlantic: Race, Disability and the Making of an International Eugenic Science 1800–1945," *Disability and Society*, 18 (7): 843–64.

Mitchell, David T., and Sharon L. Snyder (2015), *The Biopolitics of Disability. Neoliberalism, Ablenationalism, and Peripheral Embodiment*, Ann Arbor: University of Michigan Press.

Mitchell, Ross E. (2005), "A Brief Summary of Estimates for the Size of the Deaf Population in the USA Based on Available Federal Data and Published Research," Gallaudet Research Institute, February 15. Available online: https://research.gallaudet.edu/Demographics/deaf-US.php.

Moalem, Sharon, and Jonathan Prince (2008), *Survival of the Sickest: The Surprising Connections Between Disease and Longevity*, New York: Harper Perennial.

Mollow, Anna (2014), "Criphystemologies: What Disability Theory Needs to Know About Hysteria," *Journal of Literary & Cultural Disability Studies*, 8 (2): 185–201.

Mollow, Anna (2017), "Unvictimizable: Toward a Fat Black Disability Studies," *African American Review*, 50 (2): 105–21.

Morris, S. (2017), Care Home Directors Convicted Over "Horrific" Learning Disability Regime. *The Guardian*, June 7. Available online: https://www.theguardian.com/society/2017/jun/07/care-home-directors-convicted-over-devon-learning-disability-regime.

Morrison, Linda (2005), *Talking Back to Psychiatry: The Psychiatric Consumer/Survivor/Ex-patient Movement*, New York: Routledge.

Morrison, Toni ([1970] 2007), *The Bluest Eye*, New York: Vintage Books.

Morrison, Toni ([1987] 2004), *Beloved*, New York: Vintage Books.

Moschos, Marlita M. (2014). "Physiology and Psychology of Vision and its Disorders: A Review," *Medical Hypothesis, Discovery and Innovation in Ophthalmology*, 3 (3): 83–90.

Mounsey, Chris (2014), "Introduction: Variability—Beyond Sameness and Difference," in Chris Mounsey (ed.), *The Idea of Disability in the Eighteenth Century*, 1–27, Lewisburg: Bucknell University Press.

Mrozik, Susanne (2007), *Virtuous Bodies: The Physical Dimensions of Morality in Buddhist Ethics*, Oxford: Oxford University Press.

Muñoz, José Esteban (2009), *Cruising Utopia: The Then and There of Queer Futurity*, New York: New York University Press.

Murphy, Michelle (2017), *The Economization of Life*, Durham: Duke University Press.

Mutu, Wangechi (2013), "The End of Eating Everything," courtesy of the artist and Gladstone Gallery, commissioned by the Nasher Museum of Art at Duke University, Durham, North Carolina, © 2013 Wangechi Mutu and Wangechi Mutu Studio.

Nelson, Alondra (2011), *Body and Soul: The Black Panther Party and the Fight Against Medical Discrimination*, Minneapolis: University of Minnesota Press.

Nicolls, George N. (2006), "Mobility," *Nick's Poetry Corner*. Available online: http://www.nickspoetry.co.uk/poet/mobility.htm.

Niebuhr, Richard (1998), "Anglo-Saxon Destiny and Responsibility," in Conrad Cherry (ed.), *God's New Israel Religious Interpretations of American Destiny*, 296–302, Chapel Hill: University of North Carolina Press.

Nirje, Bengt (1982), *The Basis and Logic of the Normalization Principle*, Sixth International Congress of IASSMD, Toronto.

Ng, Edwin (2016), *Buddhism and Cultural Studies: A Profession of Faith*, London: Palgrave Macmillan.

Nnamdi, Kojo (2019), "The Neglected Opioid Crisis in Washington," *The Kojo Nnamdi Show*, January 10. Available online: https://thekojonnamdishow.org/shows/2019-01-10/the-neglected-opioid-crisis-in-washington.

No Ordinary Hero: The SuperDeafy Movie ([2013] 2015), [Film] Dir. Troy Kotsur, Kimstim, Inc., DVD.

Norman, Jane (2003), "Theorizing a Deaf Cinema," *BAMPFA*. February 23. Available online: https://bampfa.org/event/theorizing-deaf-cinema.

Oliver, Michael (1993), *"What's So Wonderful about Walking?" Inaugural Professorial Lecture*, London: University of Greenwich.

Ong, Walter J. (2005), *Ramus, Method and The Decay of Dialogue: From the Art of Discourse to the Art of Reason*, Chicago: University of Chicago Press.

Orenji deizu (*Orange Days*) (2011), [TV series] Created by Eriko Kitagawa, aired April 11–June 20, 2011, on TBS.

Padden, Carol (2004), "Translating Veditz," *Sign Language Studies*, 4 (3): 244–60.

Park, Jin Y. (ed.) (2006), *Buddhism and Deconstruction*, New York: Rowman and Littlefield.

Park, Jin Y. (2011), *Buddhism and Postmodernity: Zen, Huayan, and the Possibility of Buddhist Postmodern Ethics*, Lanham: Lexington.

Parker, Richard (1998), *Beneath the Equator: Cultures of Desire, Male Homosexuality, and Emerging Gay Communities in Brazil*, Abingdon: Routledge.

Passanante Elman, Julie (2014), *Chronic Youth: Disability, Sexuality, and U.S. Media Cultures of Rehabilitation*, New York: New York University Press.

Patsavas, Aly (2014), "Toward a Cripistemology of Pain," *Journal of Literary & Cultural Disability Studies*, 8 (2): 203–18.

Pharr, Suzanne (1997), *Homophobia: A Weapon of Sexism*, Berkeley: Chardon Press.

Philo, Chris (2014), "Foreword," in Murray K. Simpson (ed.), *Modernity and the Appearance of Idiocy: Intellectual Disability as a Regime of Truth*, New York and Lampeter: Edwin Mellen Press.

Pickens, Therí (ed.) (2017), Special Issue on Blackness and Disability, *African American Review* 50 (2).

Pitts-Taylor, Victoria (2016), *The Brain's Body: Neuroscience and Corporeal Politics*, Durham: Duke University Press.

Plemya (The Tribe) (2014), [Film] Dir. Myroslav Slaboshpytskyi Austin: Drafthouse Films, DVD.

Price, Margaret (2011), *Mad at School: Rhetorics of Mental Disability in Academic Life*, Ann Arbor: University of Michigan Press.

Price, Margaret (2015), "The Bodymind Problem and the Possibilities of Pain," *Hypatia: A Journal of Feminist Philosophy*, 30 (1): 268–84.

Puar, Jasbir (2012), "Coda: The Cost of Getting Better: Suicide, Sensation, Switchpoints," *GLQ*, 18 (1): 149–58.

Puar, Jasbir (2017), *The Right to Maim: Debility, Capacity, Disability*, Durham: Duke University Press.

Reid, D. Kim, and Jan Weatherly Valle (2004), "The Discursive Practice of Learning Disability: Implications for Instruction and Parent–School Relations," *Journal of Learning Disabilities*, 37 (6): 466–81.

Rembis, Michael (2014), "The New Asylums: Madness and Mass Incarceration in the Neoliberal Era," in Liat Ben-Moshe, Chris Chapman, and Allison Carey (eds.), *Disability Incarcerated: Imprisonment and Disability in the United States and Canada*, 139–59, New York: Palgrave Macmillan.

Rembis, Michael (2017), *A Secret Worth Knowing: Living Mad Lives in the Shadow of the Asylum*, Paper delivered at the Disability and the Emotions Seminar Series, Centre for Culture and Disability Studies, Liverpool Hope University, May 10.

Ritchie, Andrea (2017), *Invisible No More: Police Violence against Black Women and Women of Color*, Boston: Beacon Press.

Rose, Nikolas, and Joelle Abi-Rached (2013), *Neuro: The New Brain Sciences and the Management of the Mind*, Princeton: Princeton University Press.

Rosenhan, David L. (1973), "On Being Sane in Insane Places," *Science*, 179 (4070): 250–8.

Rosky, Clifford J. (2003), "To Be Male: Homophobia, Sexism, and the Production of 'Masculine' Boys'," in Martha Albertson Finemann and Michael Thomson (eds.), *Exploring Masculinities: Feminist Legal Theory Reflections*, 285–310, Aldershot: Ashgate.

Rosner, David, and Gerald Markowitz ([1991] 2006), *Deadly Dust: Silicosis and the On-Going Struggle to Protect Workers' Health*, Ann Arbor: University of Michigan Press.

Rounsaville, Bruce et al. (2002), "Basic Nomenclature Issues for DSM-V," in D. J. Kupfer, M. B. First, and D. A. Regier (eds.), *A Research Agenda for DSM-V*, 1–30, Washington, D.C.: American Psychiatric Association.

Rowden, Terry (2009), *The Songs of Blind Folk: African American Musicians and the Cultures of Blindness*, Ann Arbor: University of Michigan Press.

Royal Commission on the Care and Control of the Feeble-Minded (1908), Report of the Royal Commission on the Care and Control of the Feeble-Minded, vol. VIII, London: HMSO. Available online: https://wellcomelibrary.org/item/b28038551#?c=0&m=0&s=0&cv=3&z=-2.076%2C-0.1283%2C5.4128%2C1.8331.

Ryan, L. (1918), "Plastic Surgery," *Illinois Medical Journal*, 34: 69.

Ryan, Sara (2017), *Justice for Laughing Boy: Connor Sparrowhawk—A Death by Indifference*, London and Philadelphia: Jessica Kingsley Publishers.

Sacks, Oliver (1989), *Seeing Voices: A Journey into the World of the Deaf*, Berkeley and Los Angeles: University of California Press.

Safi, Michael (2018), "'I'm Born to Do This': Condemned by Caste, India's Sewer Cleaners Condemned to Death," *The Guardian*, March 4. Available online: https://www.theguardian.com/world/2018/mar/04/im-born-to-do-this-condemned-by-caste-indias-sewer-cleaners-risk-death-daily?CMP=Share_iOSApp_Other.

Sanchez, Rebecca (2015), *Deafening Modernism: Embodied Language and Visual Poetics in American Literature*, New York: New York University Press.

Sanders, James L. (2011), "A Distinct Language and a Historic Pendulum: The Evolution of the Diagnostic and Statistical Manual of Mental Disorders," *Archives of Psychiatric Nursing*, 25 (6): 394–403.

Scarry, Elaine. *The Body in Pain: The Making and Unmaking of the World*, Oxford: Oxford University Press, 1985.

Schalk, Sami (2017), "Critical Disability Studies as Methodology," *Lateral*, 6 (1). Available online: http://csalateral.org/issue/6-1/forum-alt-humanities-critical-disability-studies-methodology-schalk.

Schalk, Sami (2018), *Bodyminds Reimagined: (Dis)ability, Race, and Gender in Black Women's Speculative Fiction*, Durham: Duke University Press.

Scherer, Bee (2014), "Crossings and Dwellings: Being Behind Transphobia," *Queering Paradigms Blog*, August 11. Available online: http://queeringparadigms.com/2014/08/11/crossings-and-dwellings-being-behind-transphobia.

Scherer, Bee (2016a), "Variable Bodies, Buddhism and (No-)Selfhood: Towards Dehegemonised Embodiment," in Chris Mounsey and Stan Booth (eds.), *The Variable Body in History*, 247–63, Oxford: Peter Lang.

Scherer, Bee (2016b), "Variant Dharma: Buddhist Queers, Queering Buddhisms," in Bee Scherer (ed.), *Queering Paradigms VI: Interventions, Ethics and Glocalities*, 253–73, Oxford: Peter Lang.

Scherer, Bee (2017), "Queerthinking Religion: Queering Religious Paradigms," *Scholar & Feminist Online*, 14 (2). Available online: http://sfonline.barnard.edu/queer-religion/queerthinking-religion-queering-religious-paradigms.

Schuchman, John S. (1988), *Hollywood Speaks: Deafness and the Film Entertainment Industry*, Urbana and Chicago: University of Illinois Press.

Schumm, Darla Y., and Michael Stoltzfus (2007), "Chronic Illness and Disability: Narratives of Suffering and Healing in Buddhism and Christianity," *Journal of Religion, Disability & Health*, 11 (3): 5–21.

Schwartz, Regina M. (1997), *The Curse of Cain: The Violent Legacy of Monotheism*, Chicago: University of Chicago Press.

Scott, Robert A. (1969), *The Making of Blind Men*, New York: Russell Sage Foundation.

Scull, Andrew (2015), *Madness in Civilization: A Cultural History of Insanity, from the Bible to Freud, from the Madhouse to Modern Medicine*, Princeton: Princeton University Press.

Sedgwick, Eve K. (2004), "Queer and Now," in *Tendencies*, 1–19, London and New York: Routledge.

Serlin, David (2004), *Replaceable You: Engineering the Body in Postwar America*, Chicago: University of Chicago Press.

Shakespeare, Tom (2006), *Disability Rights and Wrongs*, London and New York: Routledge.

Shakespeare, Tom (2013), *Disability Rights and Wrongs Revisited*, London and New York: Routledge.

Shakespeare, Tom (2017), *Disability: The Basics*, London and New York: Routledge.

Shakespeare, William (2004), *The Tragedy of Richard III*, New York: Folger Library.

Shepherd, Ben (2000), *A War of Nerves: Soldiers and Psychiatrists*, London: Jonathan Cape.

Shildrick, Margrit (1997), *Leaky Bodies and Boundaries: Feminism, Postmodernism and (Bio) ethics*, Abingdon: Routledge.

Shildrick, Margrit (2009), *Dangerous Discourses of Disability, Subjectivity and Sexuality*, New York: Palgrave Macmillan.

Shorter, Ed (1994), *From the Mind into the Body: The Cultural Origins of Psychosomatic Symptoms*, New York: The Free Press.

Siebers, Tobin (2002), "Tender Organs, Narcissism, and Identity Politics," in Sharon Snyder, Brenda Jo Brueggemann, and Rosemarie Garland-Thomson (eds.), *Disability Studies: Enabling the Humanities*, 40–55, New York: The Modern Language Association of America.

Siebers, Tobin (2008), *Disability Theory*, Ann Arbor: University of Michigan Press.

Sign ([2016] 2017), [Short film] Dir. Kenan-Bolger, London: Peccadillo Pictures, DVD.

Signage (2007), [Short film] Dir. Rick Hammerly, Hammerly, Streaming.

Sign Gene (2017), [Film] Dir. Emilio Insolera, Pluin Productions, Theatrical Release.

The Silent Child (2017), [Short film] Dir. Chris Overton, London: Slick Films, 2017, Web.

Simpson, Murray K. (2014), *Modernity and the Appearance of Idiocy: Intellectual Disability as a Regime of Truth*, New York and Lampeter: Edwin Mellen Press.

Simpson, Murray K. (2018), "Power, Ideology and Structure: The Legacy of Normalization for Intellectual Disability," *Social Inclusion*, 6 (2): 12–21.

Singer, Peter, and Helga Kuhse (1988), *Should the Baby Live: The Problem of Handicapped Infants*, Oxford: Oxford University Press.

Sinha, Indra (2007), *Animal's People*, London: Simon & Schuster.

Skinner, Burrhus Frederic (2014), *Verbal Behavior*, Cambridge, MA: B. F. Skinner Foundation.

Sontag, Susan ([1978] 2001), *Illness as Metaphor and AIDS and Its Metaphors*, London: Picador.

Spandler, Helen, Jill Anderson, and Bob Sapey (eds.) (2015), *Madness, Distress and the Politics of Disablement*, Bristol: Policy Press.

Spinney, Justin, Rachel Aldred, and Katrina Brown (2015), "Geographies of citizenship and Everyday (Im)mobility," *Geoforum*, 64: 325–32.

Spivakovsky, Claire (2017), "Governing Freedom through Risk: Locating the Group Home in the Archipelago of Confinement and Control," *Punishment & Society*, 19 (3): 366–83.

The Stand (1994), [TV miniseries] Dir. Mick Garris, aired May 8–12 on ABC.

Stevens, Andy (1997), "Recording the History of an Institution: The Royal Eastern Counties Institution at Colchester," in D. Atkinson, M. Jackson, and J. Walmsley (eds.), *Forgotten Lives: Exploring the History of Learning Disability*, 47–64, Kidderminster: BILD.

Stewart, David (2017), *Researching the Uncomfortable*, Paper presented at the Social History of Learning Disability Conference, Open University, July 20.

Stiker, Henri-Jacques (1999), *A History of Disability*, Ann Arbor: University of Michigan Press.

Stone, Deborah A. (1984), *The Disabled State*, Philadelphia: Temple University Press.

Summerfield, Ellen, and Sandra Lee (2006), *Seeing the Big Picture: A Cinematic Approach to Understanding Cultures in America* (rev. ed.), Ann Arbor: University of Michigan Press.

Sweet Nothing in My Ear (aired April 20, 2008), [TV movie] Dir. Joseph Sachs, on CBS.

Switched at Birth (2011–17), [TV series], created by Lizzy Weiss, aired June 6, 2011–April 11, 2017, on Freeform.

Swift, Jonathan (1712), *A Proposal for Correcting, Improving and Ascertaining the English Tongue: In a Letter to the Most Honourable Robert, Earl of Oxford and Mortimer, Lord High Treasurer of Great Britain*, London: Benj. Tooke.

Taylor, Sunaura (2011), "Beasts of Burden: Disability Studies and Animal Rights," *Qui Parle*, 19 (2), 191–222.

Taylor, Sunaura (2017), *Beasts of Burden: Animal and Disability Liberation*, New York: The New Press.

Telford-Smith, Telford, and W. H. Coupland (1856), *The Education of the Imbecile and the Improvement of Invalid Youth*, Edinburgh: Home and School for Invalid and Imbecile Children.

Thanissaro, Bhikku (1997), Affirming the Truths of the Heart: The Buddhist Teachings in Samvega & Pasada. Available online: https://www.accesstoinsight.org/lib/authors/thanissaro/affirming.html.

The Hammer (2010), [Film] Dir. Orin Kaplan, ARC Entertainment, DVD.

The Shape of Water (2017), [Film] Dir. Guillermo Del Toro, Los Angeles: 20th Century Fox, DVD.

The Piano (1993), [Film] Dir. Jane Campion, Vancouver: Lionsgate, Blu-ray.

Theoharis, Jeanne (2015), "How History Got the Rosa Parks Story Wrong," *The Washington Post*. Available online: https://www.washingtonpost.com/posteverything/wp/2015/12/01/how-history-got-the-rosa-parks-story-wrong/?utm_term=.cb9fcb4d4b42.

This Close (2018), [TV series] created by Shoshanna Stern and Josh Feldman, Sundance Now.

This is Normal (2013), [Short film] Dir. Justin Giddings and Ryan Walsh, streaming.

Thompson, Hannah (2017), *Reviewing Blindness in French Fiction*, London: Palgrave Macmillan.

Thumma, Scott, and Edward R. Gray (eds.) (2005), *Gay Religion*, Walnut Creek: AltaMira Press.

Titchkosky, Tanya (2003), "Governing Embodiment: Technologies of Constituting Citizens with Disabilities," *Canadian Journal of Sociology*, 28 (4): 517–42.

Titchkosky, Tanya (2014), "Monitoring Disability: The Question of the 'Human' in 'Human Rights Projects'," in Cathy Schlund-Vials and Michael Gill (eds.), *Disability, Human Rights, and the Limits of Humanitarianism*, 119–36, Burlington: Ashgate Press.

Titchkosky, Tanya (2015), "Life with Dead Metaphors: Impairment Rhetoric in Social Justice Praxis," *JLCDS Journal of Literary and Cultural Disability Studies*, 9 (1): 1–18.

Titchkosky, Tanya, and Katie Aubrecht (2015), "WHO's MIND, Whose Future? Mental Health Projects as Colonial Logics," *Social Identities*, 21 (1): 69–84.

Titchkosky, Tanya, Devon Healey, and Rod Michalko (2019), "Understanding Blindness Simulation and the Culture of Sight." *Journal of Literary and Cultural Disability Studies*. Vol 13(2), 123–139.

Tollifson, Joan (1996), *Bare-Bones Meditation: Waking Up from the Story of My Life*, New York: Harmony.

Tremain, Shelley (2015), "Foucault, Governmentality, and Critical Disability Theory," in Shelley Tremain (ed.), *Foucault and the Government of Disability*, 1–24, Ann Arbor: University of Michigan Press.

Trent, James W. (1994), *Inventing the Feeble Mind: A History of Intellectual Disability in the United States*, Berkeley, Los Angeles, and London: University of California Press.

Tunstall, Kate E. (2011), *Blindness and Enlightenment: An Essay*, New York: Bloomsbury Publishing.

UN General Assembly (2007), *Convention on the Rights of Persons with Disabilities: resolution/adopted by the General Assembly*, A/RES/61/106. Available online: https://www. un.org/development/desa/disabilities/convention-on-the-rights-of-persons-with-disabilities. html#Fulltext.

Unlocking the Past (2010a), Bath Routines. Available online: https://web.archive.org/ web/20100929091035/http://www.unlockingthepast.org.uk:80/index/archives/view_ archives/89.

Unlocking the Past (2010b), Refusing Bath. Available online: https://web.archive.org/ web/20100929164634/http://www.unlockingthepast.org.uk:80/index/archives/view_ archives/90.

US Department of Health and Human Services (1999), *Mental Health: A Report of the Surgeon General*. Rockville: US Department of Health and Human Services. Available online: https:// profiles.nlm.nih.gov/ps/access/NNBBHS.pdf.

Versa Effect (2011), [Film] Dir. Mark Wood, ASL Films, DVD.

Volosinov, Valentin, Ladislav Matejka, and I. R. Titunik (1973), *Marxism and the Philosophy of Language*, New York: Seminar Press.

Voronka, Jijian (2008), "Re/Moving Forward: Spacing Mad Degeneracy at the Queen Street Site," *Resources for Feminist Research*, 33 (1&2): 45–61.

Vygotsky, Lev Semenovich (2012), *Thought and Language*, Cambridge, MA: MIT Press.

Walters, Mark, Rupert Brown, and Susann Wiedlitzka (2016), *Causes and Motivations of Hate Crime*, Manchester: Equality and Human Rights Commission.

Wang Youxuan (2001), *Buddhism and Deconstruction: Towards a Comparative Semiotics*, Richmond: Curzon Press.

Ward, Geoffrey C., and Ken Burns (2017), *The Vietnam War: An Intimate History*, New York: Alfred A. Knopf Books.

Warin, Megan, Tanya Zivkovic, Vivienne Moore, Paul Ward, and Michelle Jones (2015), "Short Horizons and Obesity Futures: Disjunctures between Public health Interventions and Everyday Temporalities," *Social Science & Medicine*, 128: 309–15.

Washington, Harriet A. (2006), *Medical Apartheid: The Dark History of Medical Experimentation on Black Americans from Colonial Times to the Present*, New York: Penguin.

Watson, Nick, and Brian Woods (2005), "No Wheelchairs Beyond This Point: A Historical Examination of Wheelchair Access in the Twentieth Century," *Social Policy & Society*, 4 (1): 97–105.

Watts, Ivan Eugene, and Nirmala Erevelles (2004), "These Deadly Times: Reconceptualizing School Violence by Using Critical Race Theory and Disability Studies," *American Educational Research Journal* 41 (2): 271–99.

Webster, Noah (1959), *Webster's New Twentieth Century Dictionary of the English Language*, 2nd edn., Cleveland: The World Publishing Company.

Weheliye, Alexander G. (2014), *Habeas Viscus: Racializing Assemblages, Biopolitics, and Black Feminist Theories of the Human*, Durham: Duke University Press.

Weiwei, Ai (2018), "The Refugee Crisis Isn't about Refugees. It's about Us," *The Guardian*, February 2. Available online: https://www.theguardian.com/commentisfree/2018/feb/02/ refugee-crisis-human-flow-ai-weiwei-china?CMP=Share_iOSApp_Other.

Wendell, Susan (2001), "Unhealthy Disabled: Treating Chronic Illnesses as Disabilities,"
    Hypatia 16 (4): 17–33.

Wilcox, Melissa M. (2009), *Queer Women and Religious Individualism*, Bloomington: Indiana
    University Press.

Wolfensberger, Wolf (1972), *Normalization: The Principle of Normalization in Human
    Services*, Toronto: National Institute of Mental Retardation.

Wonderstruck (2017), [Film] Dir. Todd Haynes, Los Angeles: Amazon Studios, DVD.

Woods, Brian, and Nick Watson (2003), "A Short History of Powered Wheelchairs," *Assistive
    Technology*, 15 (2): 164–80.

Woodward, Anna (2018), *Poetry in Motion*, York University. Available online: http://www.
    annawoodford.co.uk/installations/poetry-in-motion.

Woodward, James (1982), *How You Gonna Get to Heaven If You Can't Talk with Jesus: On
    Depathologizing Deafness*, Silver Spring: T. J. Publishers.

Woolf, Virginia (1981), *To the Lighthouse*, New York: Harcourt, Inc.

Words (2010), [Short film] Dir. Anup Bhandari, A. Bhandari, streaming.

World Health Organization (2015), "Healthy Eyes for Everyone," in *Blindness Prevention*.
    Available online: http://www.wpro.who.int/mediacentre/factsheets/blindness/en.

World Health Organization (2017), "Blindness: The Global Picture," in *Blindness: Vision 2020
    The Global Initiative for the Elimination of Avoidable Blindness*.

Wright, David (1996), "'Childlike in His Innocence.' Lay Attitudes to 'Idiots' and 'Imbeciles'
    in Victorian England," in David Wright and Anne Digby (eds.), *From Idiocy to Mental
    Deficiency. Historical Perspectives on People with Learning Difficulties*, 118–33, London:
    Routledge.

Wright, David, and Anne Digby (eds.) (1996), *From Idiocy to Mental Deficiency. Historical
    Perspectives on People with Learning Difficulties*, London: Routledge.

Wylie, Gillian (2017), "Neo-abolitionism and Transnational Advocacy Networks," in Eilís
    Ward and Gillian Wylie (eds.), *Feminism, Prostitution and the State: The Politics of Neo-
    Abolitionism*, 12–28, Abingdon and New York: Routledge.

Yuan, David Y. (1997), "Disfigurement and Reconstruction in Oliver Wendell Holmes's 'The
    Human Wheel, Its Spokes and Felloes'," in D. T. Mitchell and S. L. Snyder (eds.), *The Body
    and Physical Difference: Discourses of Disability*, 71–87, Ann Arbor: University of Michigan
    Press.

Zalewski, Marysia, and Anne Sisson Runyan (2013), "Taking Feminist Violence Seriously
    in Feminist International Relations," *International Feminist Journal of Politics*, 15 (3):
    293–313.

Zehfuss, Maja (2011), "Targeting: Precision and the Production of Ethics," *European Journal of
    International Relations*, 17 (3): 543–56.

Žižek, Slavoj (1989), *The Sublime Object of Ideology*, London: Verso.

Žižek, Slavoj (2004), *Absolute Recoil: Towards a New Foundation of Dialectical Materialism*,
    London: Verso.

INDEX